JOURNEY TO **STAR WARS: THE LAST JEDI**

STAR WARS

CAPTAIN PHASMA

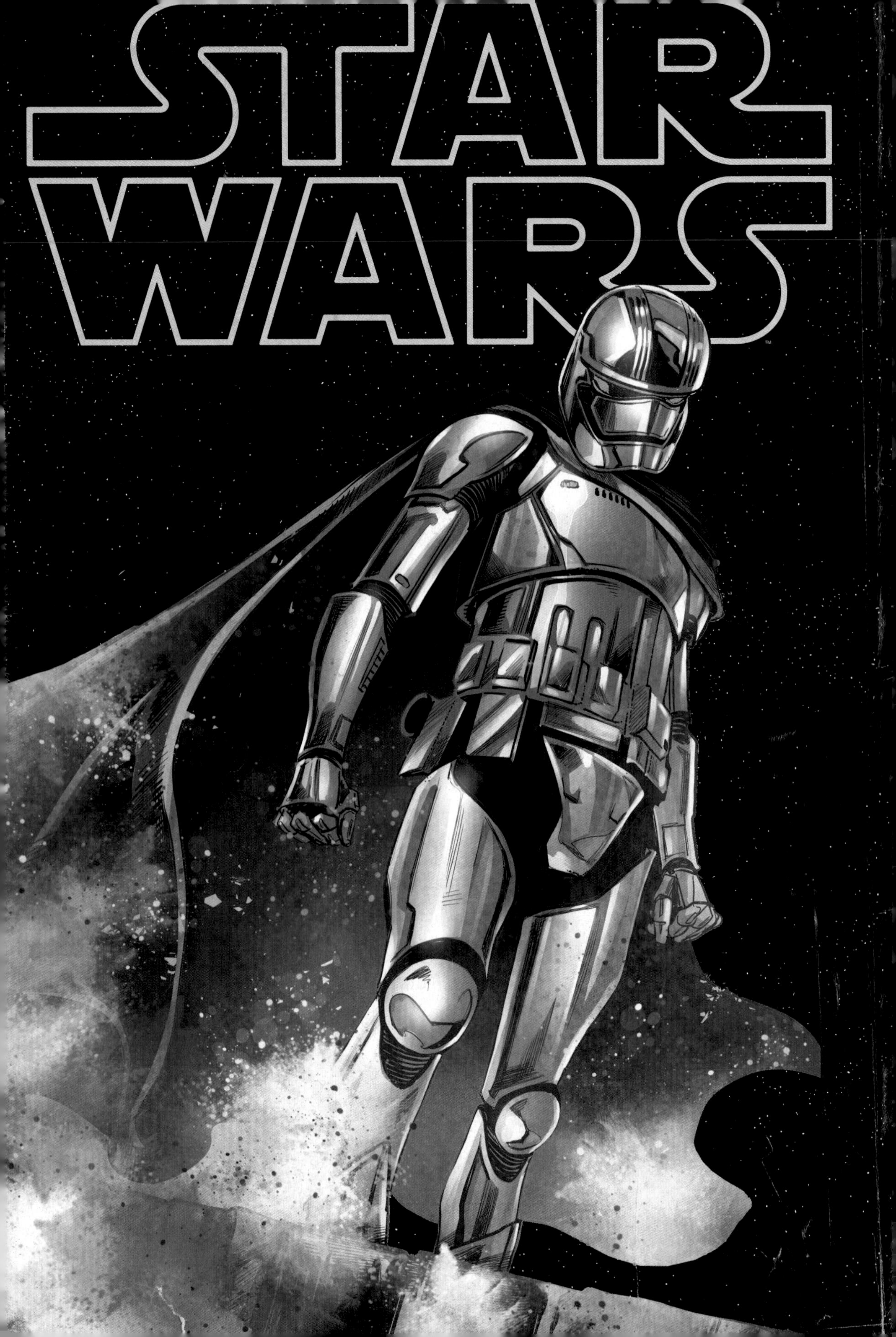
STAR WARS

JOURNEY TO **STAR WARS: THE LAST JEDI**

CAPTAIN PHASMA

Writer	**KELLY THOMPSON**
Artist	**MARCO CHECCHETTO**
Color Artist	**ANDRES MOSSA**
Letterer	**VC's CLAYTON COWLES**
Cover Art	**PAUL RENAUD**
Assistant Editor	**HEATHER ANTOS**
Editor	**JORDAN D. WHITE**
Executive Editor	**C.B. CEBULSKI**

Editor in Chief	**AXEL ALONSO**
Chief Creative Officer	**JOE QUESADA**
President	**DAN BUCKLEY**

For Lucasfilm:

Senior Editor	**FRANK PARISI**
Creative Director	**MICHAEL SIGLAIN**
Lucasfilm Story Group	**JAMES WAUGH, LELAND CHEE, MATT MARTIN**

Collection Editor	**JENNIFER GRÜNWALD**
Assistant Editor	**CAITLIN O'CONNELL**
Associate Managing Editor	**KATERI WOODY**
Editor, Special Projects	**MARK D. BEAZLEY**
VP Production & Special Projects	**JEFF YOUNGQUIST**
SVP Print, Sales & Marketing	**DAVID GABRIEL**
Book Designer	**ADAM DEL RE**

STAR WARS: JOURNEY TO STAR WARS: THE LAST JEDI — CAPTAIN PHASMA. Contains material originally published in magazine form as JOURNEY TO STAR WARS: THE LAST JEDI — CAPTAIN PHASMA #1-4. First printing 2017. ISBN# 978-0-7851-9455-2. Published by MARVEL WORLDWIDE, INC., a subsidiary of MARVEL ENTERTAINMENT, LLC. OFFICE OF PUBLICATION: 135 West 50th Street, New York, NY 10020. STAR WARS and related text and illustrations are trademarks and/or copyrights, in the United States and other countries, of Lucasfilm Ltd. and/or its affiliates. © & TM Lucasfilm Ltd. No similarity between any of the names, characters, persons, and/or institutions in this magazine with those of any living or dead person or institution is intended, and any such similarity which may exist is purely coincidental. Marvel and its logos are TM Marvel Characters, Inc. **Printed in Canada.** DAN BUCKLEY, President, Marvel Entertainment; JOE QUESADA, Chief Creative Officer; TOM BREVOORT, SVP of Publishing; DAVID BOGART, SVP of Business Affairs & Operations, Publishing & Partnership; C.B. CEBULSKI, VP of Brand Management & Development, Asia; DAVID GABRIEL, SVP of Sales & Marketing, Publishing; JEFF YOUNGQUIST, VP of Production & Special Projects; DAN CARR, Executive Director of Publishing Technology; ALEX MORALES, Director of Publishing Operations; SUSAN CRESPI, Production Manager; STAN LEE, Chairman Emeritus. For information regarding advertising in Marvel Comics or on Marvel.com, please contact Vit DeBellis, Integrated Sales Manager, at vdebellis@marvel.com. For Marvel subscription inquiries, please call 888-511-5480. **Manufactured between 9/8/2017 and 10/10/2017 by SOLISCO PRINTERS, SCOTT, QC, CANADA.**

10 9 8 7 6 5 4 3 2 1

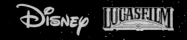

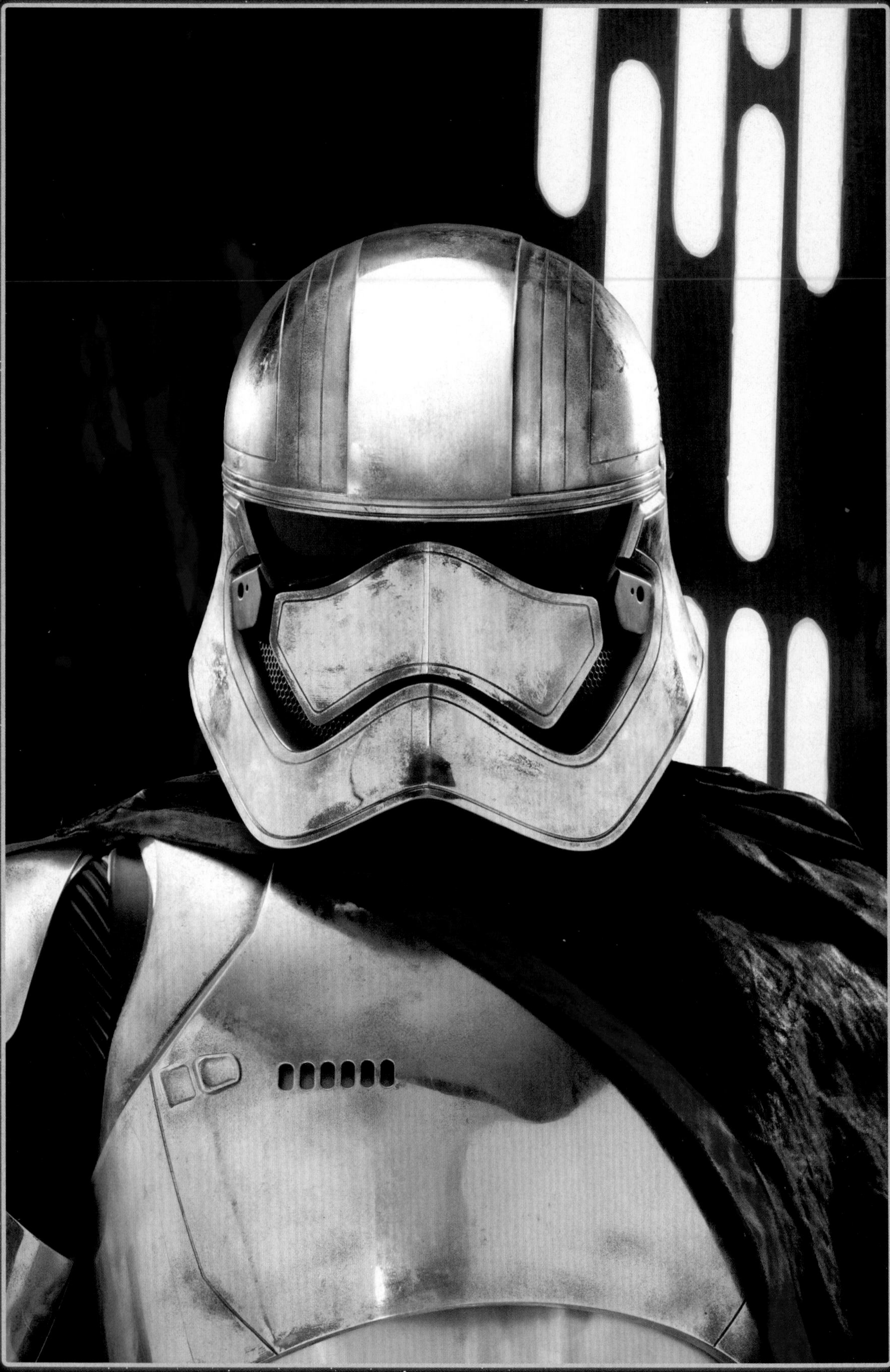

#1 Movie Variant

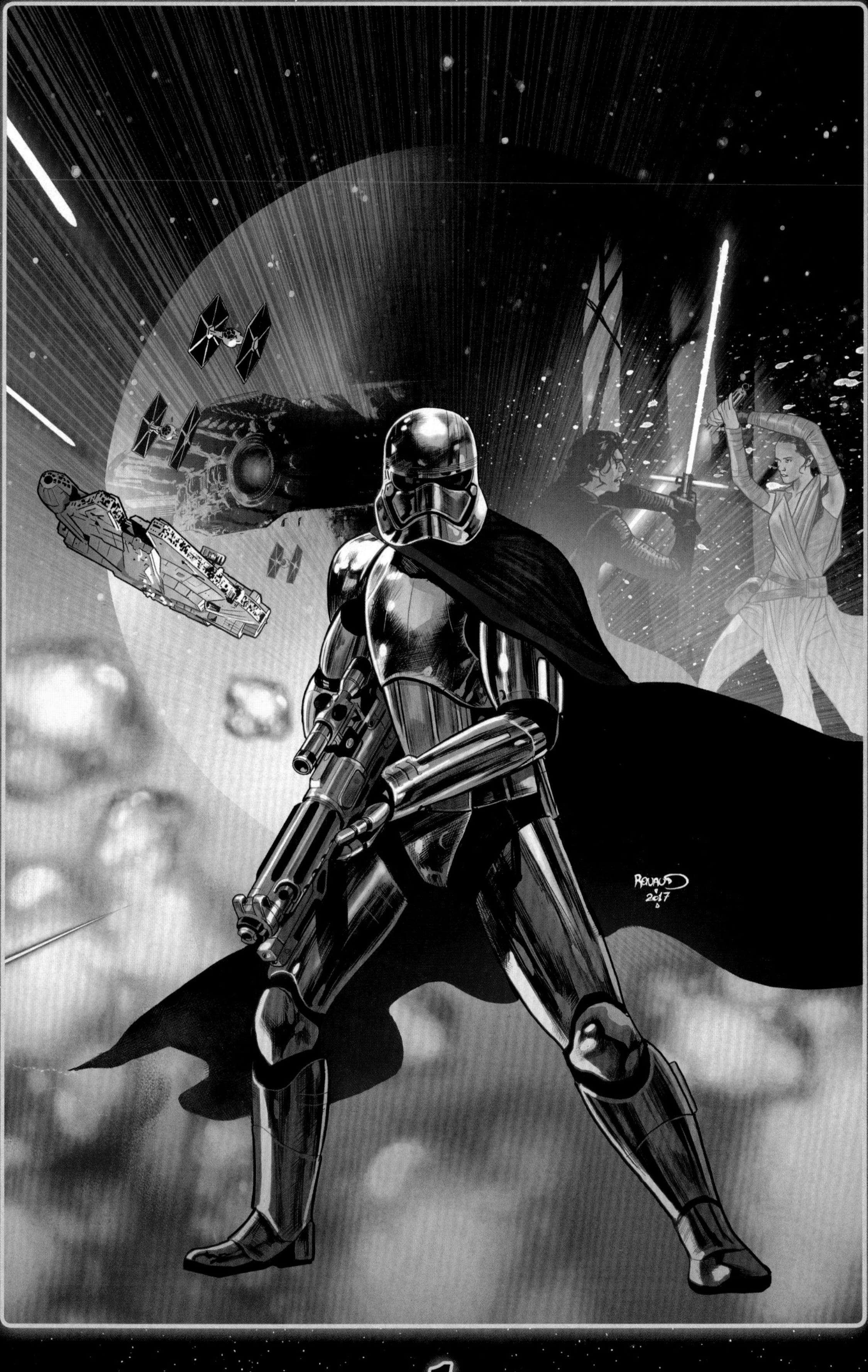
RENAUD
2017

Book I
CAPTAIN PHASMA

General Organa's Resistance forces have mounted a direct attack on the First Order's most powerful weapon, Starkiller Base.

A small assault team consisting of Han Solo, Chewbacca, and former stormtrooper FN-2187, now a Resistance fighter known as Finn, has infiltrated the base to lower its defense shields.

While Starkiller's planet-destroying superweapon is charging, Captain Phasma is forced at blasterpoint to lower the base's defensive shields, allowing Resistance forces to attack in full. The trio then forces Captain Phasma into a garbage chute.

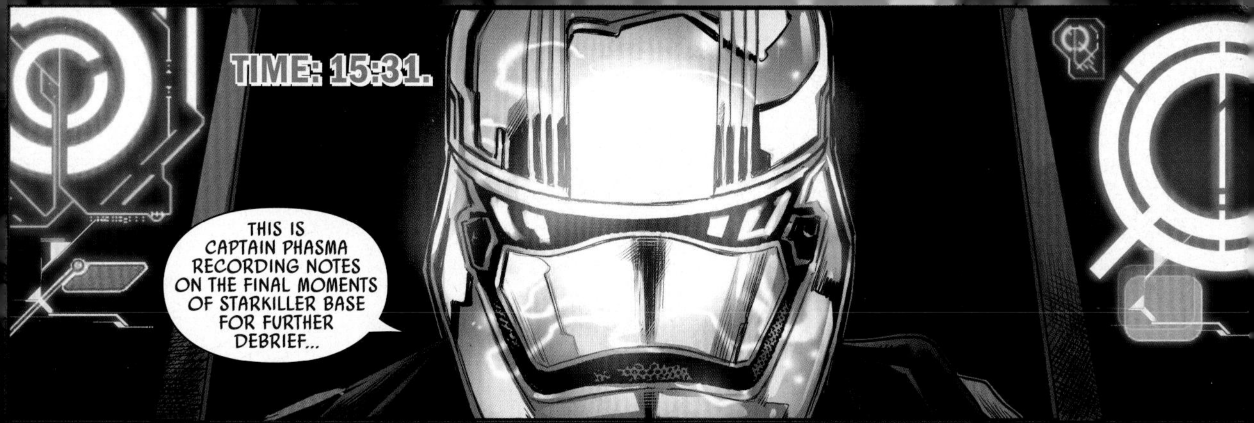
TIME: 15:31.
THIS IS CAPTAIN PHASMA RECORDING NOTES ON THE FINAL MOMENTS OF STARKILLER BASE FOR FURTHER DEBRIEF...

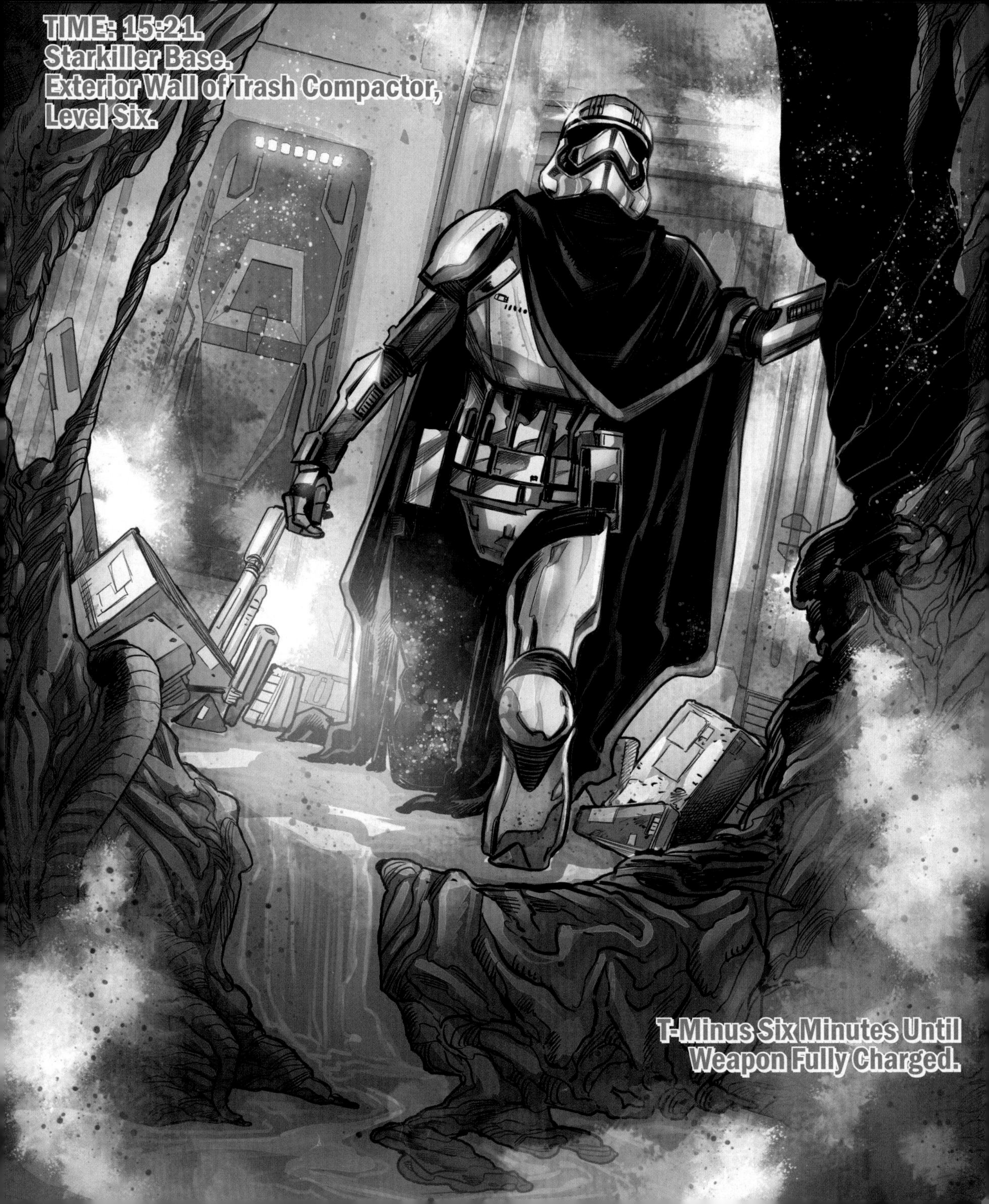
TIME: 15:21.
Starkiller Base.
Exterior Wall of Trash Compactor, Level Six.
T-Minus Six Minutes Until Weapon Fully Charged.

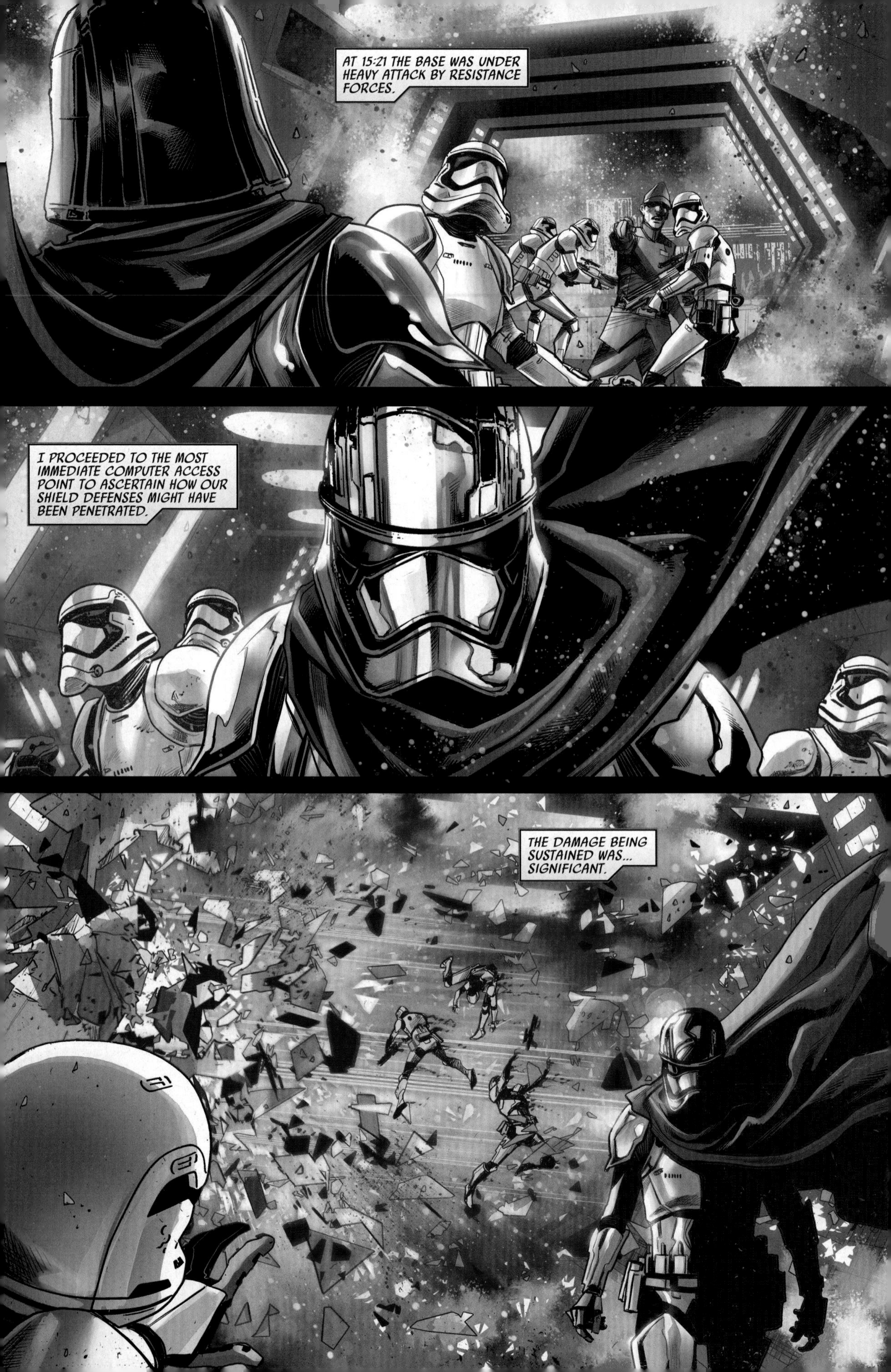
AT 15:21 THE BASE WAS UNDER HEAVY ATTACK BY RESISTANCE FORCES.
I PROCEEDED TO THE MOST IMMEDIATE COMPUTER ACCESS POINT TO ASCERTAIN HOW OUR SHIELD DEFENSES MIGHT HAVE BEEN PENETRATED.
THE DAMAGE BEING SUSTAINED WAS... SIGNIFICANT.

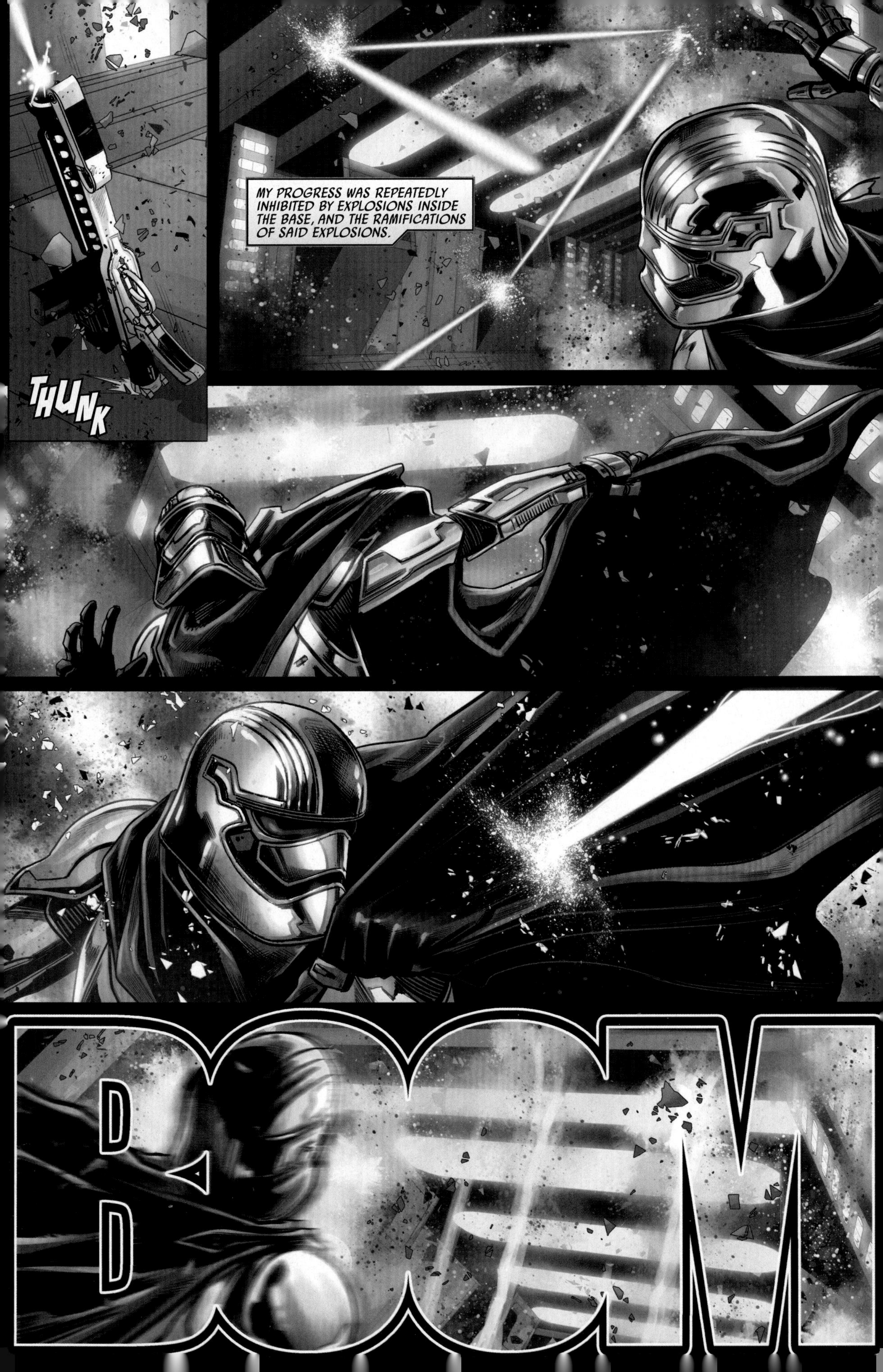
MY PROGRESS WAS REPEATEDLY INHIBITED BY EXPLOSIONS INSIDE THE BASE, AND THE RAMIFICATIONS OF SAID EXPLOSIONS.
THUNK
BOOM

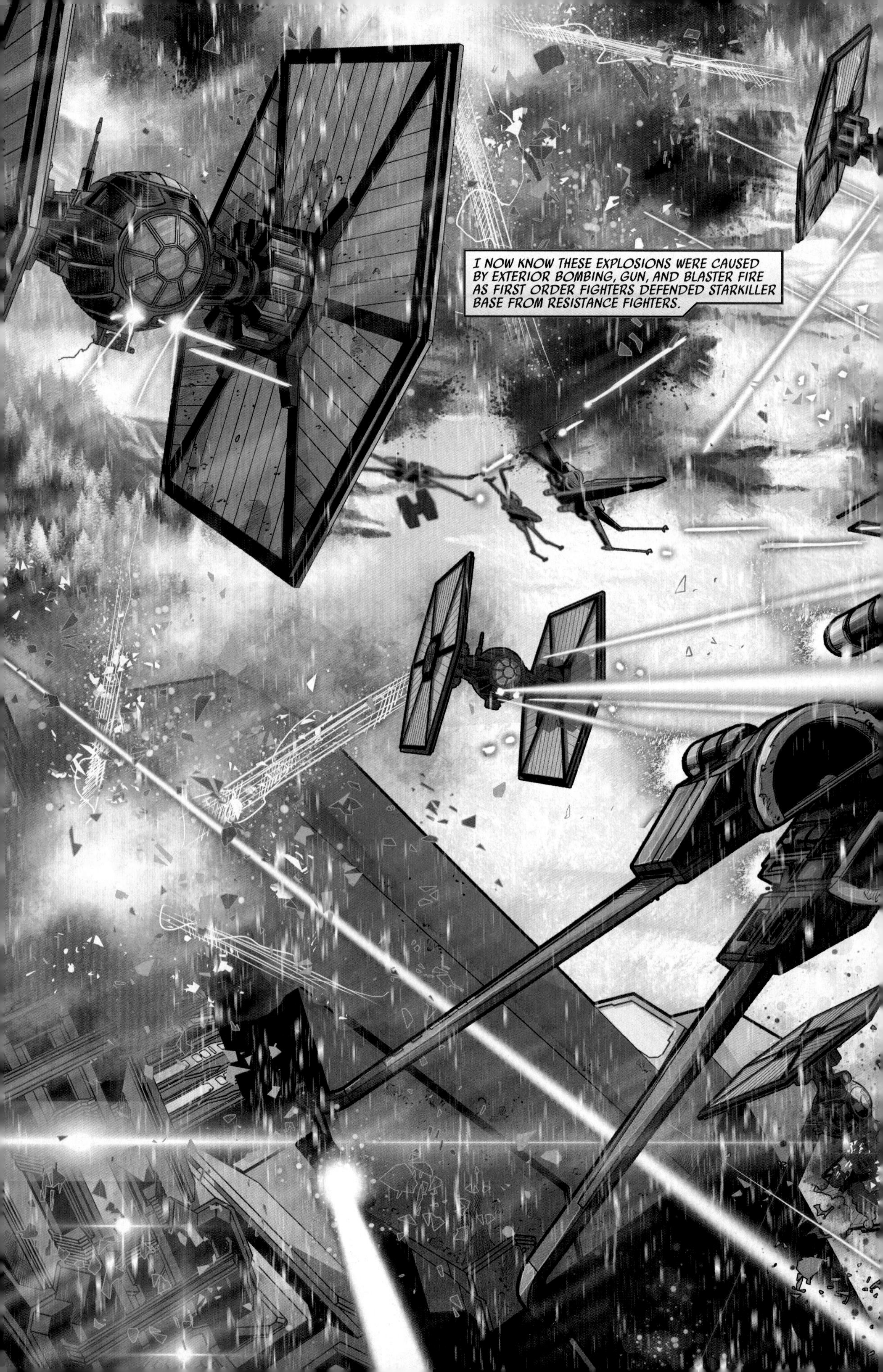
I NOW KNOW THESE EXPLOSIONS WERE CAUSED BY EXTERIOR BOMBING, GUN, AND BLASTER FIRE AS FIRST ORDER FIGHTERS DEFENDED STARKILLER BASE FROM RESISTANCE FIGHTERS.

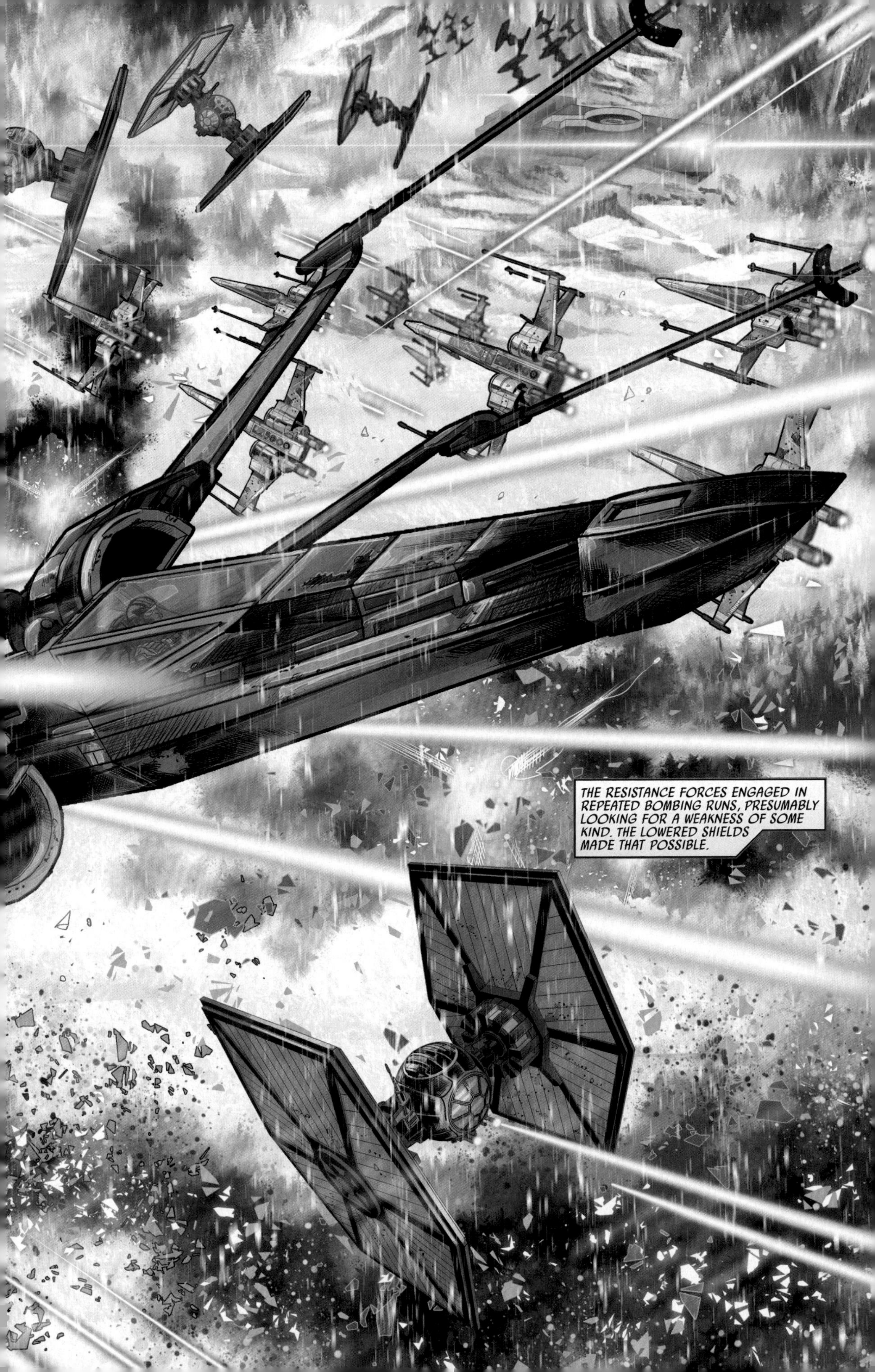
THE RESISTANCE FORCES ENGAGED IN REPEATED BOMBING RUNS, PRESUMABLY LOOKING FOR A WEAKNESS OF SOME KIND. THE LOWERED SHIELDS MADE THAT POSSIBLE.

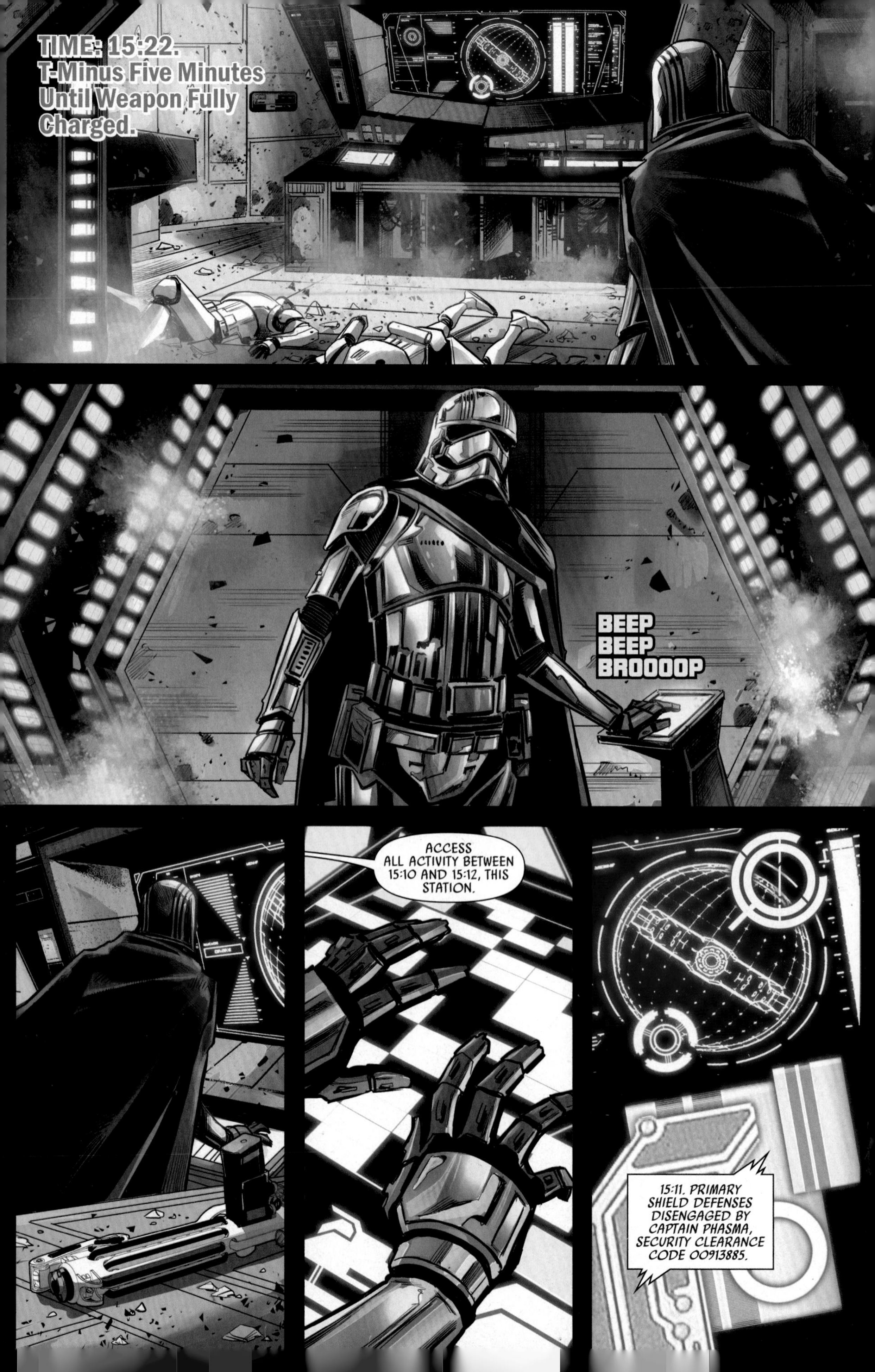
TIME: 15:22.
T-Minus Five Minutes Until Weapon Fully Charged.
BEEP BEEP BROOOOP
ACCESS ALL ACTIVITY BETWEEN 15:10 AND 15:12, THIS STATION.
15:11. PRIMARY SHIELD DEFENSES DISENGAGED BY CAPTAIN PHASMA, SECURITY CLEARANCE CODE 00913885.

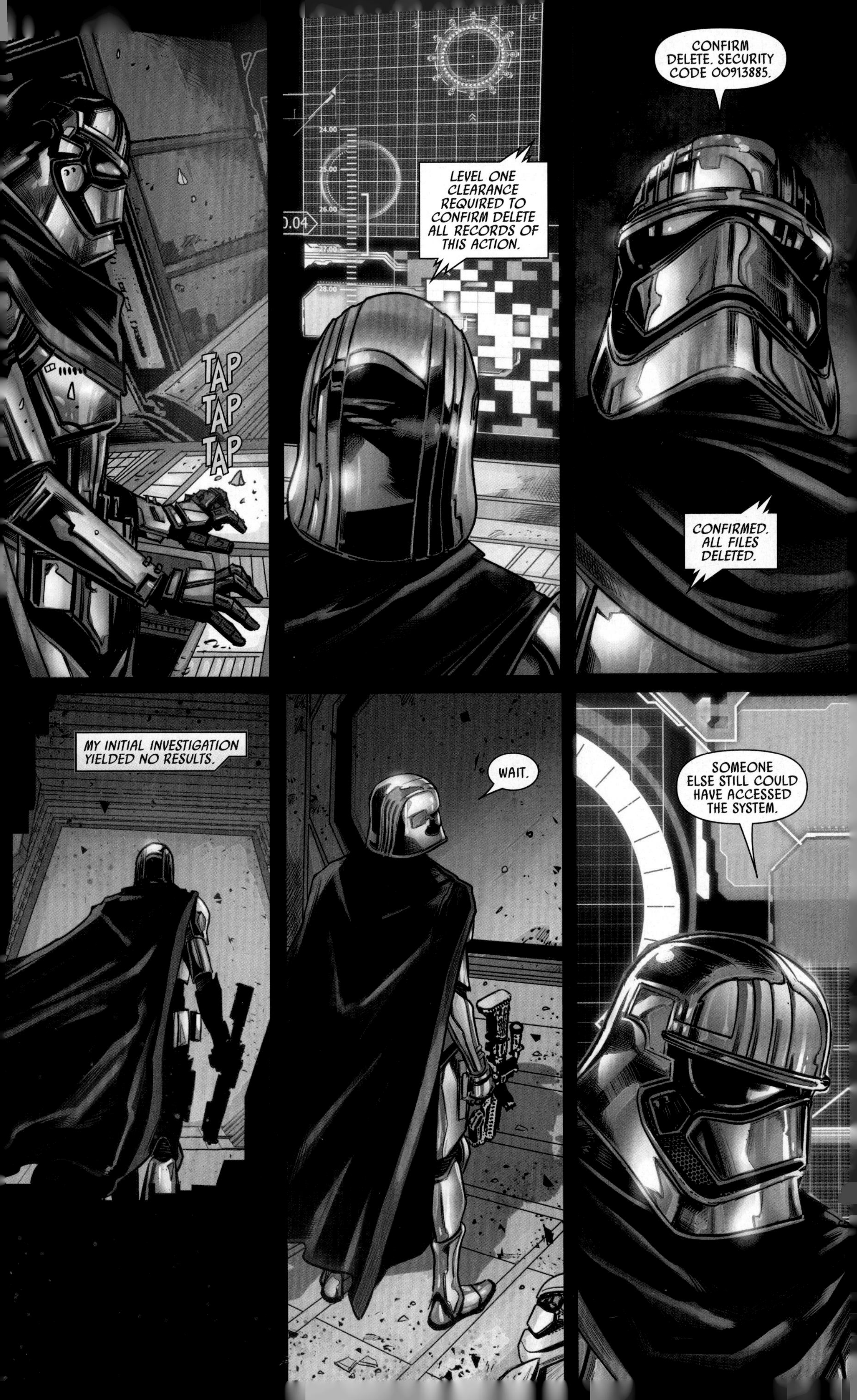
TAP
TAP
TAP
LEVEL ONE CLEARANCE REQUIRED TO CONFIRM DELETE ALL RECORDS OF THIS ACTION.
CONFIRM DELETE. SECURITY CODE 00913885.
CONFIRMED. ALL FILES DELETED.
MY INITIAL INVESTIGATION YIELDED NO RESULTS.
WAIT.
SOMEONE ELSE STILL COULD HAVE ACCESSED THE SYSTEM.

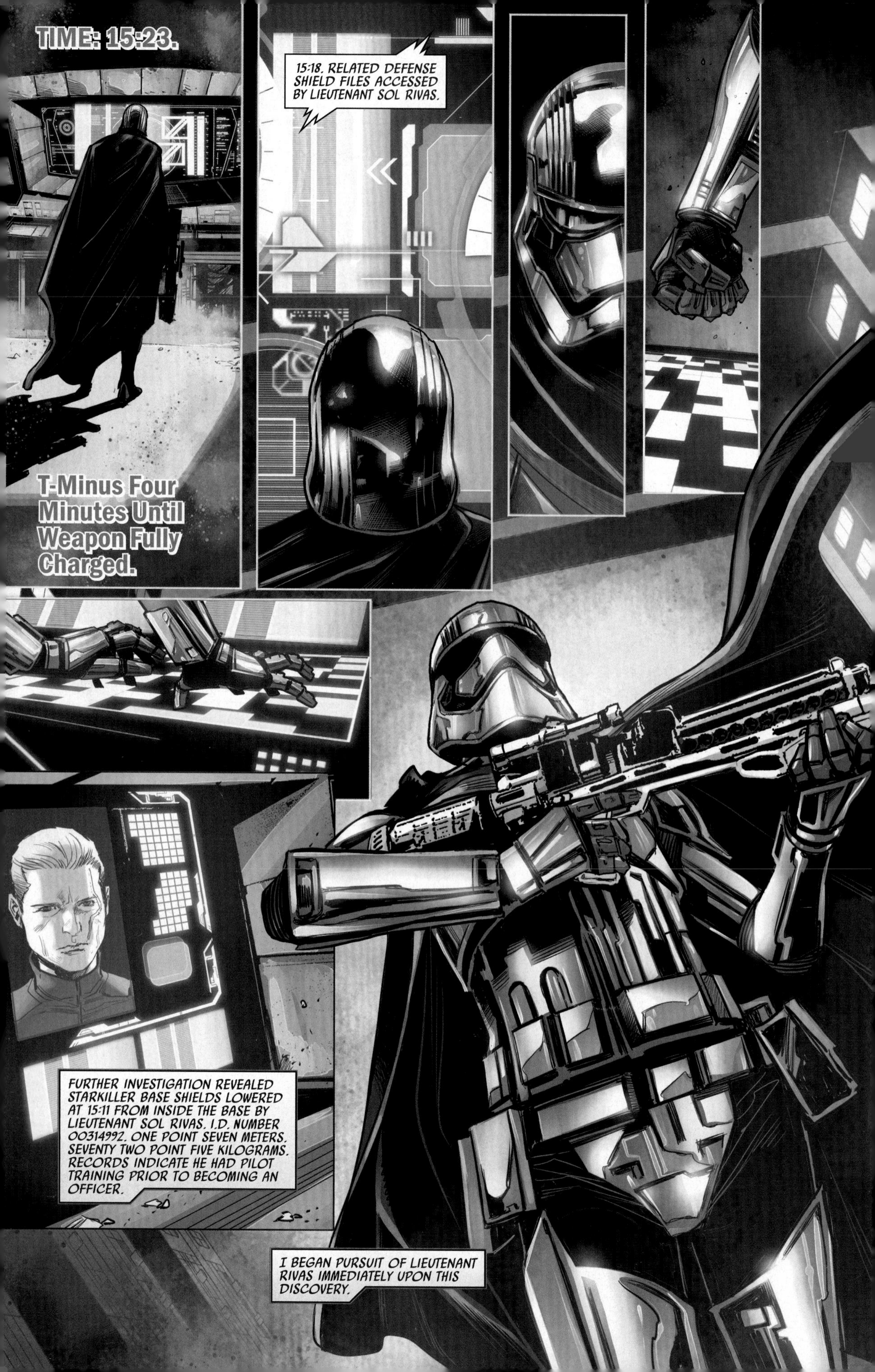
TIME: 15:23.
T-Minus Four Minutes Until Weapon Fully Charged.
15:18. RELATED DEFENSE SHIELD FILES ACCESSED BY LIEUTENANT SOL RIVAS.
FURTHER INVESTIGATION REVEALED STARKILLER BASE SHIELDS LOWERED AT 15:11 FROM INSIDE THE BASE BY LIEUTENANT SOL RIVAS. I.D. NUMBER 00314992. ONE POINT SEVEN METERS. SEVENTY TWO POINT FIVE KILOGRAMS. RECORDS INDICATE HE HAD PILOT TRAINING PRIOR TO BECOMING AN OFFICER.
I BEGAN PURSUIT OF LIEUTENANT RIVAS IMMEDIATELY UPON THIS DISCOVERY.

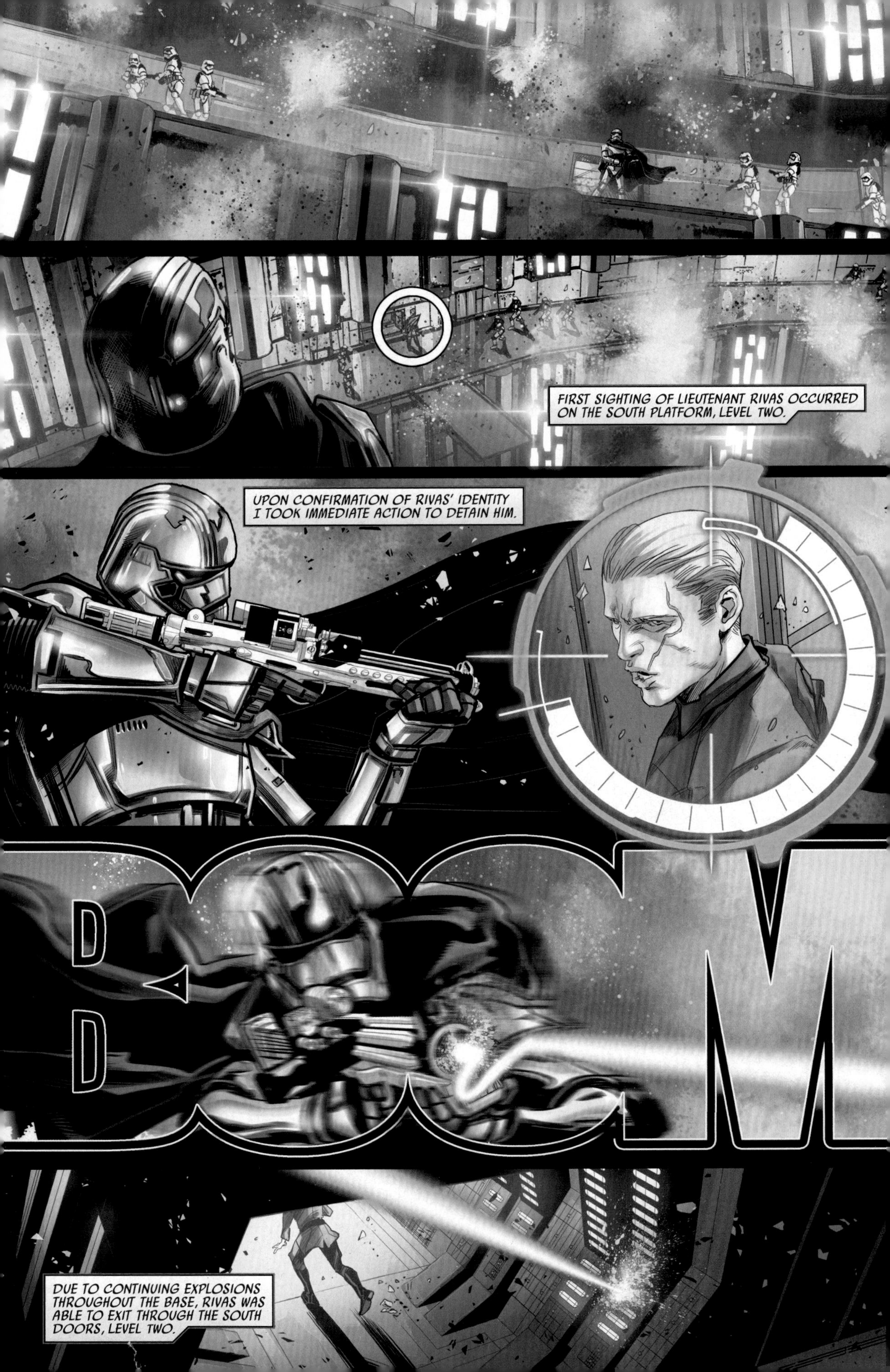
FIRST SIGHTING OF LIEUTENANT RIVAS OCCURRED ON THE SOUTH PLATFORM, LEVEL TWO.
UPON CONFIRMATION OF RIVAS' IDENTITY I TOOK IMMEDIATE ACTION TO DETAIN HIM.
DOOM
DUE TO CONTINUING EXPLOSIONS THROUGHOUT THE BASE, RIVAS WAS ABLE TO EXIT THROUGH THE SOUTH DOORS, LEVEL TWO.

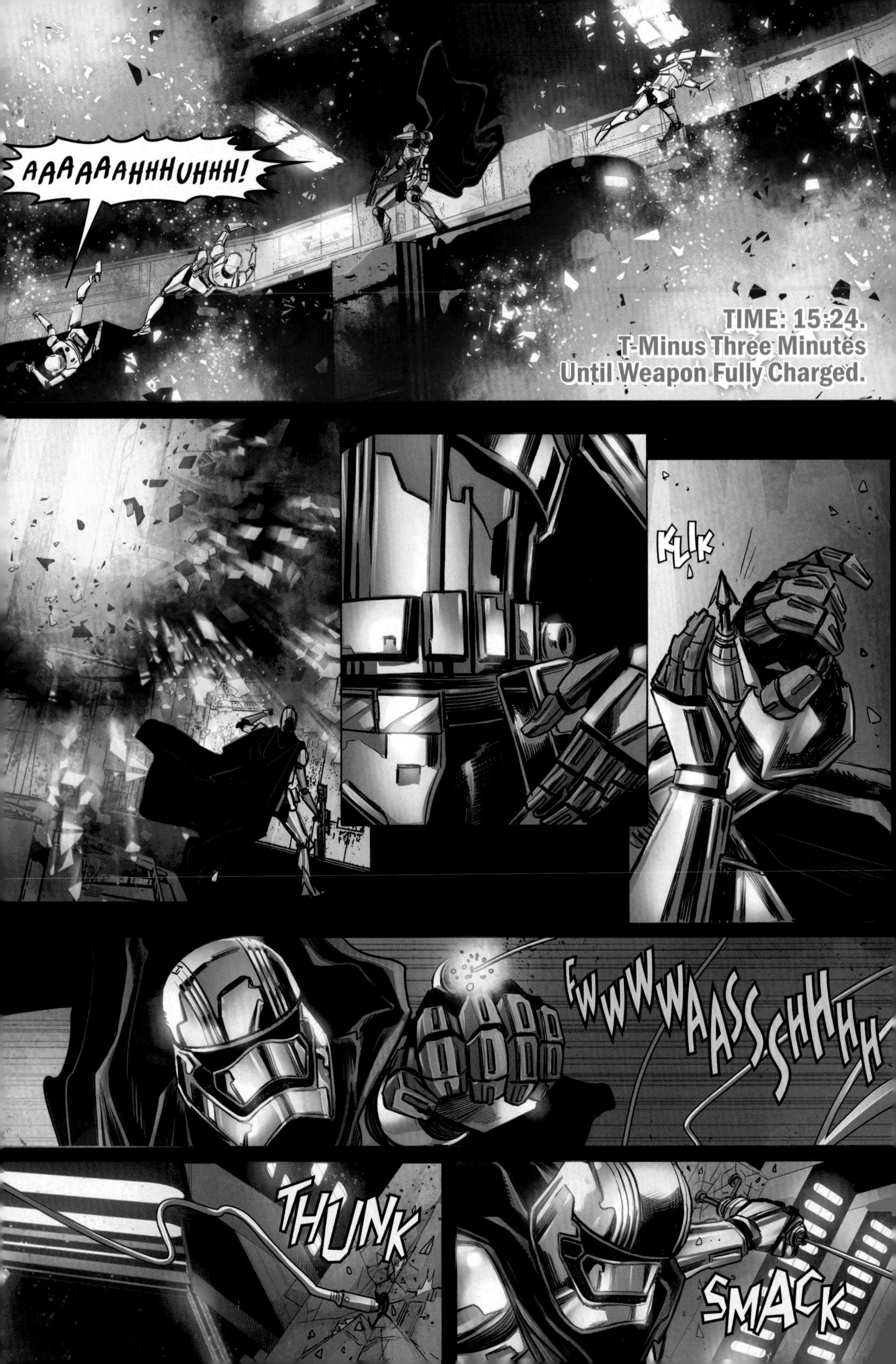
AAAAAAHHUHHH!
TIME: 15:24.
T-Minus Three Minutes
Until Weapon Fully Charged.
KLIK
FWWWWAASSHHHH
THUNK
SMACK

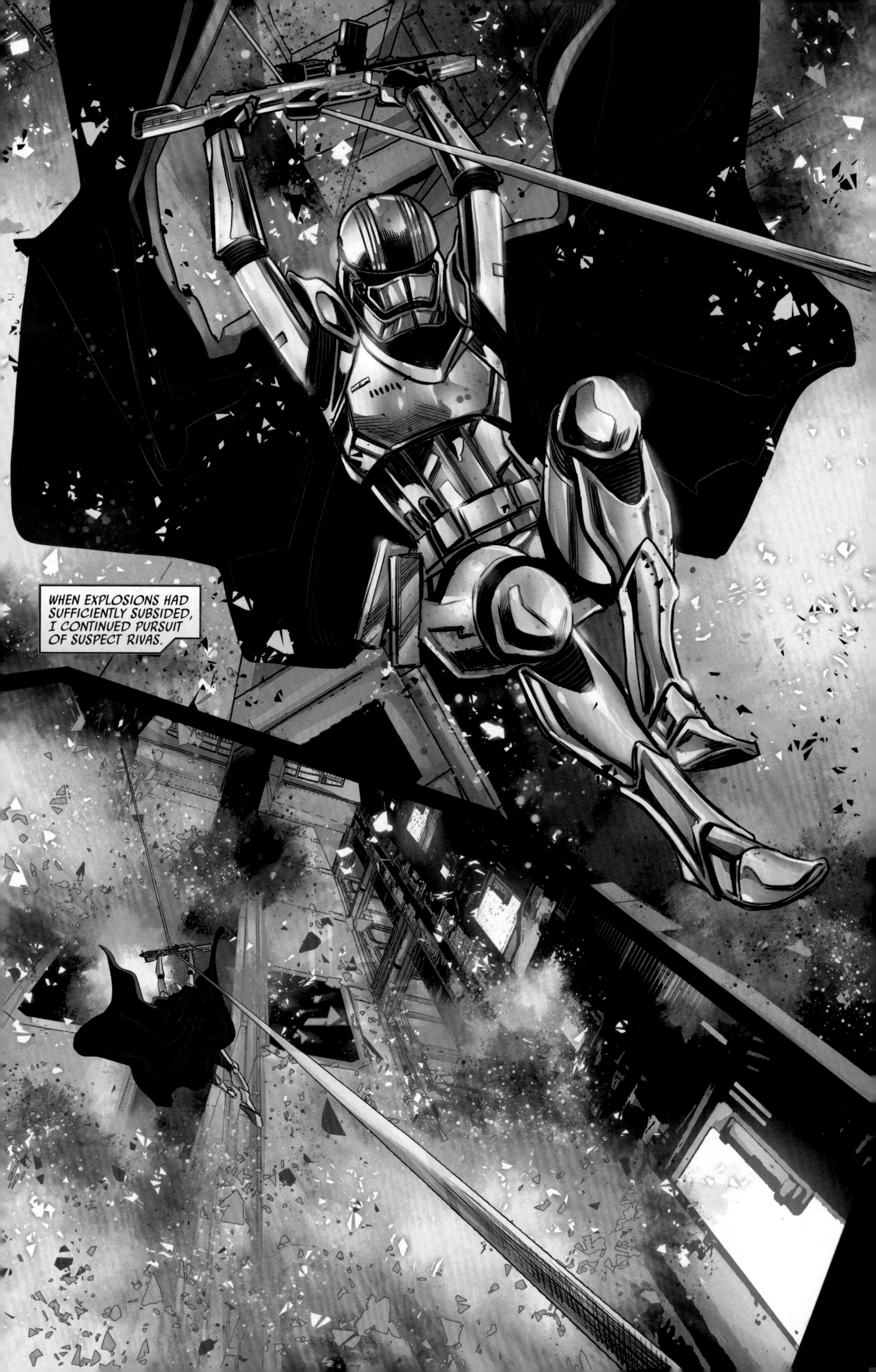
WHEN EXPLOSIONS HAD SUFFICIENTLY SUBSIDED, I CONTINUED PURSUIT OF SUSPECT RIVAS.

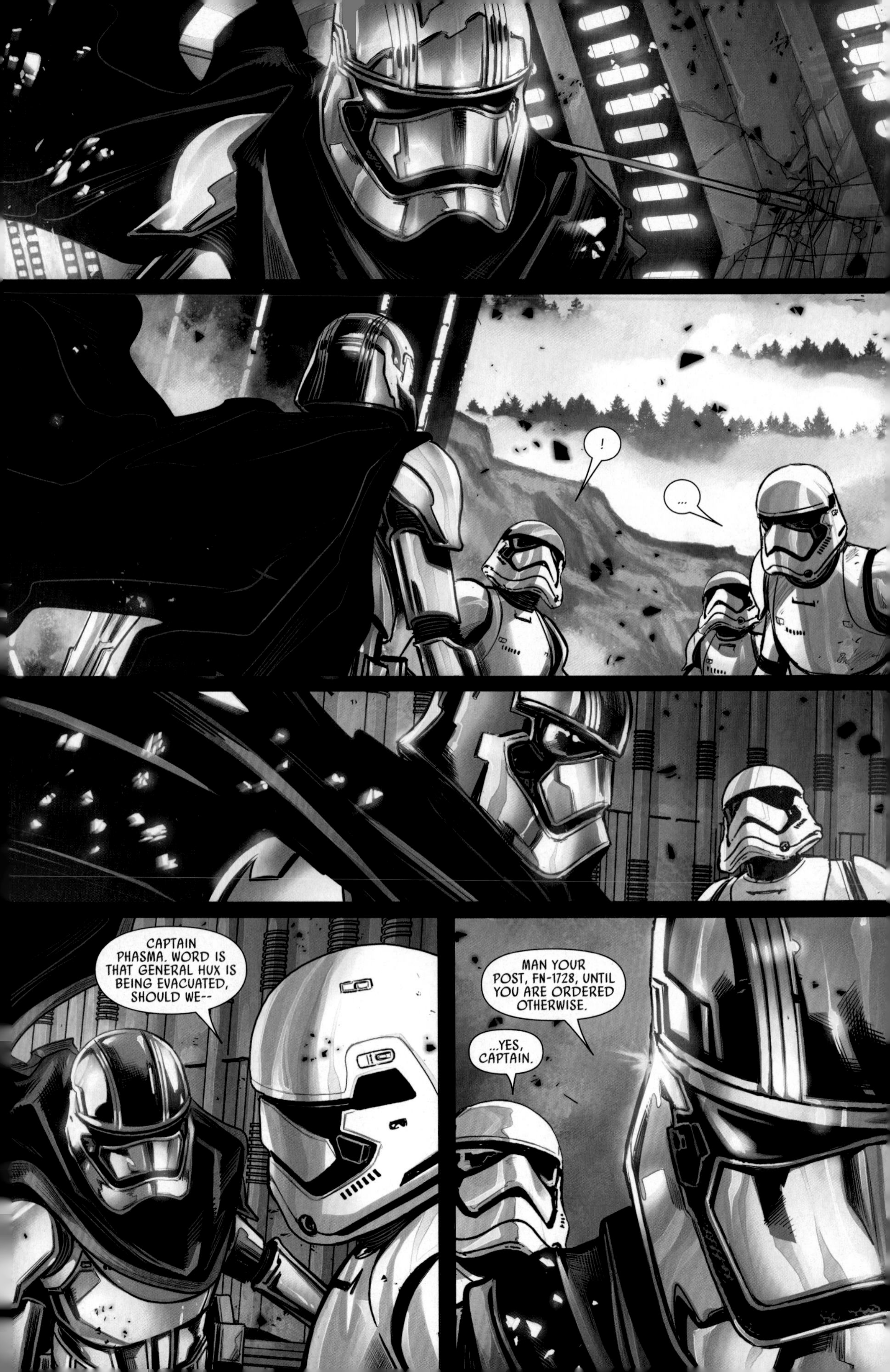
!
...
CAPTAIN PHASMA. WORD IS THAT GENERAL HUX IS BEING EVACUATED, SHOULD WE--
MAN YOUR POST, FN-1728, UNTIL YOU ARE ORDERED OTHERWISE.
...YES, CAPTAIN.

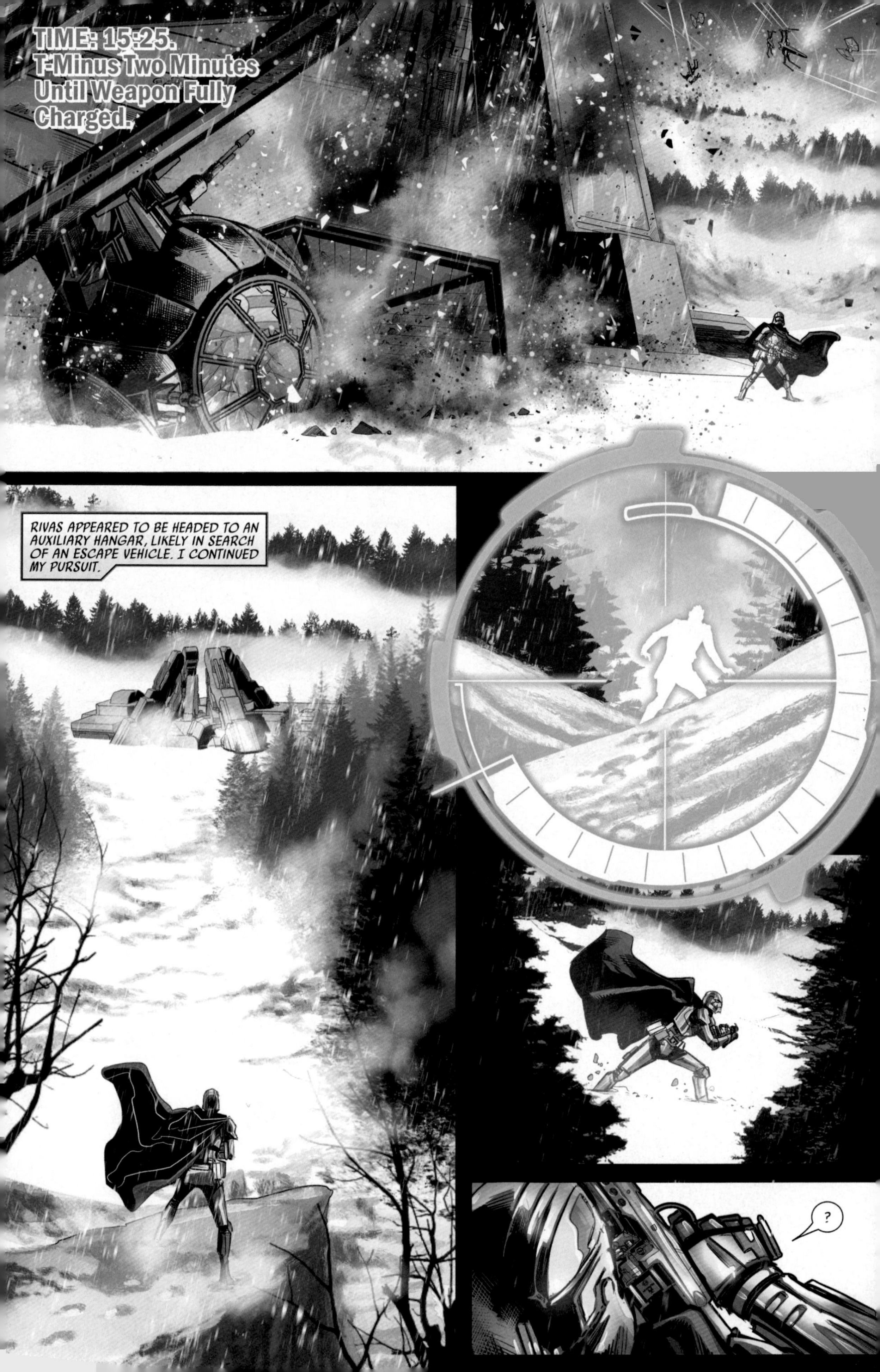
TIME: 15:25.
T-Minus Two Minutes Until Weapon Fully Charged.
RIVAS APPEARED TO BE HEADED TO AN AUXILIARY HANGAR, LIKELY IN SEARCH OF AN ESCAPE VEHICLE. I CONTINUED MY PURSUIT.
?

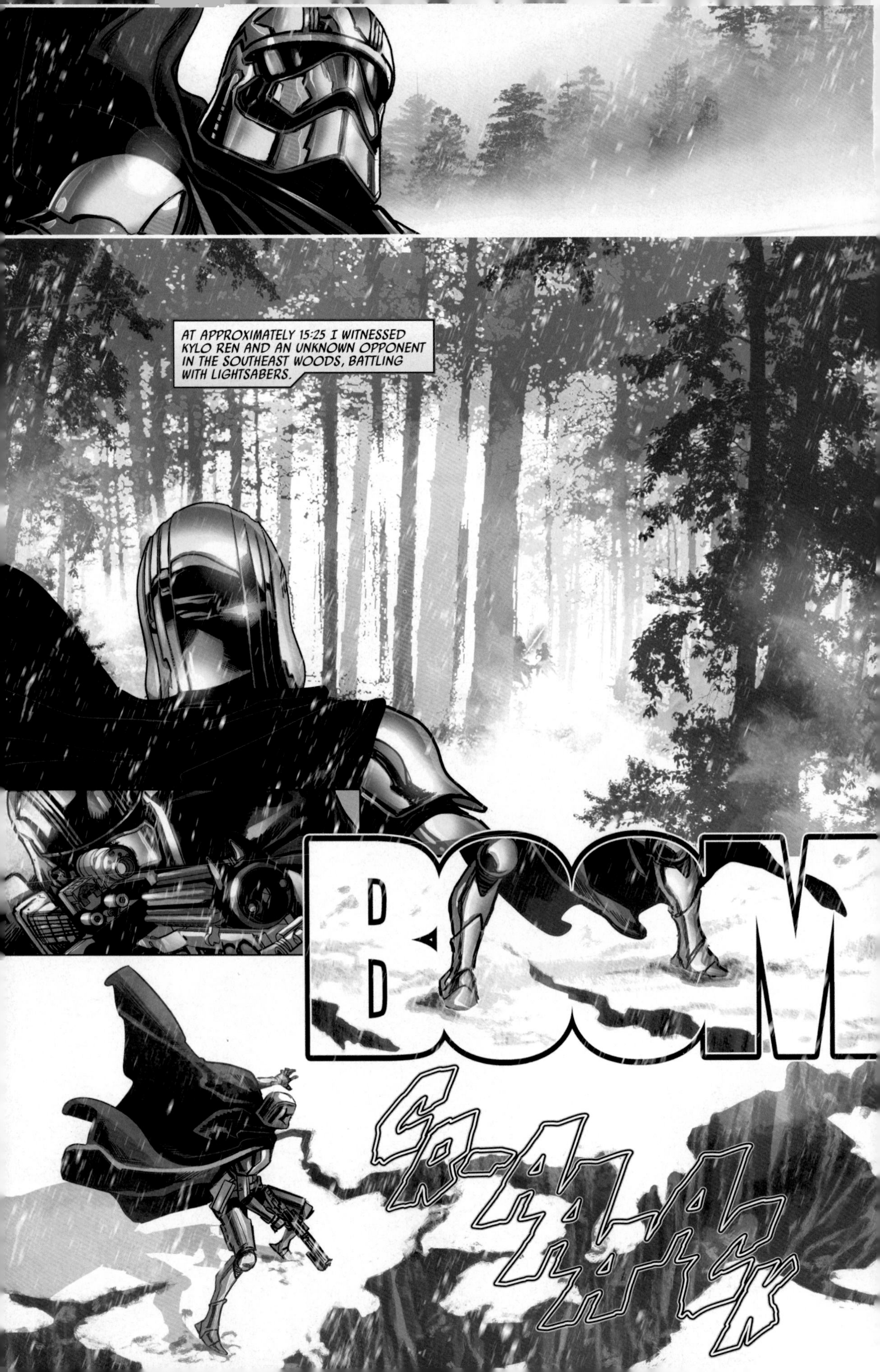
AT APPROXIMATELY 15:25 I WITNESSED KYLO REN AND AN UNKNOWN OPPONENT IN THE SOUTHEAST WOODS, BATTLING WITH LIGHTSABERS.
BOOM

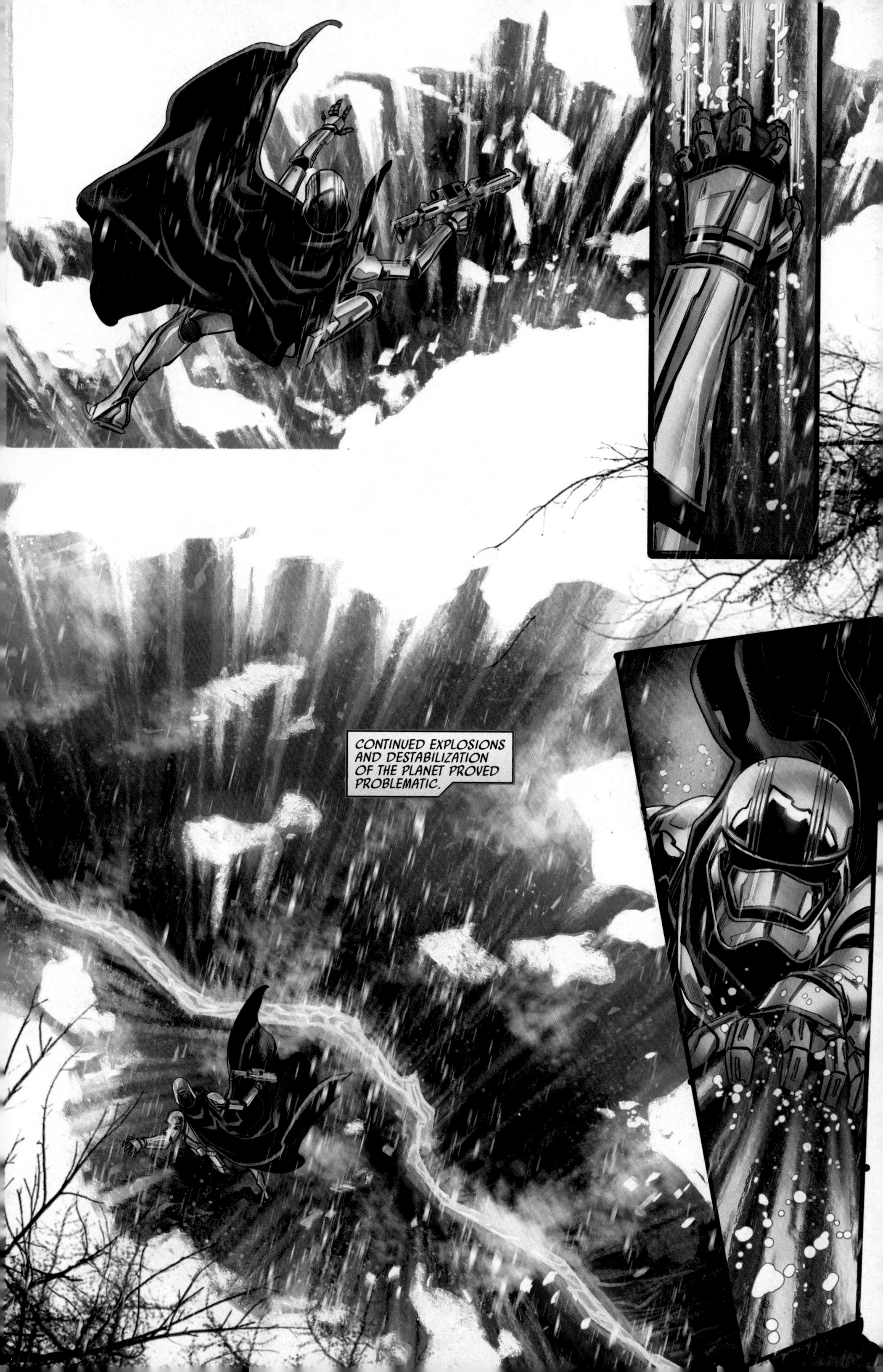
CONTINUED EXPLOSIONS AND DESTABILIZATION OF THE PLANET PROVED PROBLEMATIC.

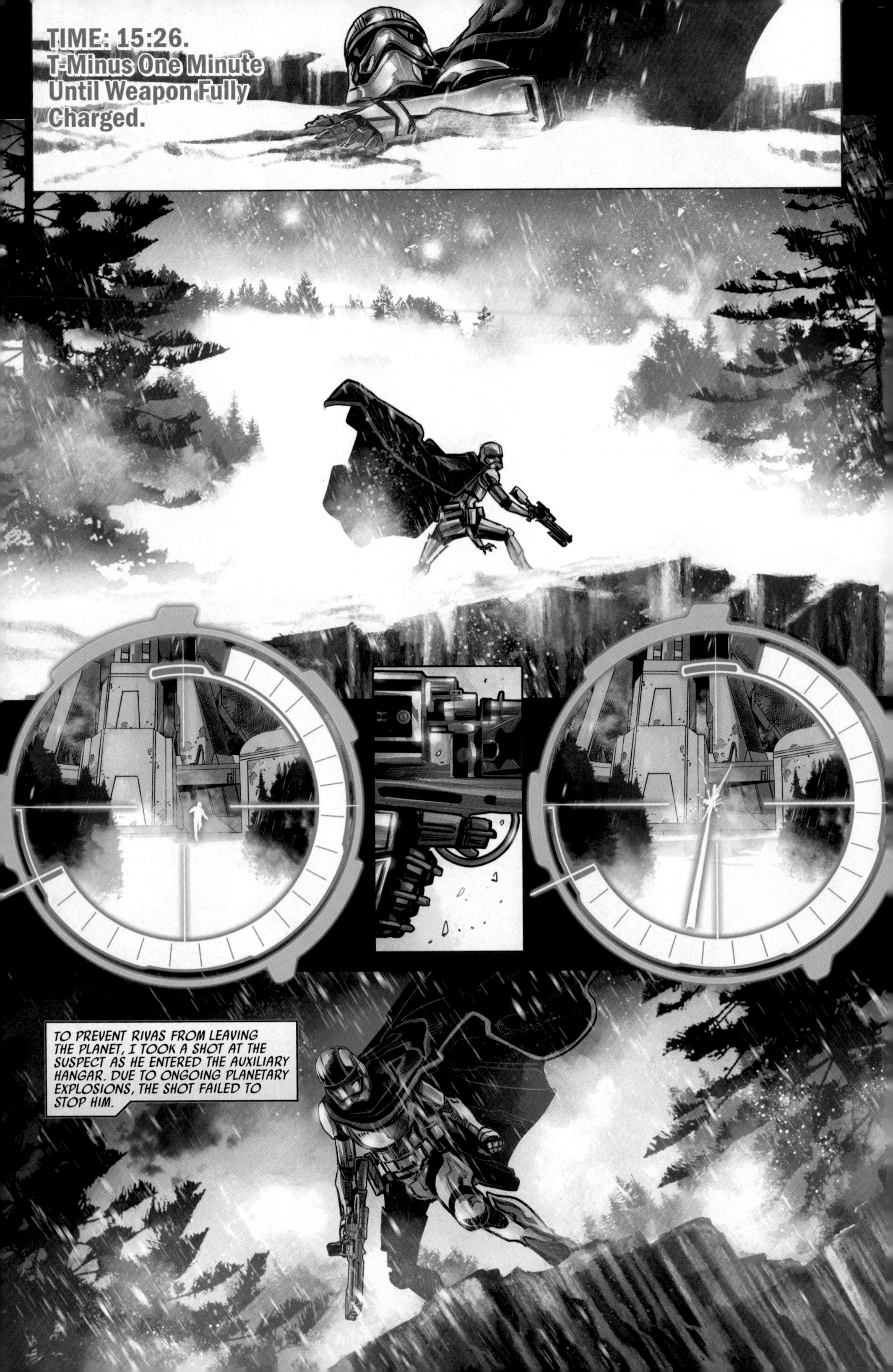
TIME: 15:26.
T-Minus One Minute Until Weapon Fully Charged.
TO PREVENT RIVAS FROM LEAVING THE PLANET, I TOOK A SHOT AT THE SUSPECT AS HE ENTERED THE AUXILIARY HANGAR. DUE TO ONGOING PLANETARY EXPLOSIONS, THE SHOT FAILED TO STOP HIM.

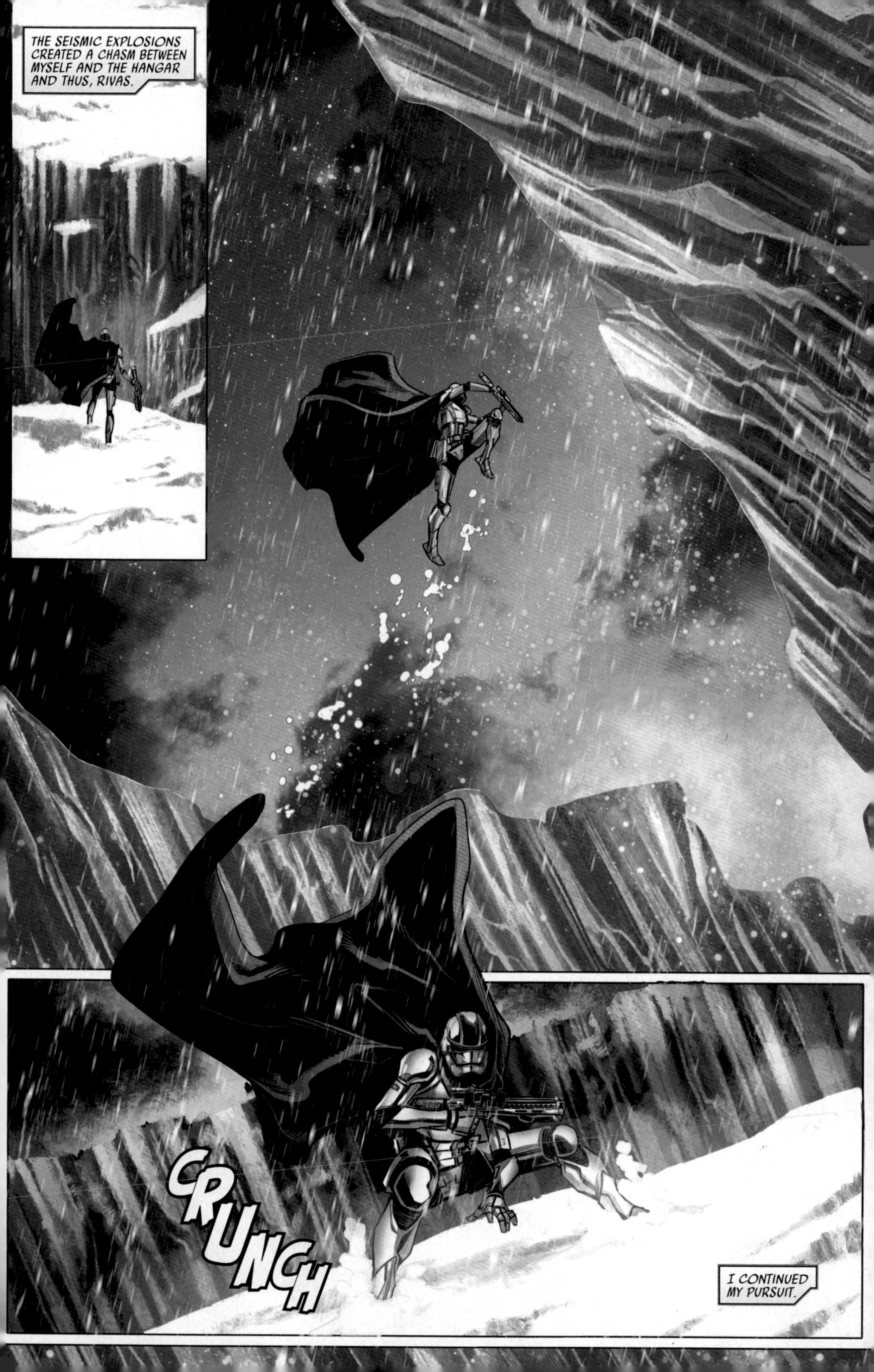
THE SEISMIC EXPLOSIONS CREATED A CHASM BETWEEN MYSELF AND THE HANGAR AND THUS, RIVAS.
CRUNCH
I CONTINUED MY PURSUIT.

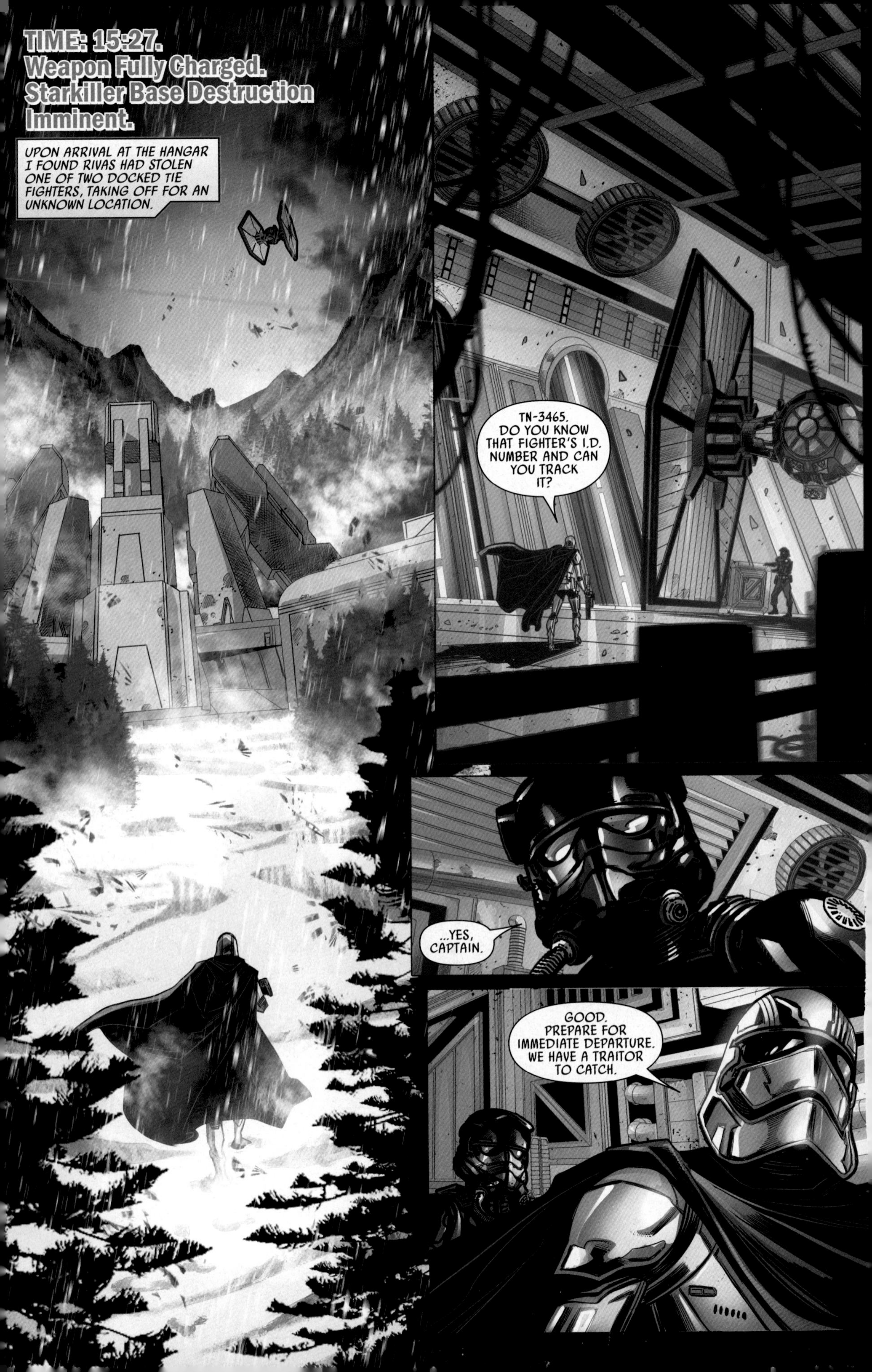
TIME: 15:27.
Weapon Fully Charged.
Starkiller Base Destruction Imminent.
UPON ARRIVAL AT THE HANGAR I FOUND RIVAS HAD STOLEN ONE OF TWO DOCKED TIE FIGHTERS, TAKING OFF FOR AN UNKNOWN LOCATION.
TN-3465. DO YOU KNOW THAT FIGHTER'S I.D. NUMBER AND CAN YOU TRACK IT?
...YES, CAPTAIN.
GOOD. PREPARE FOR IMMEDIATE DEPARTURE. WE HAVE A TRAITOR TO CATCH.

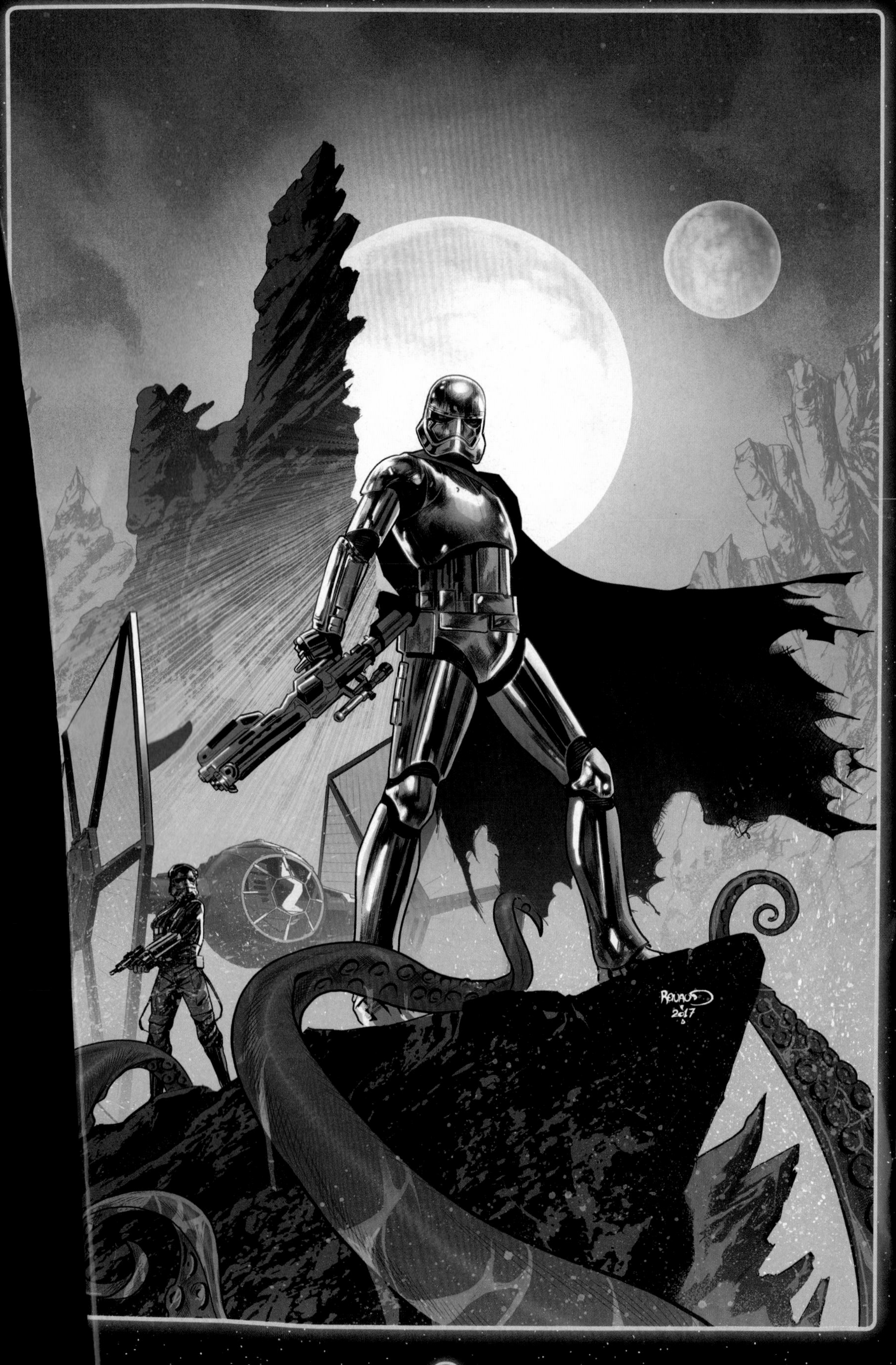

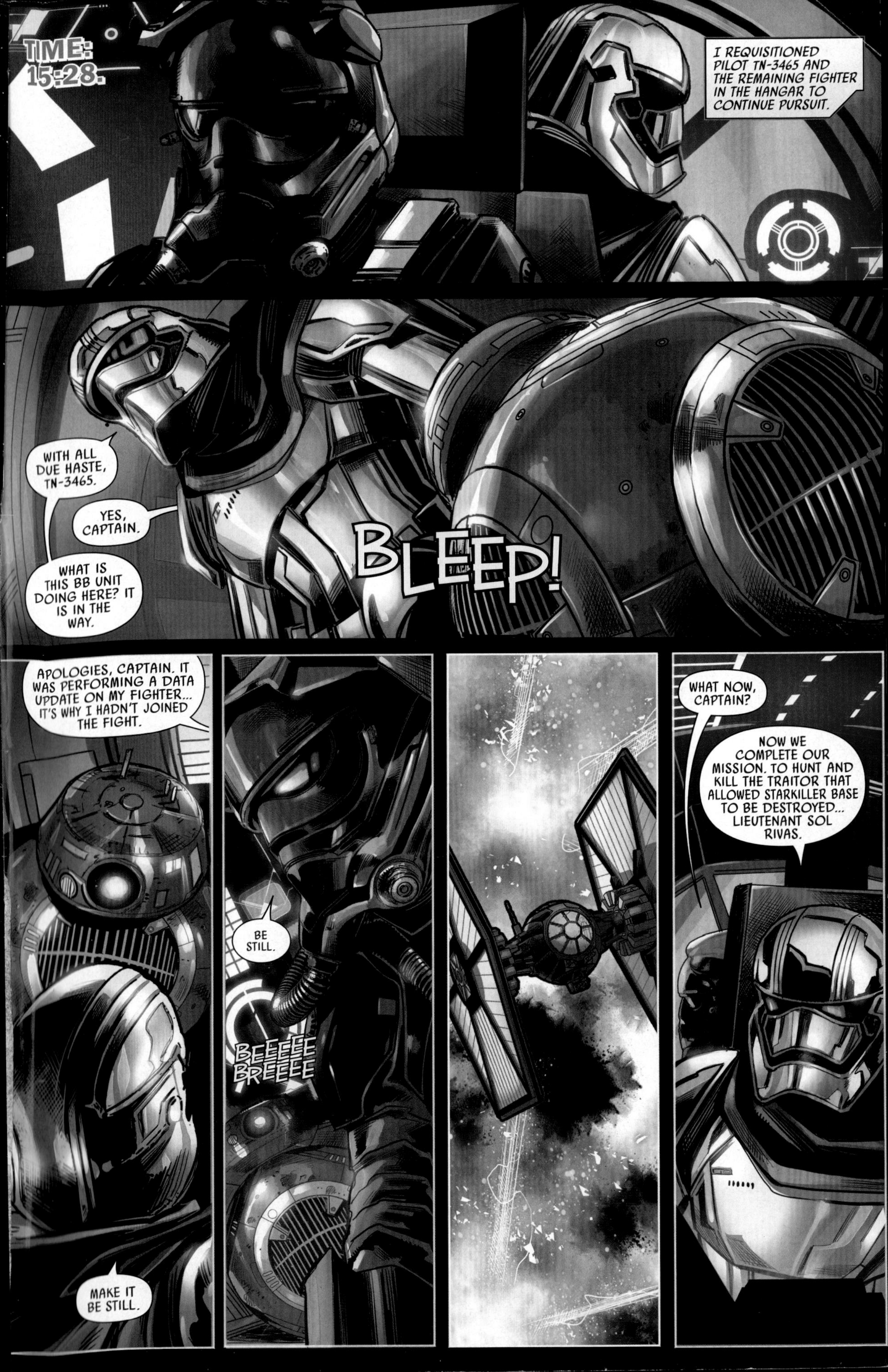
TIME: 15:28.
I REQUISITIONED PILOT TN-3465 AND THE REMAINING FIGHTER IN THE HANGAR TO CONTINUE PURSUIT.
WITH ALL DUE HASTE, TN-3465.
YES, CAPTAIN.
WHAT IS THIS BB UNIT DOING HERE? IT IS IN THE WAY.
BLEEP!
APOLOGIES, CAPTAIN. IT WAS PERFORMING A DATA UPDATE ON MY FIGHTER... IT'S WHY I HADN'T JOINED THE FIGHT.
MAKE IT BE STILL.
BE STILL.
BEEEEE BREEEE
WHAT NOW, CAPTAIN?
NOW WE COMPLETE OUR MISSION. TO HUNT AND KILL THE TRAITOR THAT ALLOWED STARKILLER BASE TO BE DESTROYED... LIEUTENANT SOL RIVAS.

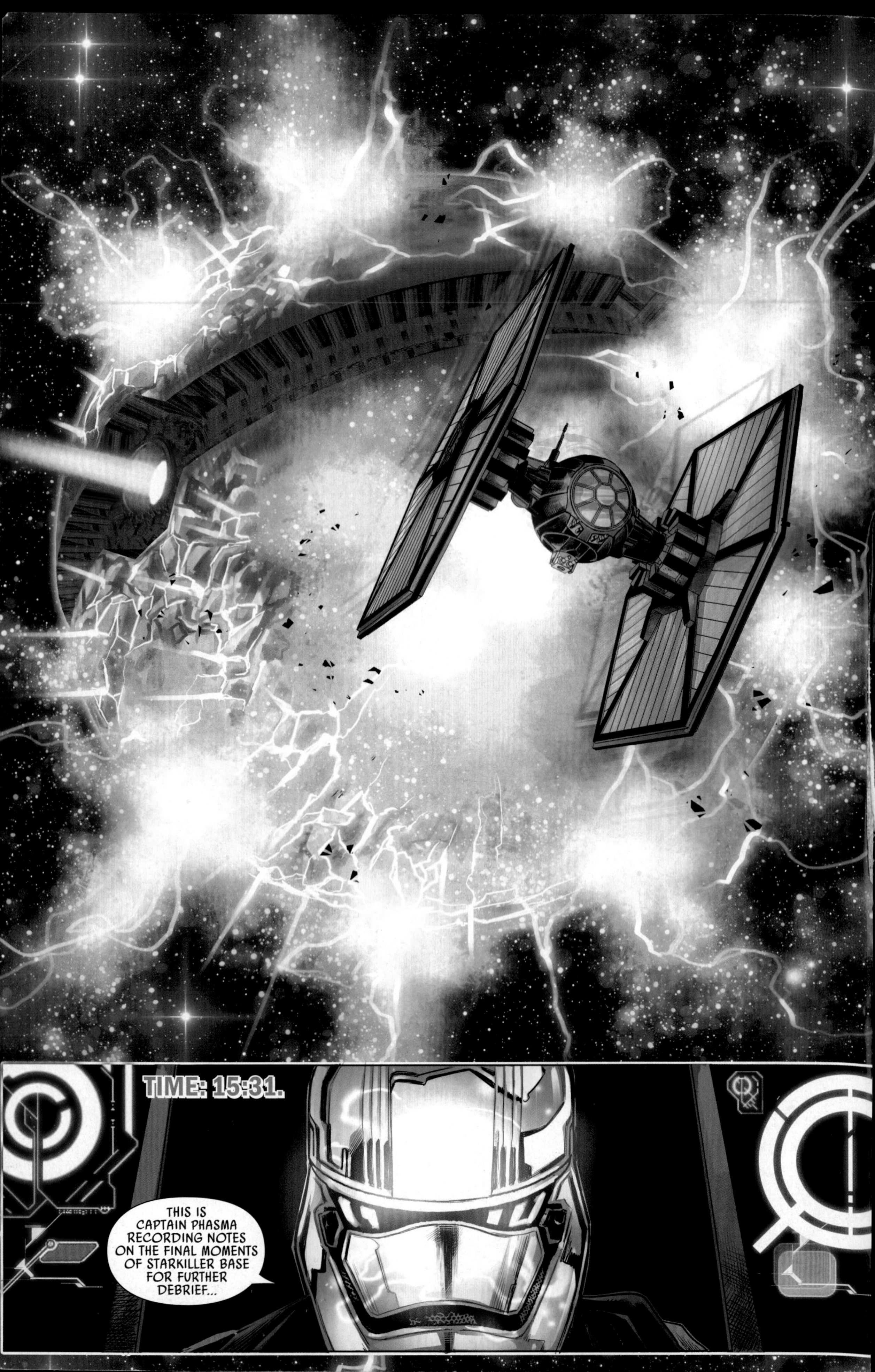
TIME: 15:31.
THIS IS CAPTAIN PHASMA RECORDING NOTES ON THE FINAL MOMENTS OF STARKILLER BASE FOR FURTHER DEBRIEF...

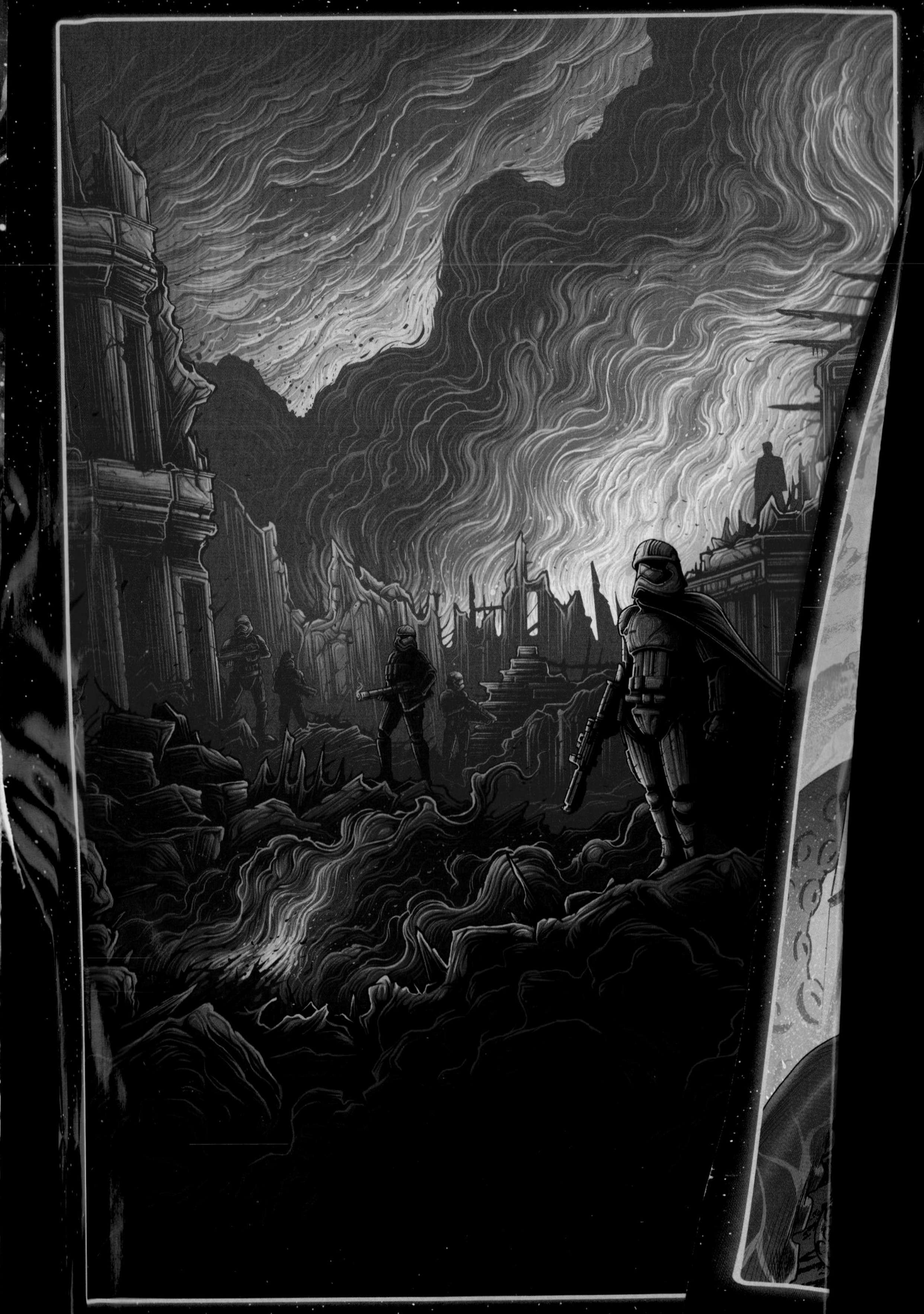

#2 Movie Variant

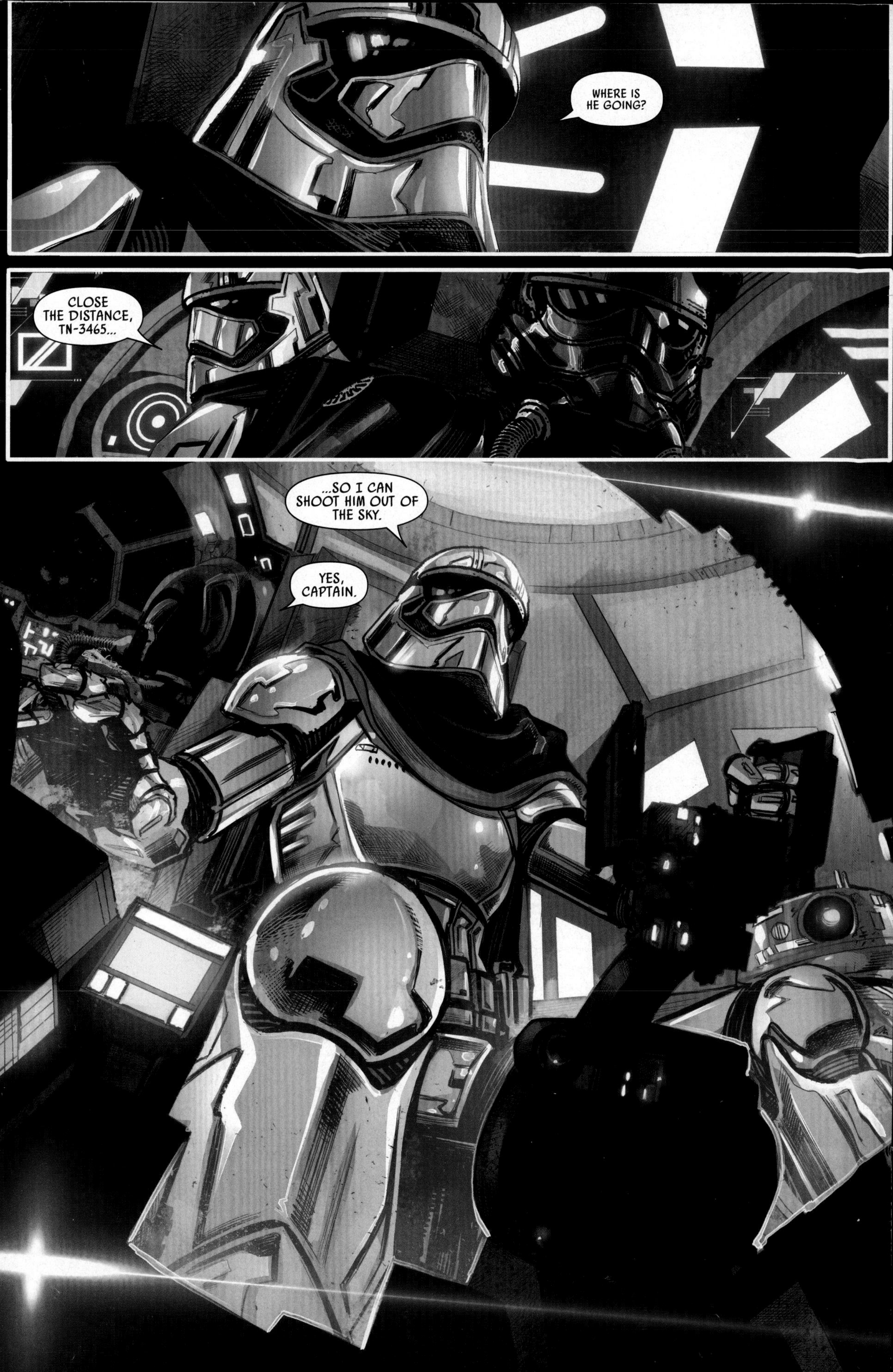
WHERE IS HE GOING?
CLOSE THE DISTANCE, TN-3465...
...SO I CAN SHOOT HIM OUT OF THE SKY.
YES, CAPTAIN.

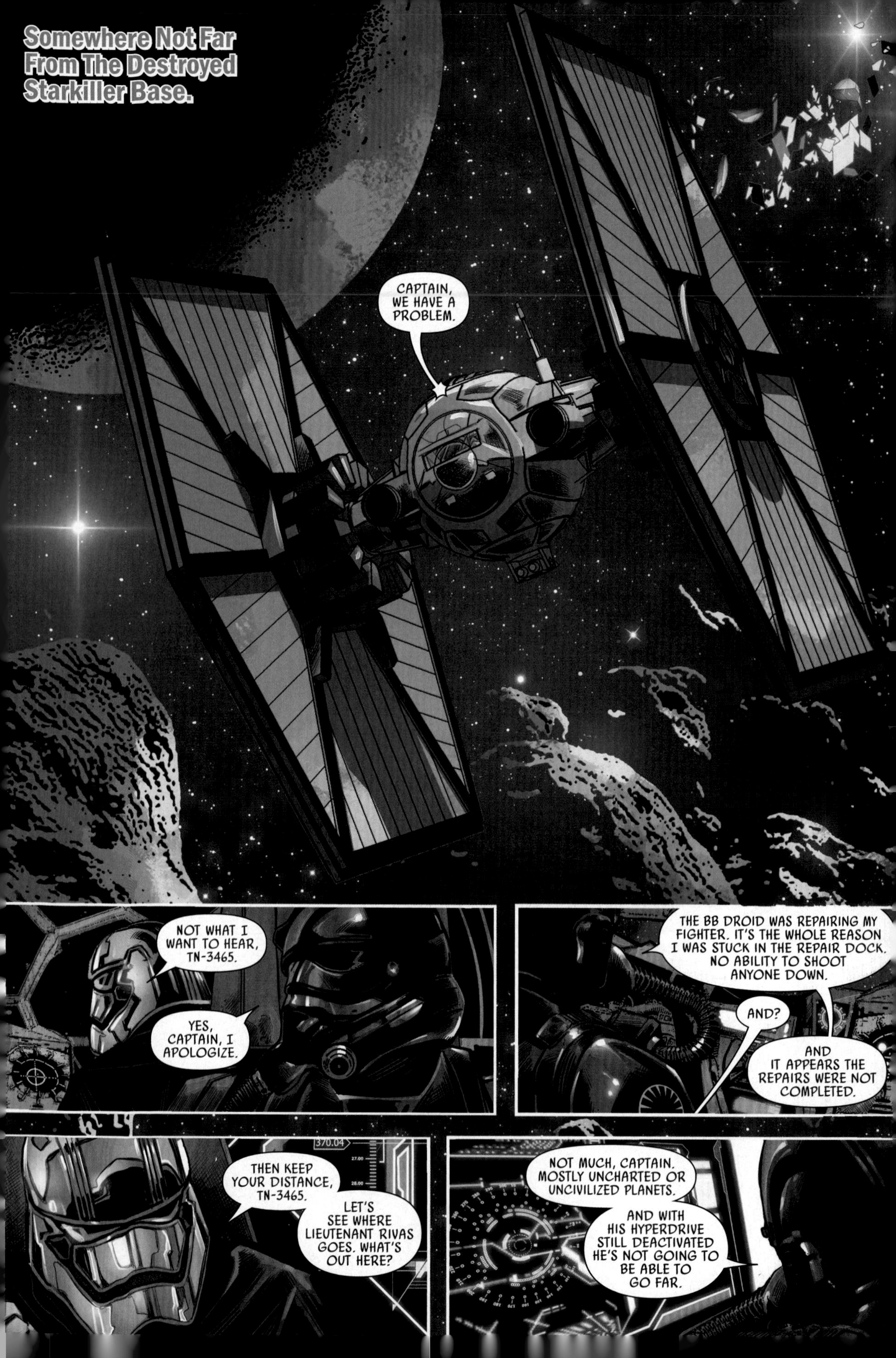
Somewhere Not Far From The Destroyed Starkiller Base.
CAPTAIN, WE HAVE A PROBLEM.
NOT WHAT I WANT TO HEAR, TN-3465.
YES, CAPTAIN, I APOLOGIZE.
THE BB DROID WAS REPAIRING MY FIGHTER. IT'S THE WHOLE REASON I WAS STUCK IN THE REPAIR DOCK. NO ABILITY TO SHOOT ANYONE DOWN.
AND?
AND IT APPEARS THE REPAIRS WERE NOT COMPLETED.
THEN KEEP YOUR DISTANCE, TN-3465.
LET'S SEE WHERE LIEUTENANT RIVAS GOES. WHAT'S OUT HERE?
NOT MUCH, CAPTAIN. MOSTLY UNCHARTED OR UNCIVILIZED PLANETS.
AND WITH HIS HYPERDRIVE STILL DEACTIVATED HE'S NOT GOING TO BE ABLE TO GO FAR.

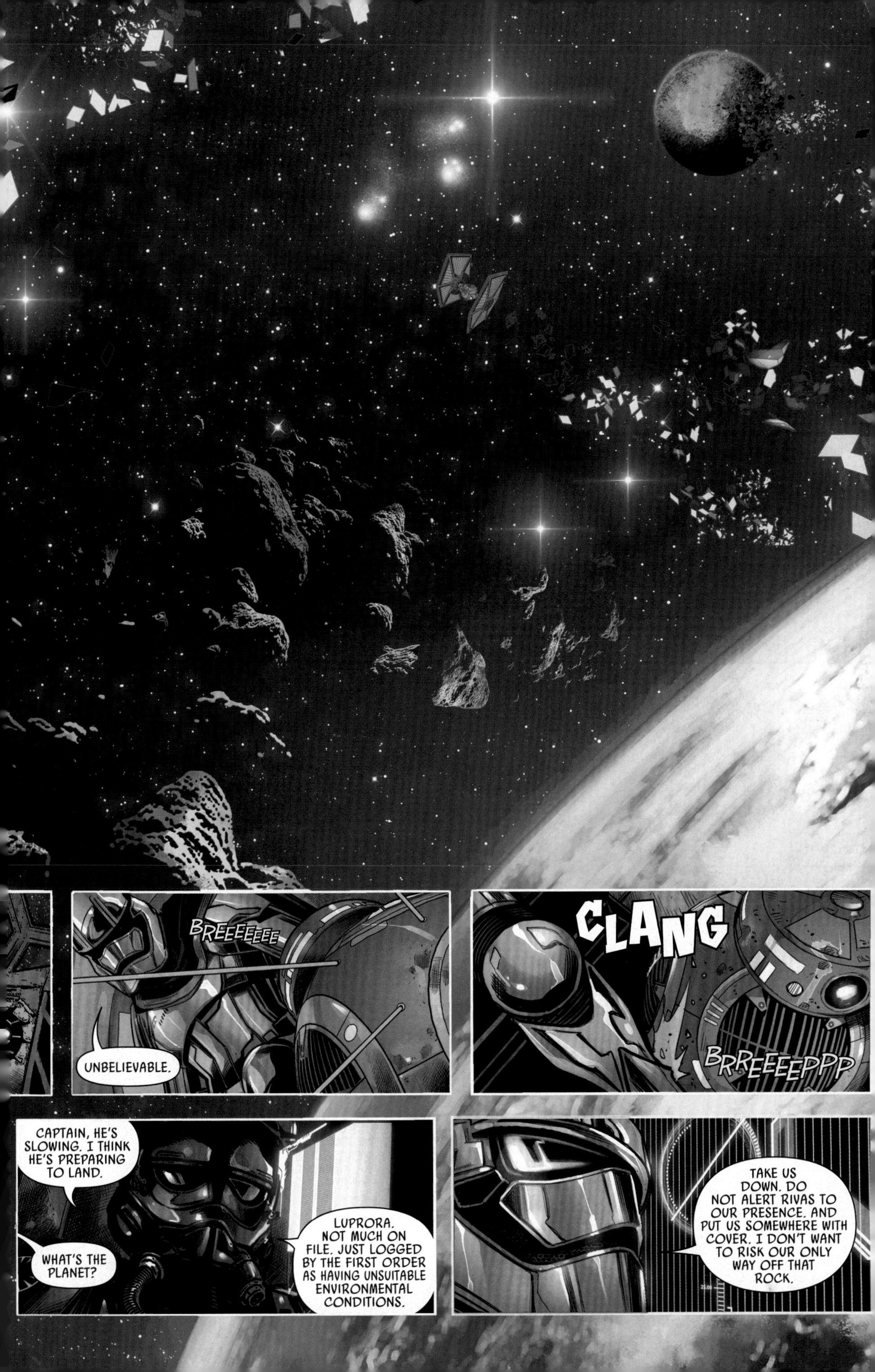
BREEEEEEE
UNBELIEVABLE.
CLANG
BRREEEEPPP
CAPTAIN, HE'S SLOWING. I THINK HE'S PREPARING TO LAND.
WHAT'S THE PLANET?
LUPRORA. NOT MUCH ON FILE. JUST LOGGED BY THE FIRST ORDER AS HAVING UNSUITABLE ENVIRONMENTAL CONDITIONS.
TAKE US DOWN. DO NOT ALERT RIVAS TO OUR PRESENCE. AND PUT US SOMEWHERE WITH COVER. I DON'T WANT TO RISK OUR ONLY WAY OFF THAT ROCK.

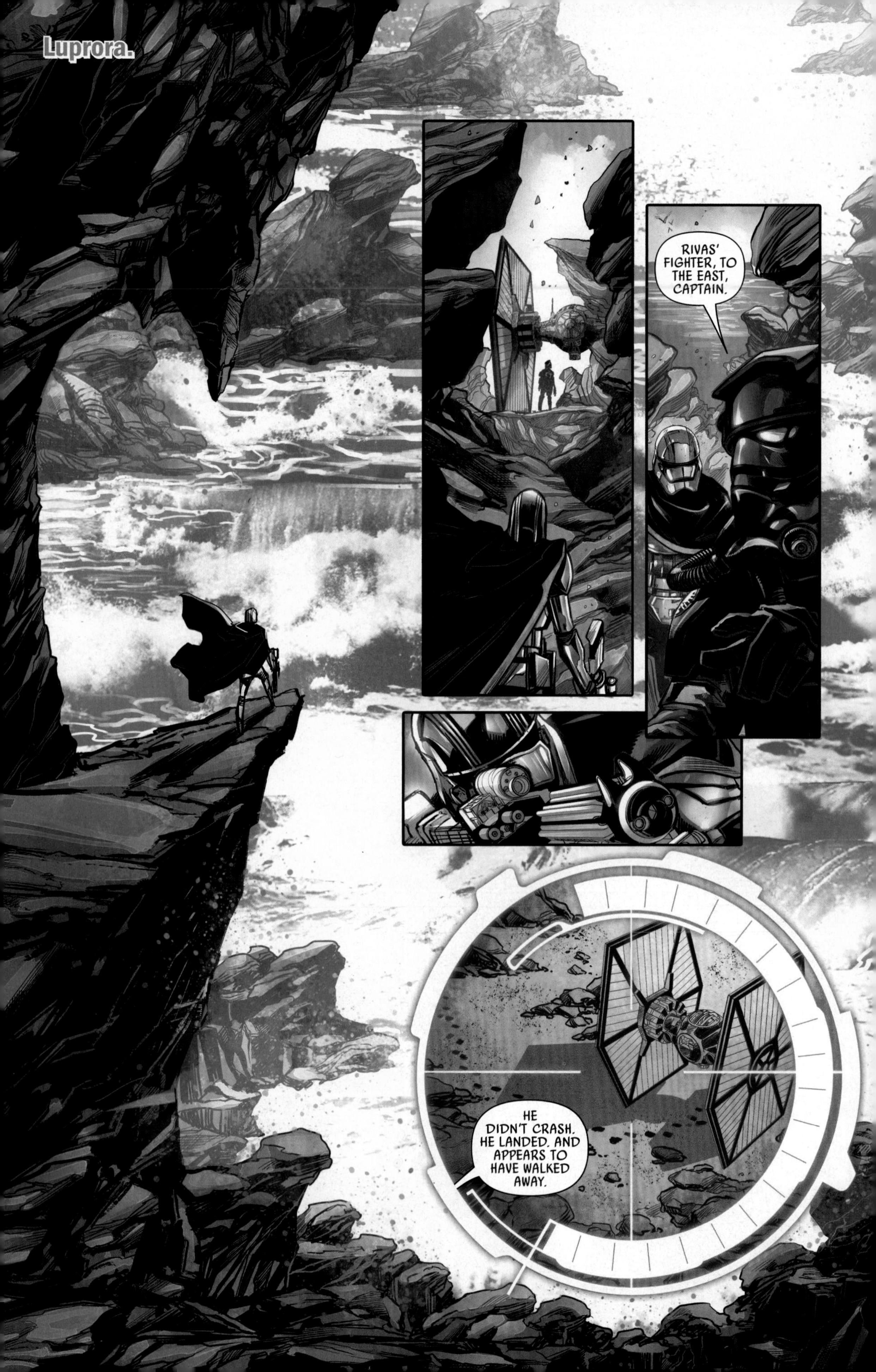
Luprora.
RIVAS' FIGHTER, TO THE EAST, CAPTAIN.
HE DIDN'T CRASH. HE LANDED. AND APPEARS TO HAVE WALKED AWAY.

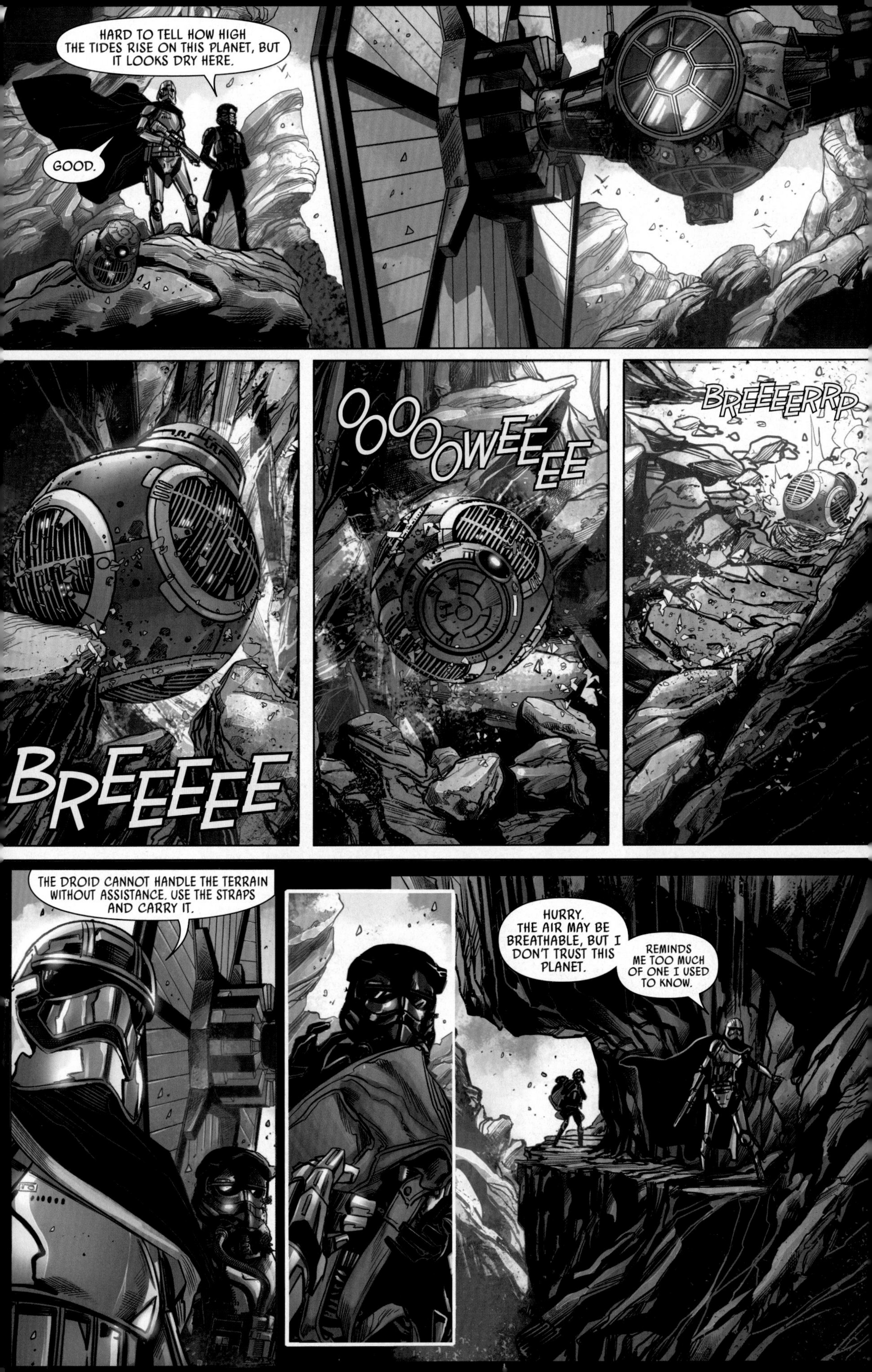
HARD TO TELL HOW HIGH THE TIDES RISE ON THIS PLANET, BUT IT LOOKS DRY HERE.
GOOD.
BREEEEE
OOOOOWEEEE
BREEEEERRP
THE DROID CANNOT HANDLE THE TERRAIN WITHOUT ASSISTANCE. USE THE STRAPS AND CARRY IT.
HURRY. THE AIR MAY BE BREATHABLE, BUT I DON'T TRUST THIS PLANET.
REMINDS ME TOO MUCH OF ONE I USED TO KNOW.

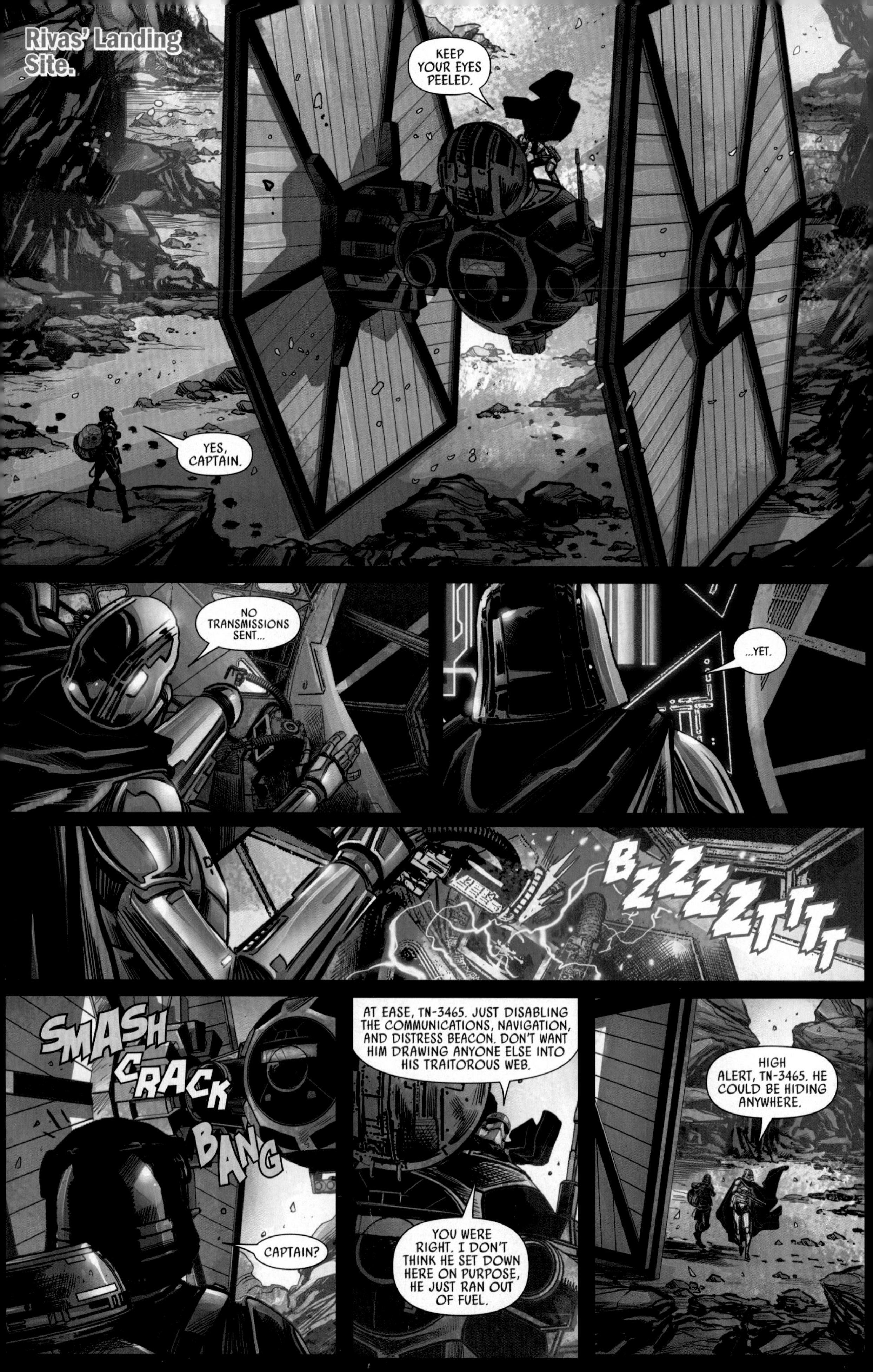
Rivas' Landing Site.
KEEP YOUR EYES PEELED.
YES, CAPTAIN.
NO TRANSMISSIONS SENT...
...YET.
BZZZZZTTTT
SMASH
CRACK
BANG
CAPTAIN?
AT EASE, TN-3465. JUST DISABLING THE COMMUNICATIONS, NAVIGATION, AND DISTRESS BEACON. DON'T WANT HIM DRAWING ANYONE ELSE INTO HIS TRAITOROUS WEB.
YOU WERE RIGHT. I DON'T THINK HE SET DOWN HERE ON PURPOSE, HE JUST RAN OUT OF FUEL.
HIGH ALERT, TN-3465. HE COULD BE HIDING ANYWHERE.

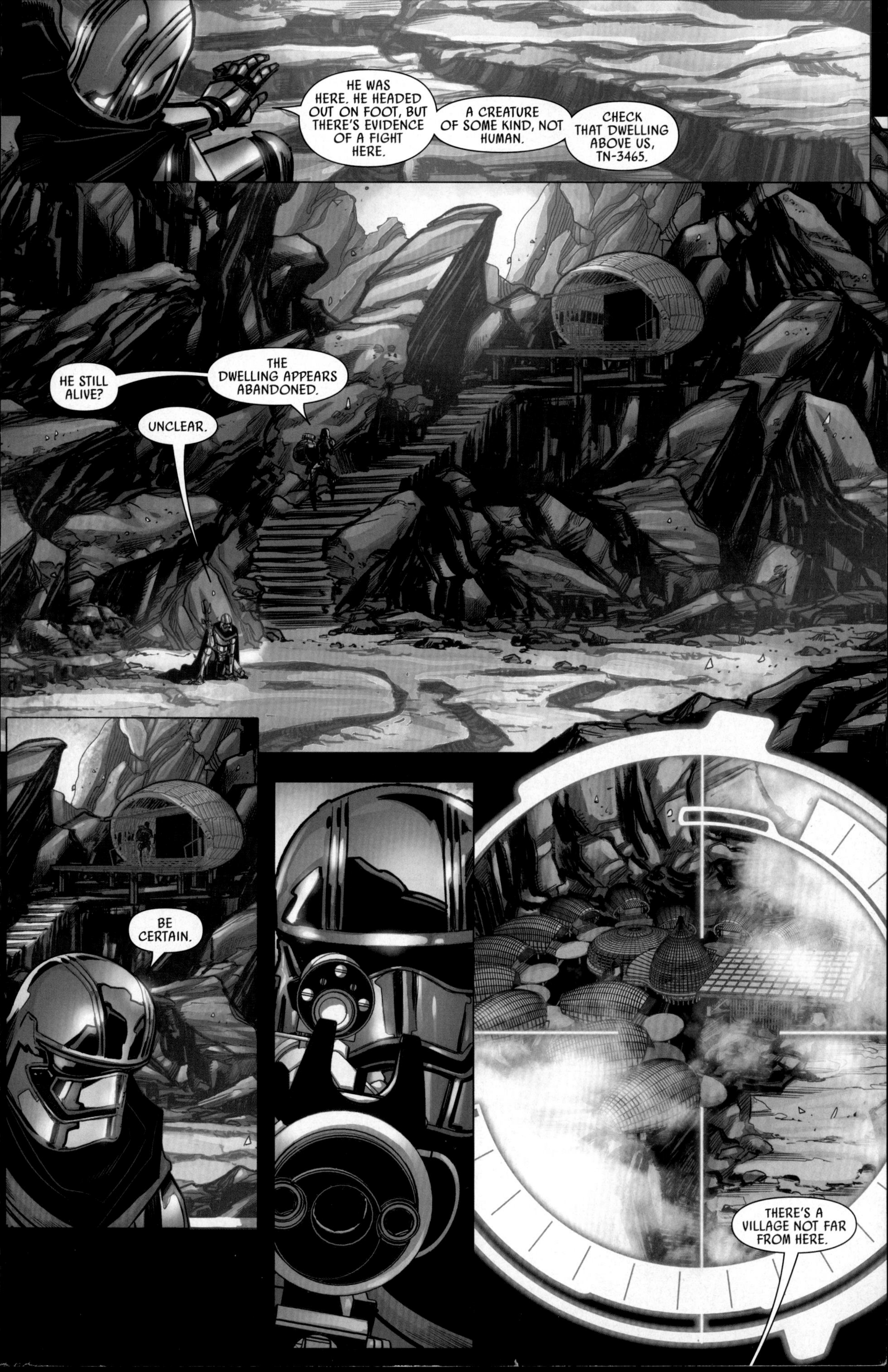
HE WAS HERE. HE HEADED OUT ON FOOT, BUT THERE'S EVIDENCE OF A FIGHT HERE.
A CREATURE OF SOME KIND, NOT HUMAN.
CHECK THAT DWELLING ABOVE US, TN-3465.
THE DWELLING APPEARS ABANDONED.
HE STILL ALIVE?
UNCLEAR.
BE CERTAIN.
THERE'S A VILLAGE NOT FAR FROM HERE.

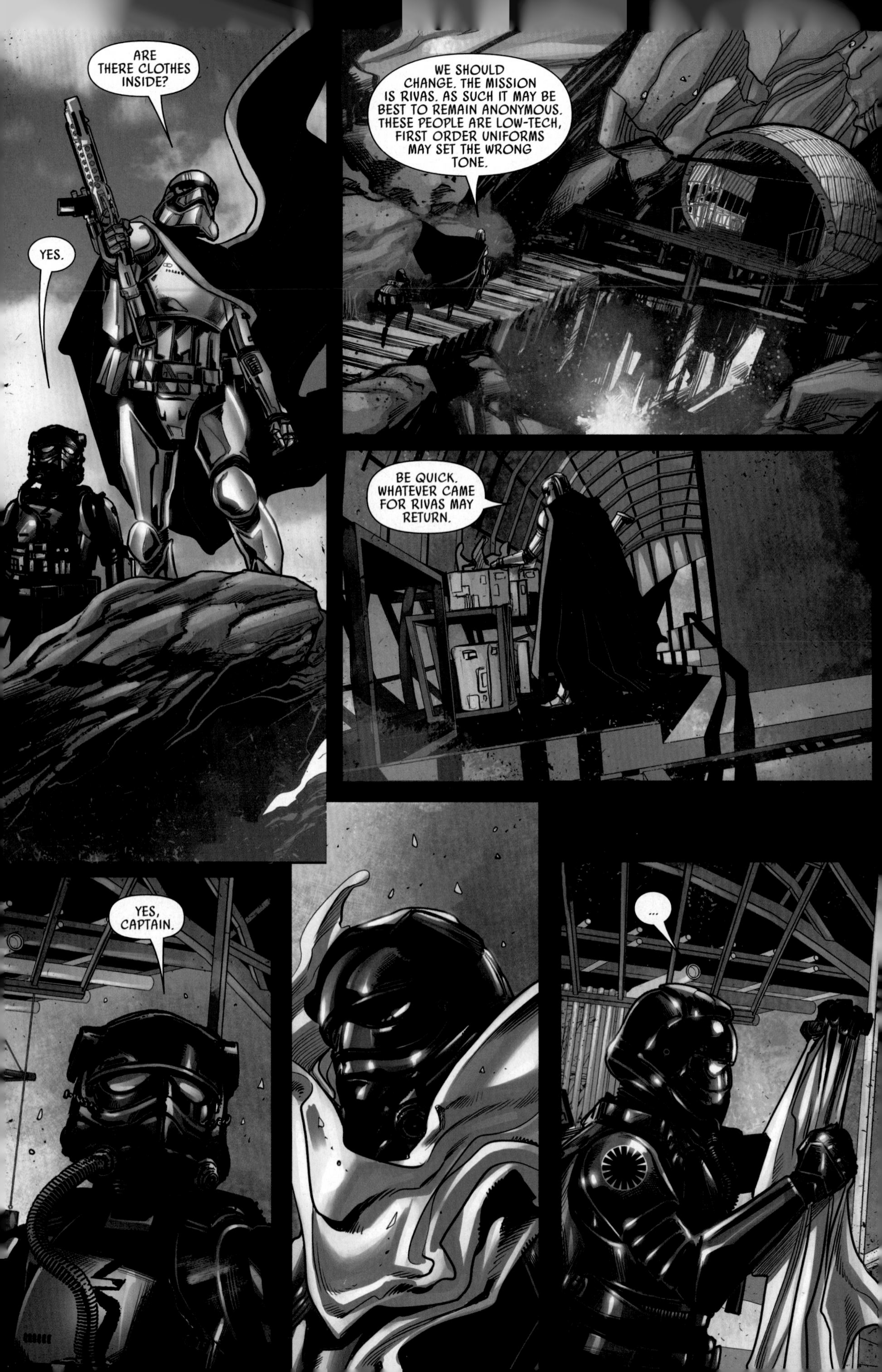
ARE THERE CLOTHES INSIDE?
YES.
WE SHOULD CHANGE. THE MISSION IS RIVAS. AS SUCH IT MAY BE BEST TO REMAIN ANONYMOUS. THESE PEOPLE ARE LOW-TECH, FIRST ORDER UNIFORMS MAY SET THE WRONG TONE.
BE QUICK. WHATEVER CAME FOR RIVAS MAY RETURN.
YES, CAPTAIN.
...

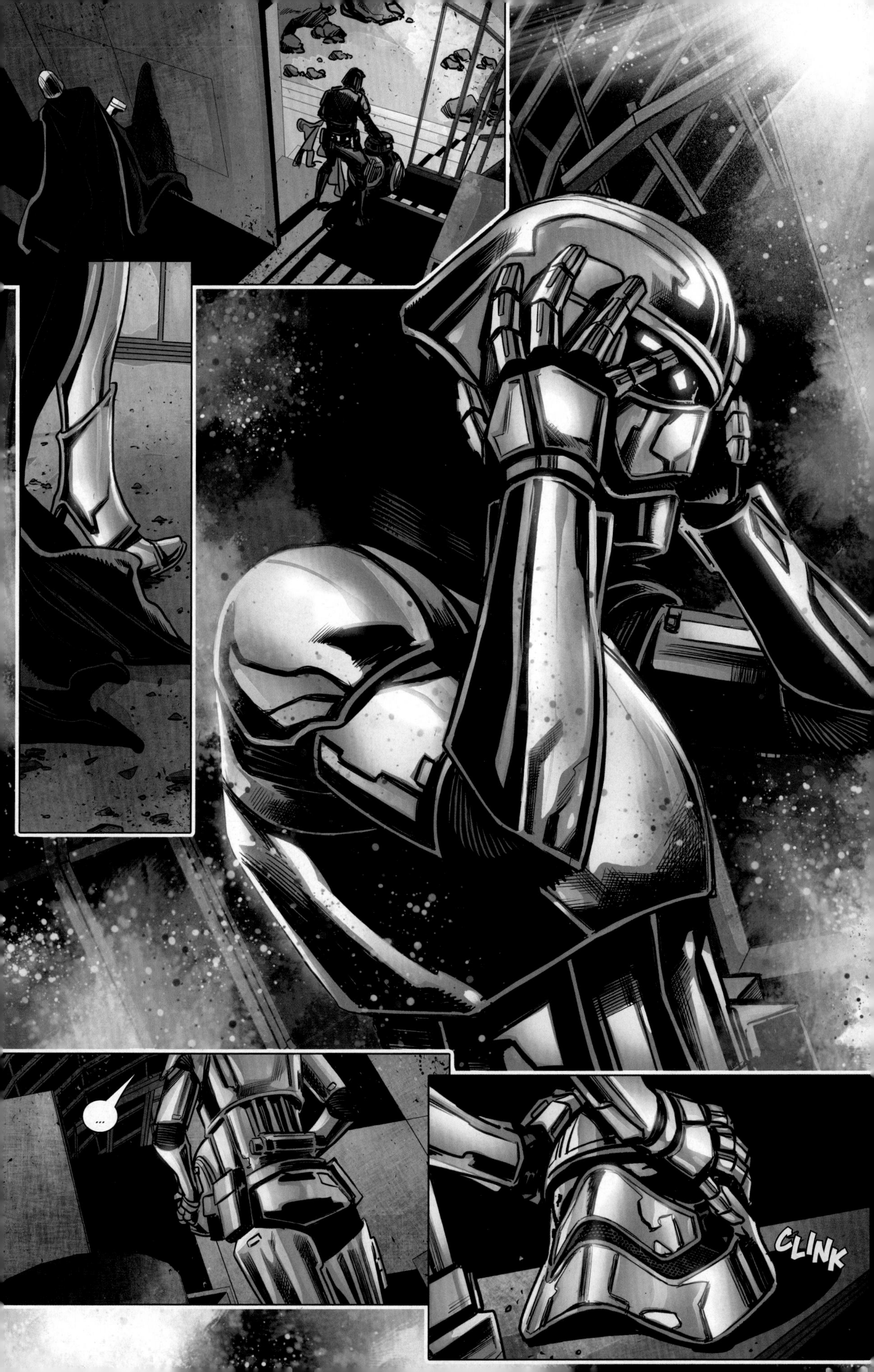
...
CLINK

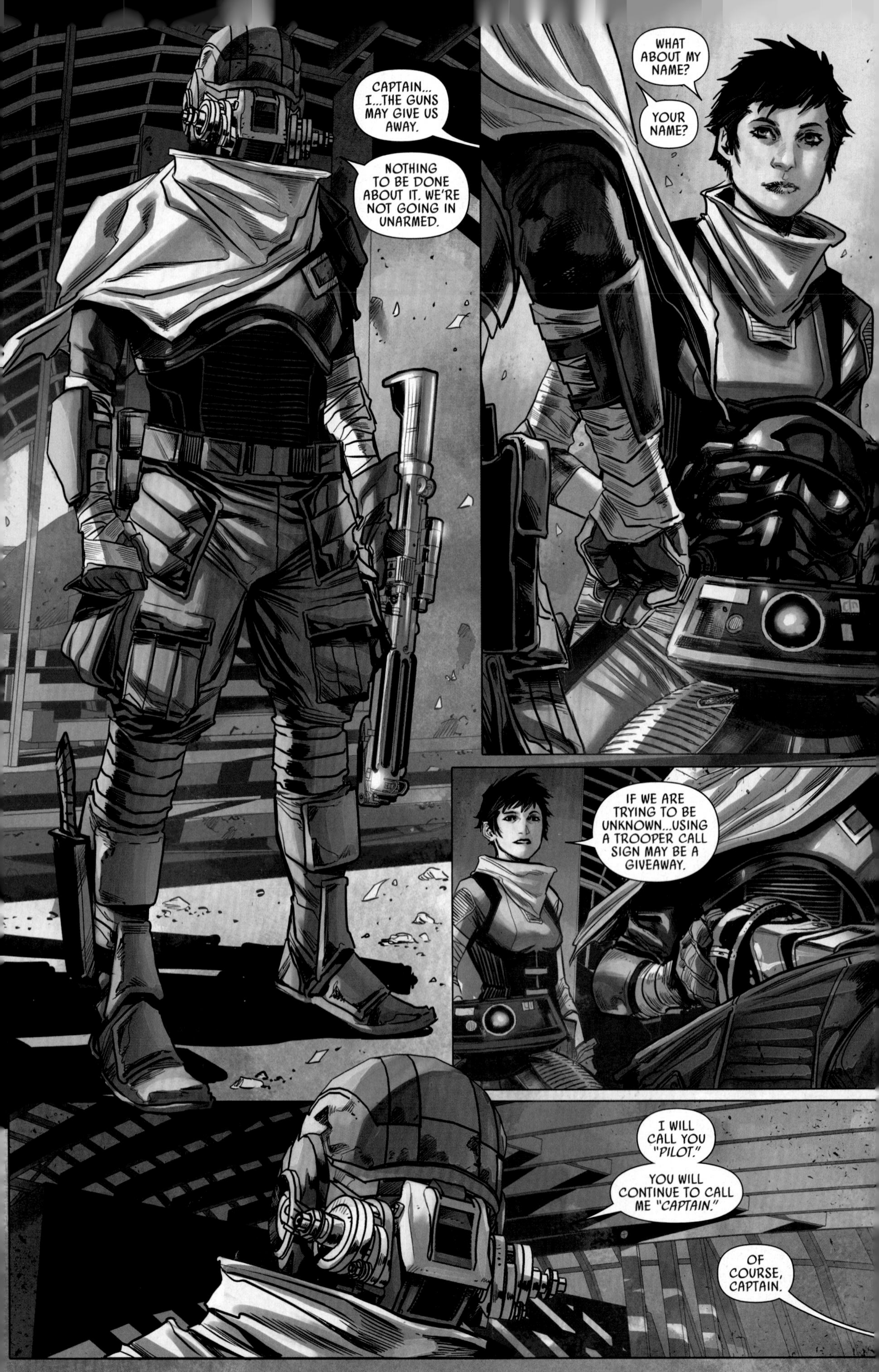
CAPTAIN... I...THE GUNS MAY GIVE US AWAY.
NOTHING TO BE DONE ABOUT IT. WE'RE NOT GOING IN UNARMED.
WHAT ABOUT MY NAME?
YOUR NAME?
IF WE ARE TRYING TO BE UNKNOWN...USING A TROOPER CALL SIGN MAY BE A GIVEAWAY.
I WILL CALL YOU "PILOT."
YOU WILL CONTINUE TO CALL ME "CAPTAIN."
OF COURSE, CAPTAIN.

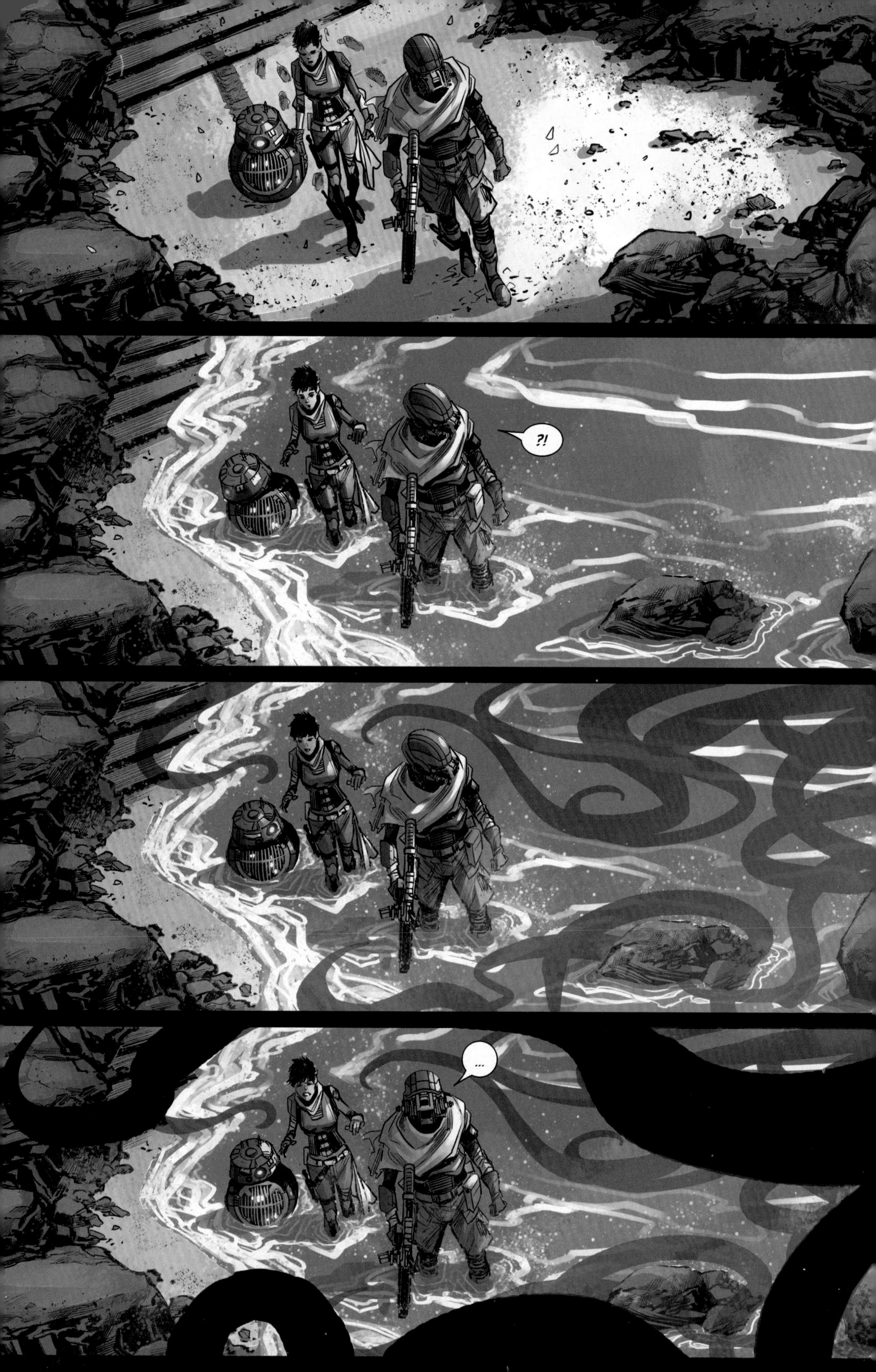
?!
...

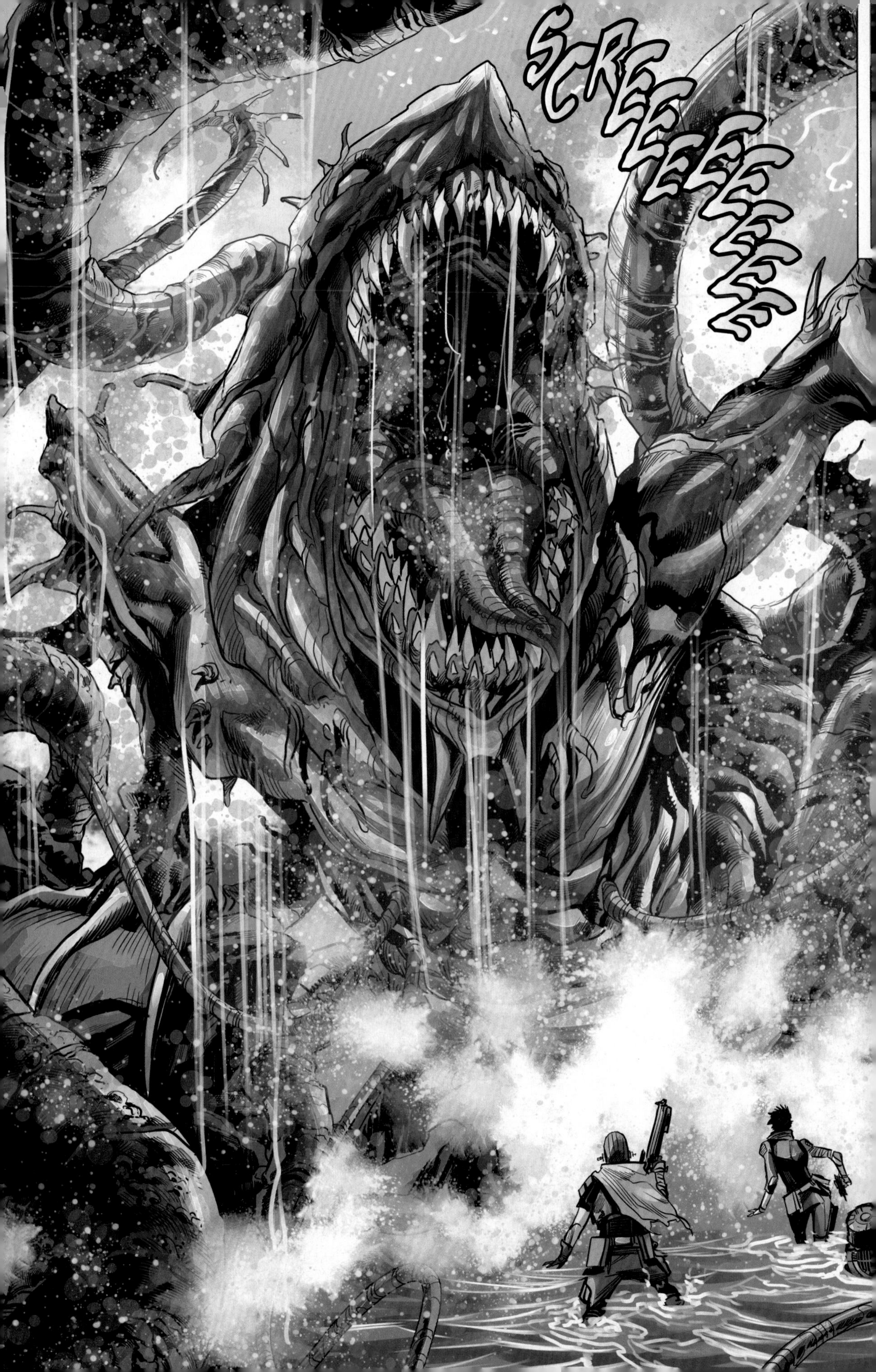
SCREEEEEEEEE

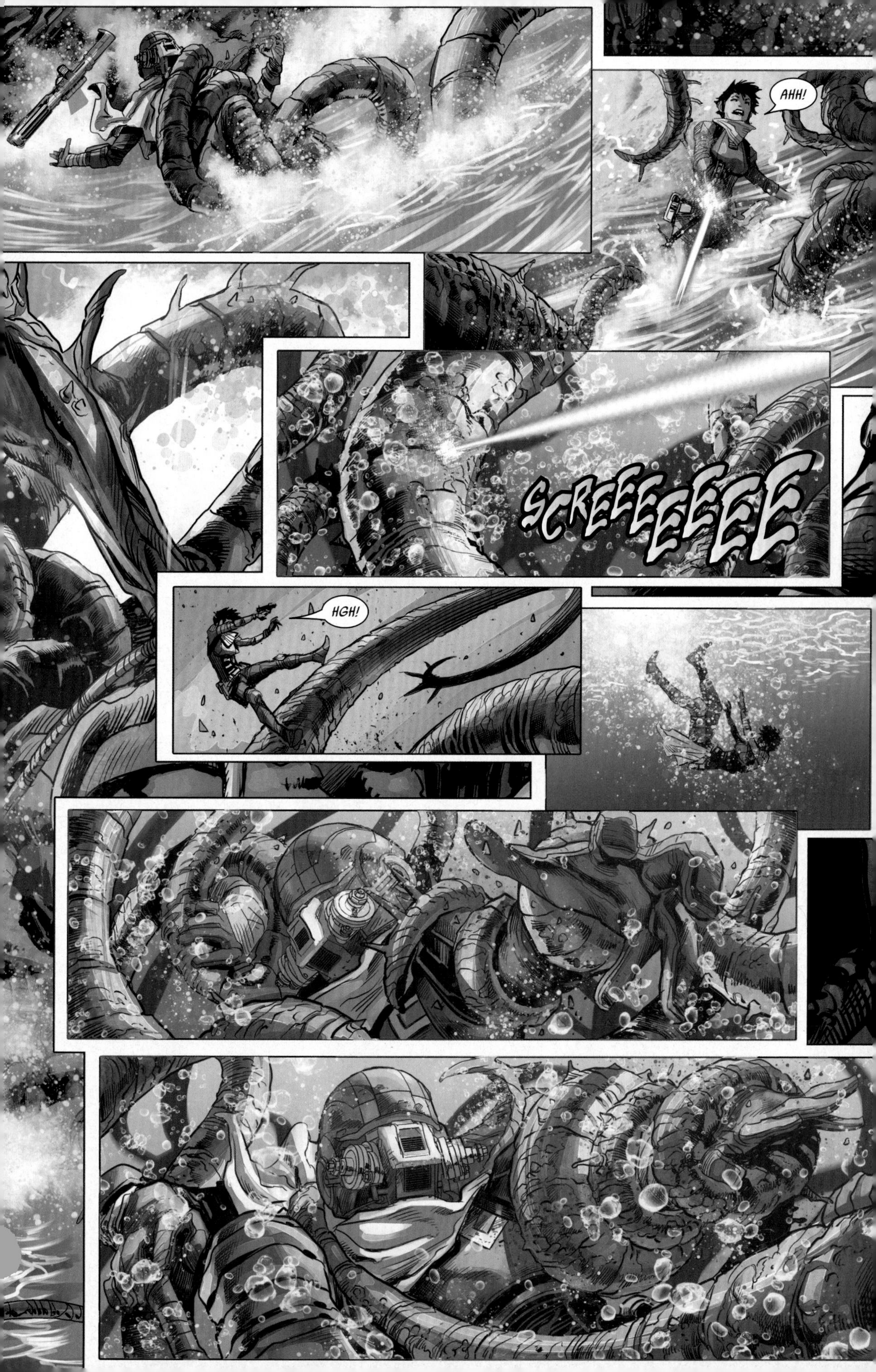
AHH!
SCREEEEEEEEE
HGH!

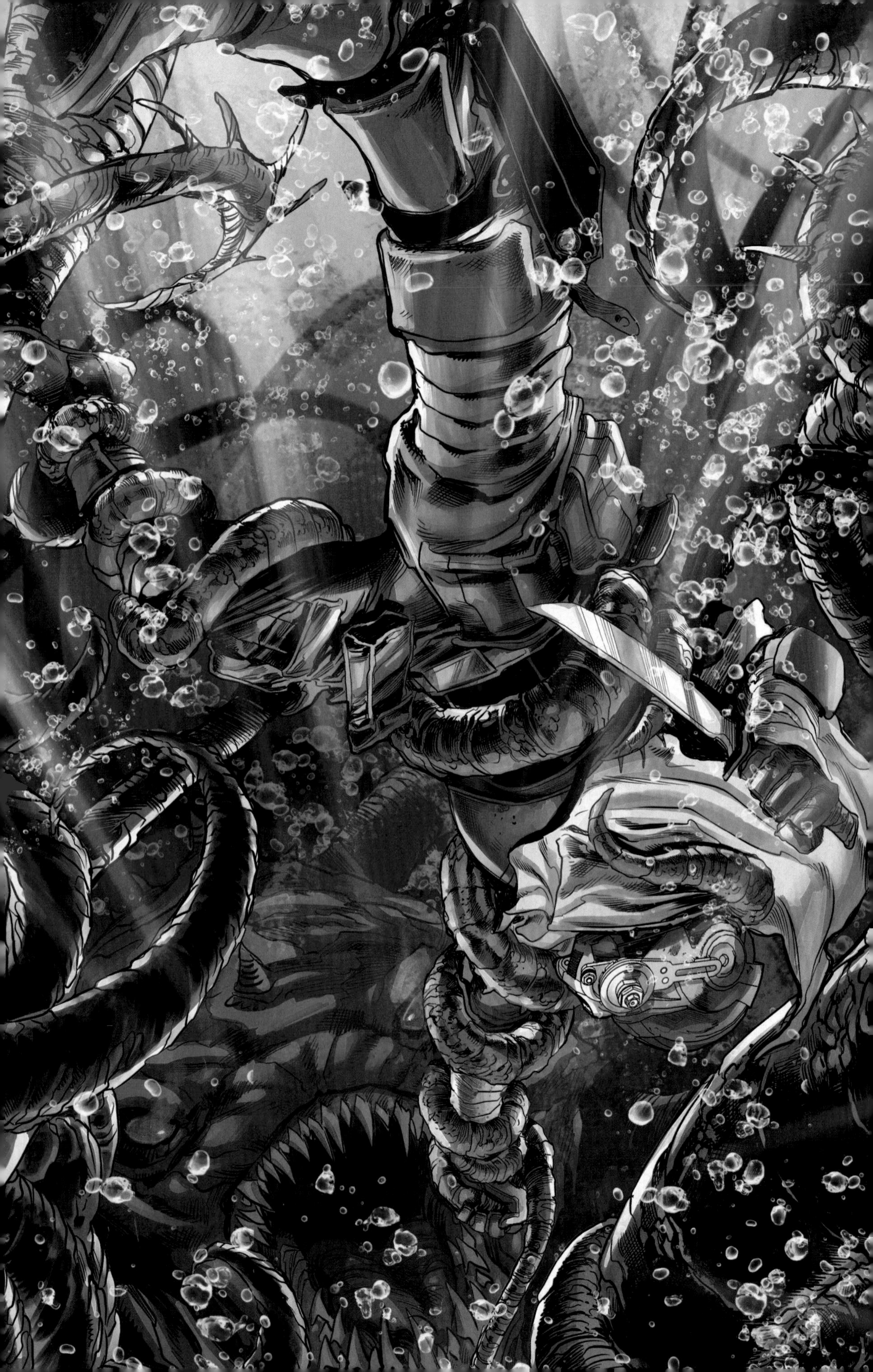

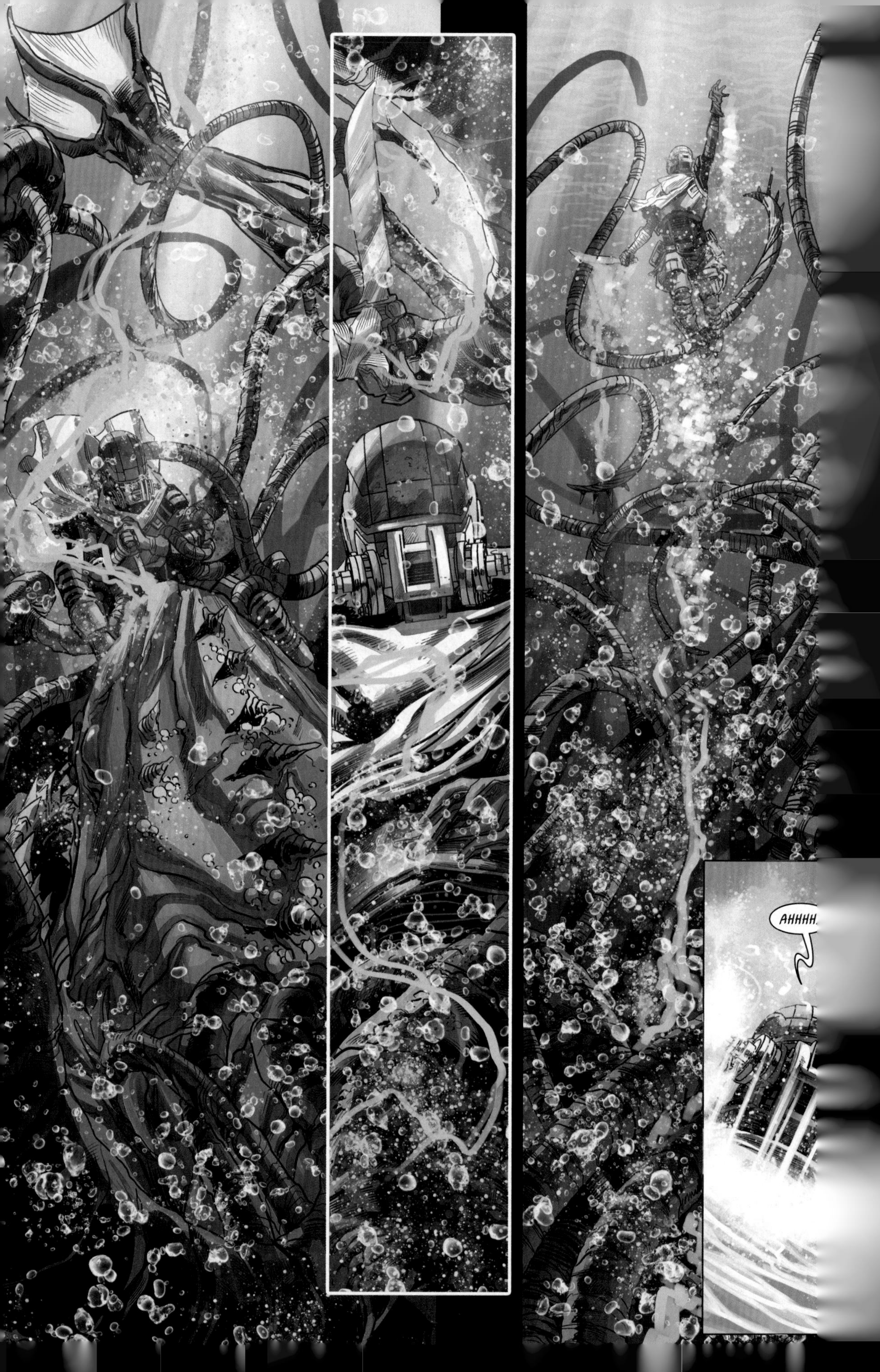
AHHHH

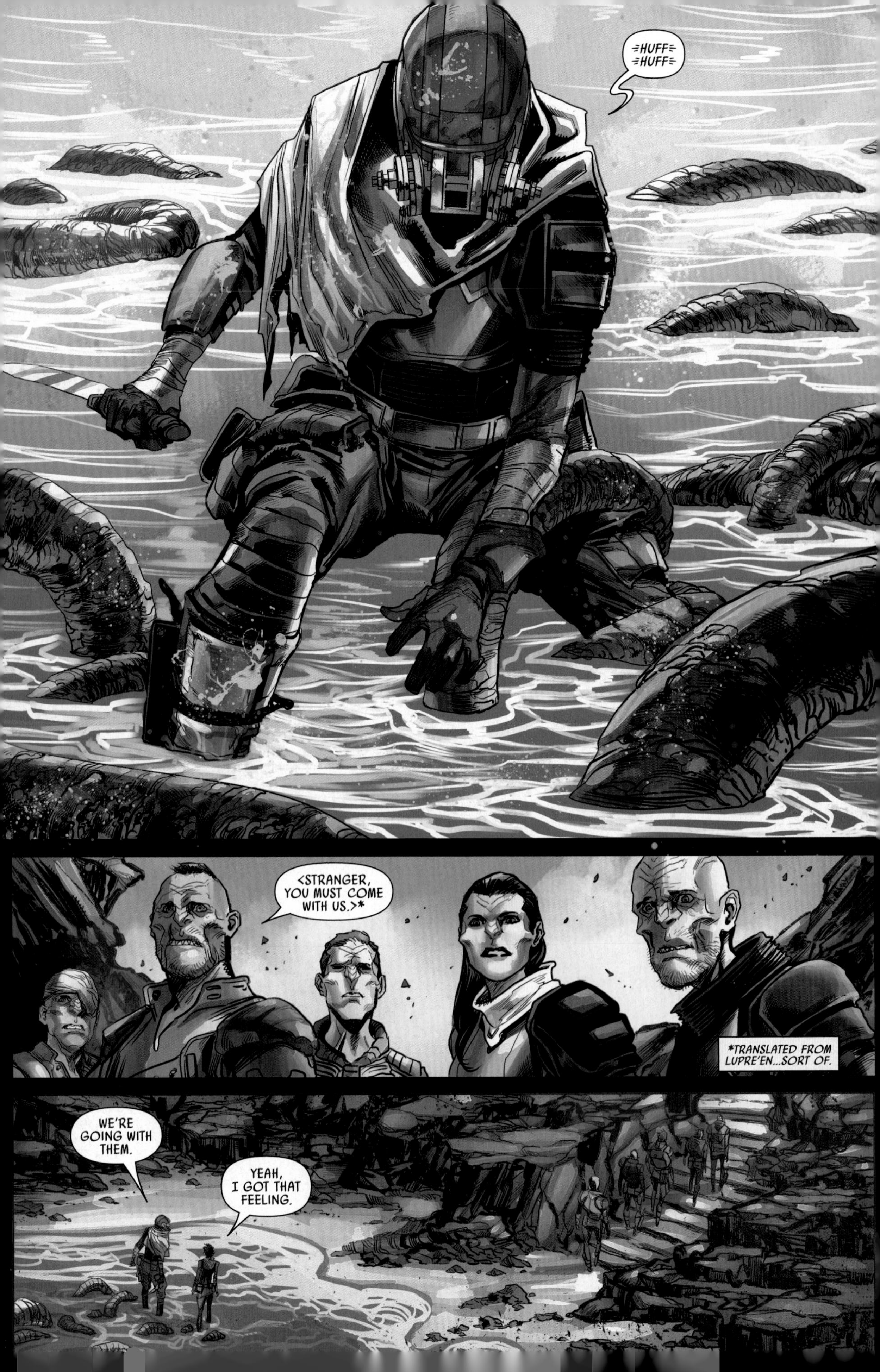
HUFF HUFF
<STRANGER, YOU MUST COME WITH US.>*
*TRANSLATED FROM LUPRE'EN...SORT OF.
WE'RE GOING WITH THEM.
YEAH, I GOT THAT FEELING.

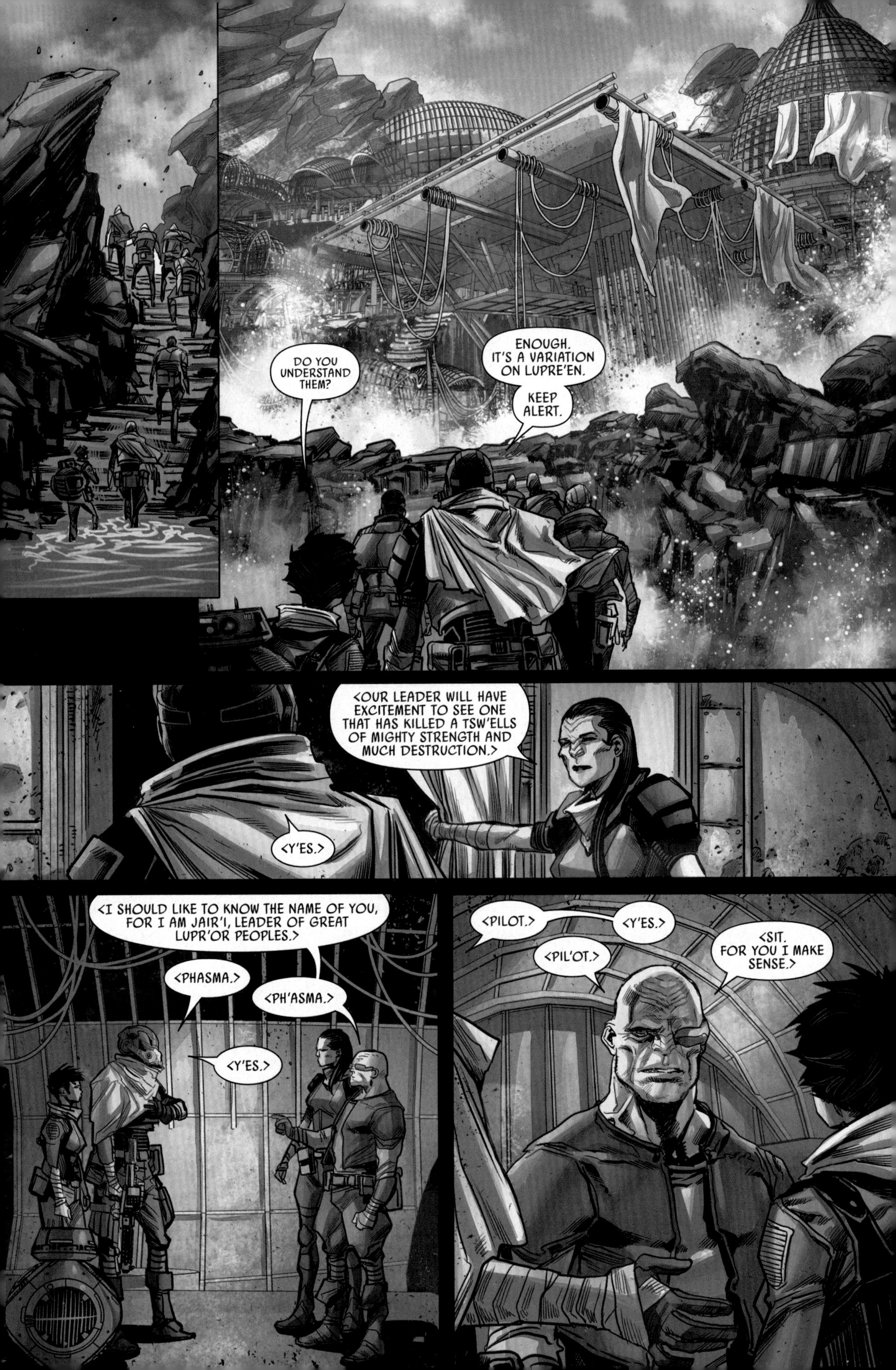
DO YOU UNDERSTAND THEM?
ENOUGH. IT'S A VARIATION ON LUPRE'EN.
KEEP ALERT.
<OUR LEADER WILL HAVE EXCITEMENT TO SEE ONE THAT HAS KILLED A TSW'ELLS OF MIGHTY STRENGTH AND MUCH DESTRUCTION.>
<Y'ES.>
<I SHOULD LIKE TO KNOW THE NAME OF YOU, FOR I AM JAIR'I, LEADER OF GREAT LUPR'OR PEOPLES.>
<PHASMA.>
<PH'ASMA.>
<Y'ES.>
<PILOT.>
<Y'ES.>
<PIL'OT.>
<SIT. FOR YOU I MAKE SENSE.>

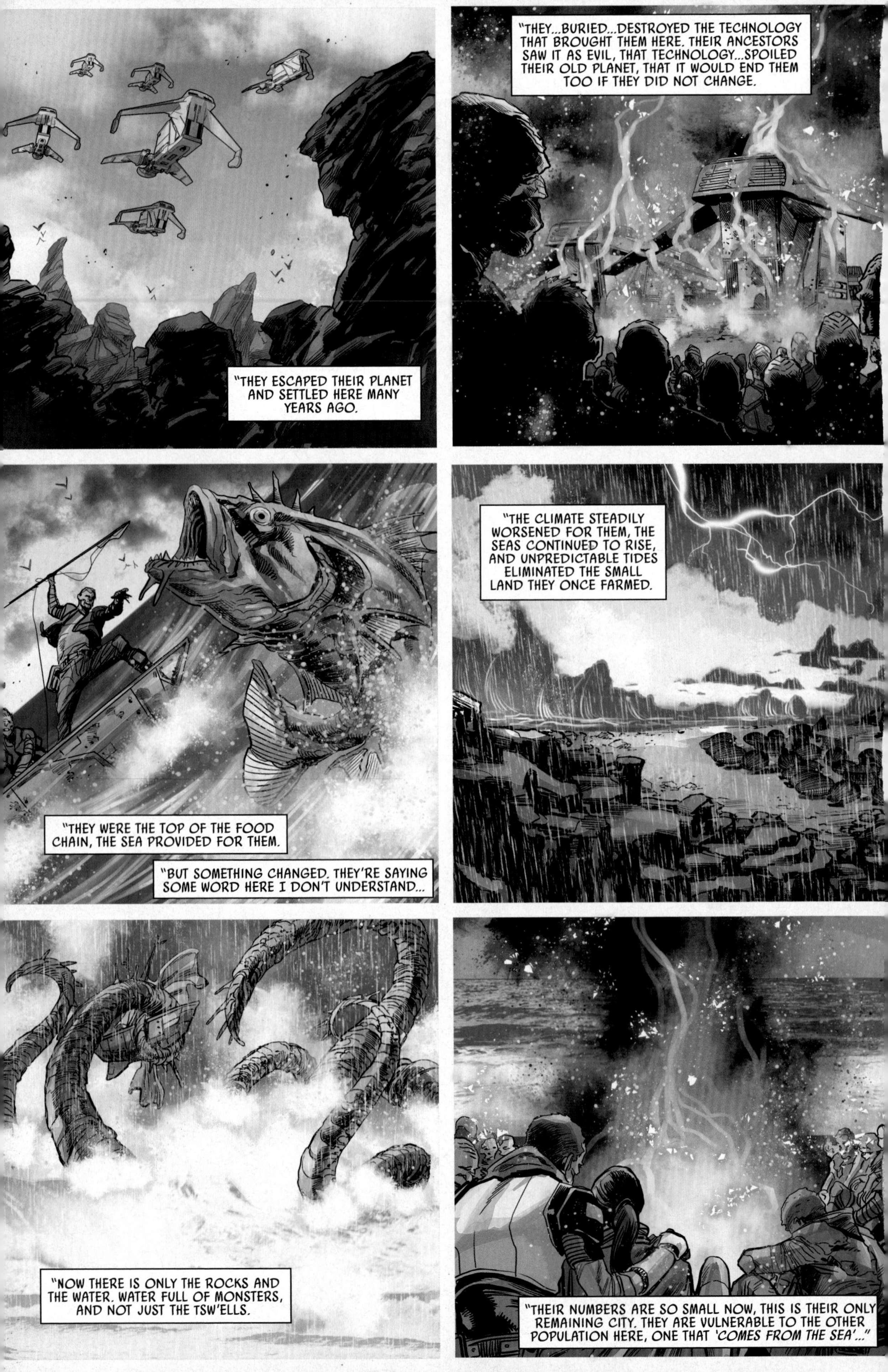

"THEY ESCAPED THEIR PLANET AND SETTLED HERE MANY YEARS AGO.
"THEY...BURIED...DESTROYED THE TECHNOLOGY THAT BROUGHT THEM HERE. THEIR ANCESTORS SAW IT AS EVIL, THAT TECHNOLOGY...SPOILED THEIR OLD PLANET, THAT IT WOULD END THEM TOO IF THEY DID NOT CHANGE.
"THEY WERE THE TOP OF THE FOOD CHAIN, THE SEA PROVIDED FOR THEM.
"BUT SOMETHING CHANGED. THEY'RE SAYING SOME WORD HERE I DON'T UNDERSTAND...
"THE CLIMATE STEADILY WORSENED FOR THEM, THE SEAS CONTINUED TO RISE, AND UNPREDICTABLE TIDES ELIMINATED THE SMALL LAND THEY ONCE FARMED.
"NOW THERE IS ONLY THE ROCKS AND THE WATER. WATER FULL OF MONSTERS, AND NOT JUST THE TSW'ELLS.
"THEIR NUMBERS ARE SO SMALL NOW, THIS IS THEIR ONLY REMAINING CITY. THEY ARE VULNERABLE TO THE OTHER POPULATION HERE, ONE THAT *'COMES FROM THE SEA'...*"

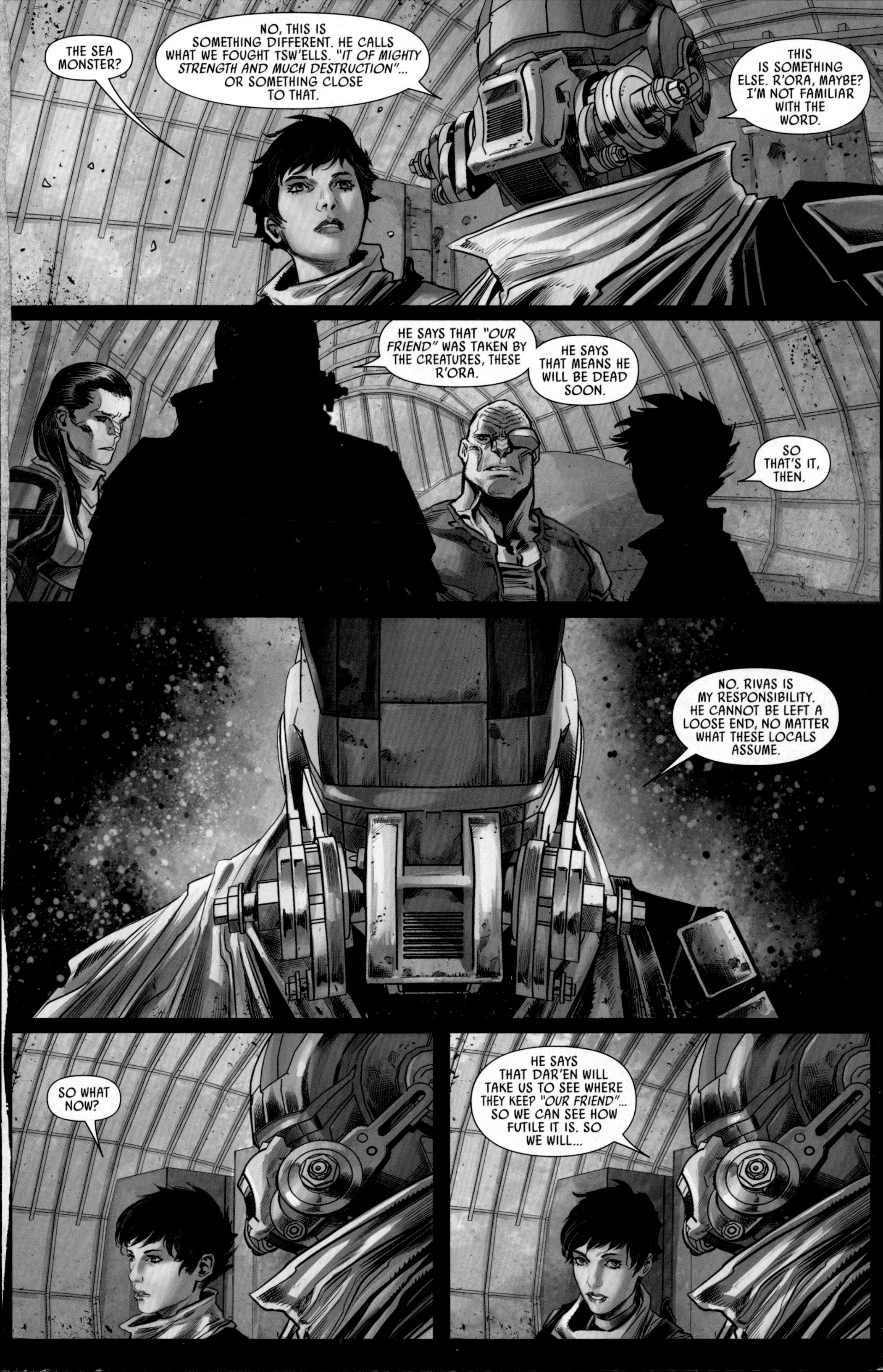
THE SEA MONSTER?
NO, THIS IS SOMETHING DIFFERENT. HE CALLS WHAT WE FOUGHT TSW'ELLS. "IT OF MIGHTY STRENGTH AND MUCH DESTRUCTION"... OR SOMETHING CLOSE TO THAT.
THIS IS SOMETHING ELSE. R'ORA, MAYBE? I'M NOT FAMILIAR WITH THE WORD.
HE SAYS THAT "OUR FRIEND" WAS TAKEN BY THE CREATURES, THESE R'ORA.
HE SAYS THAT MEANS HE WILL BE DEAD SOON.
SO THAT'S IT, THEN.
NO. RIVAS IS MY RESPONSIBILITY. HE CANNOT BE LEFT A LOOSE END, NO MATTER WHAT THESE LOCALS ASSUME.
SO WHAT NOW?
HE SAYS THAT DAR'EN WILL TAKE US TO SEE WHERE THEY KEEP "OUR FRIEND"... SO WE CAN SEE HOW FUTILE IT IS. SO WE WILL...

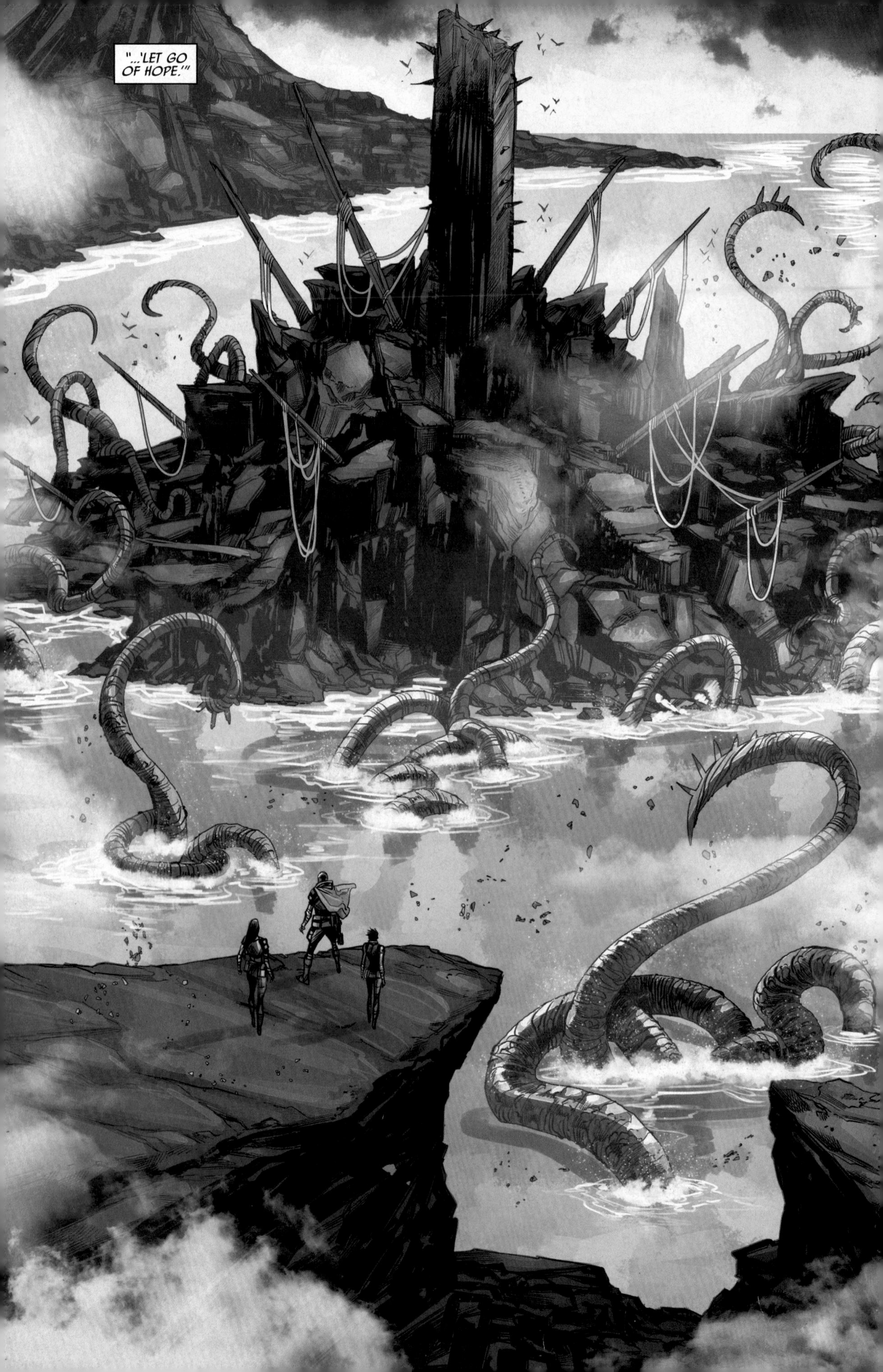
"...'LET GO OF HOPE.'"

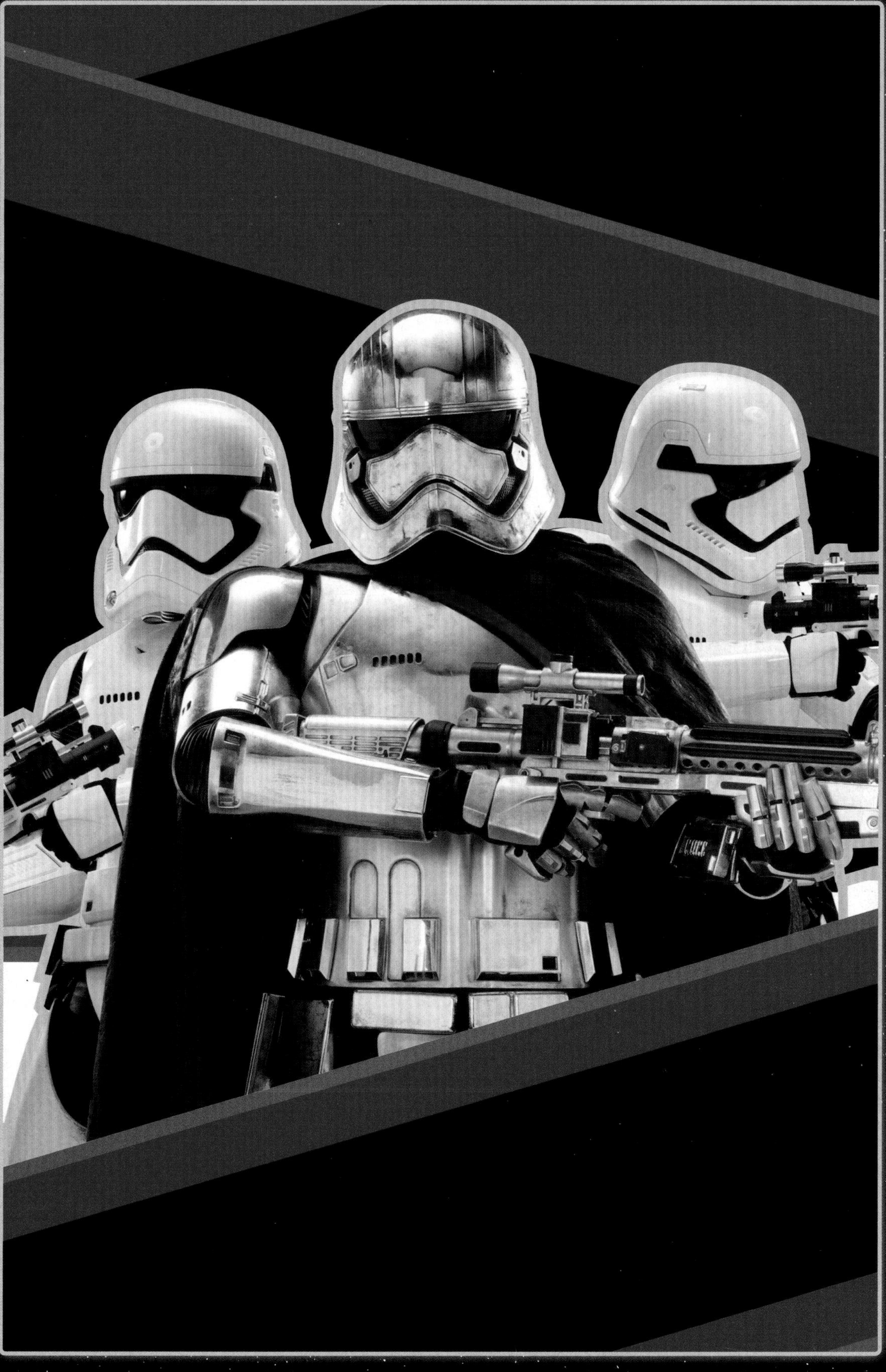

#3 Movie Variant

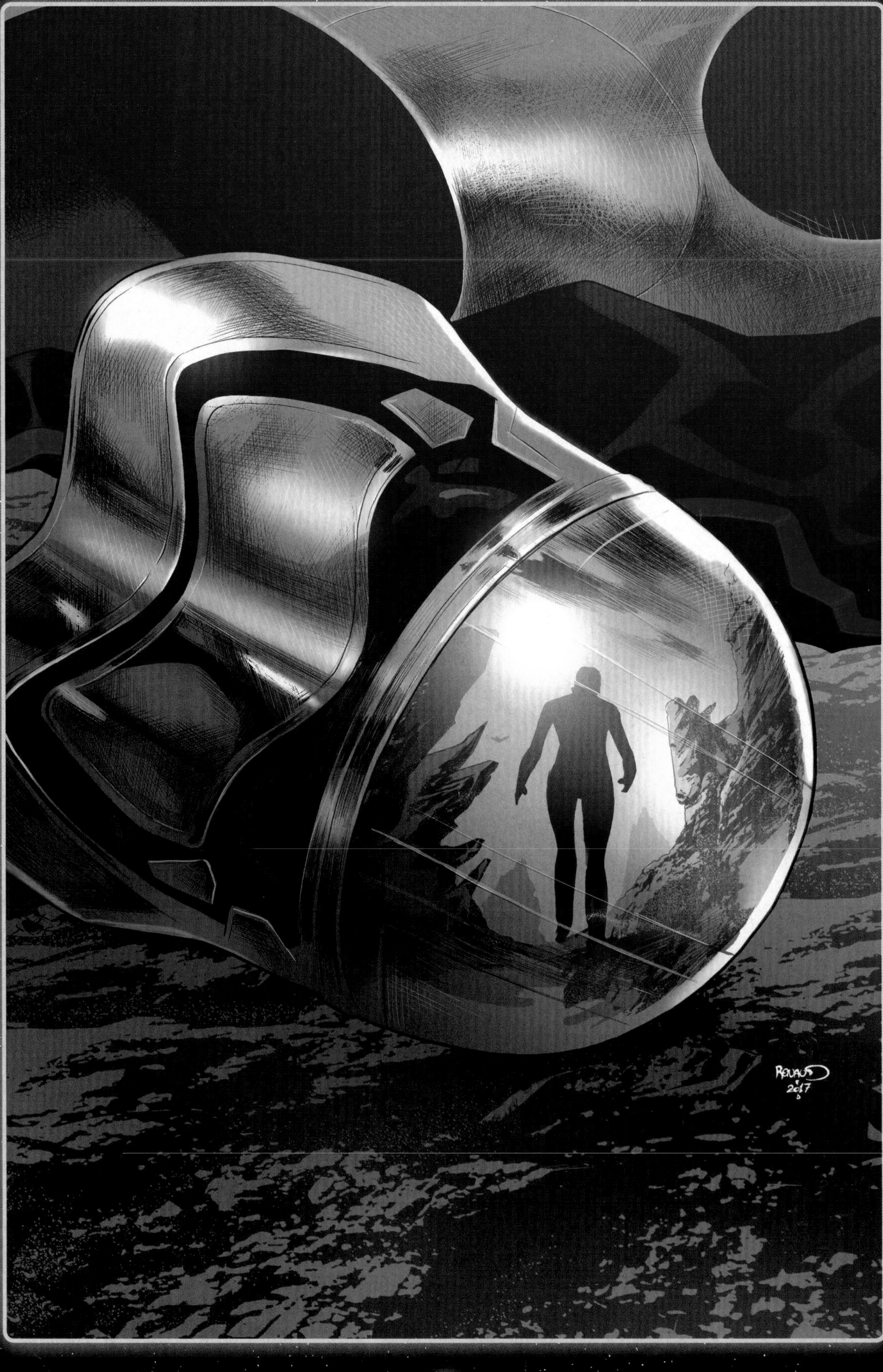

3

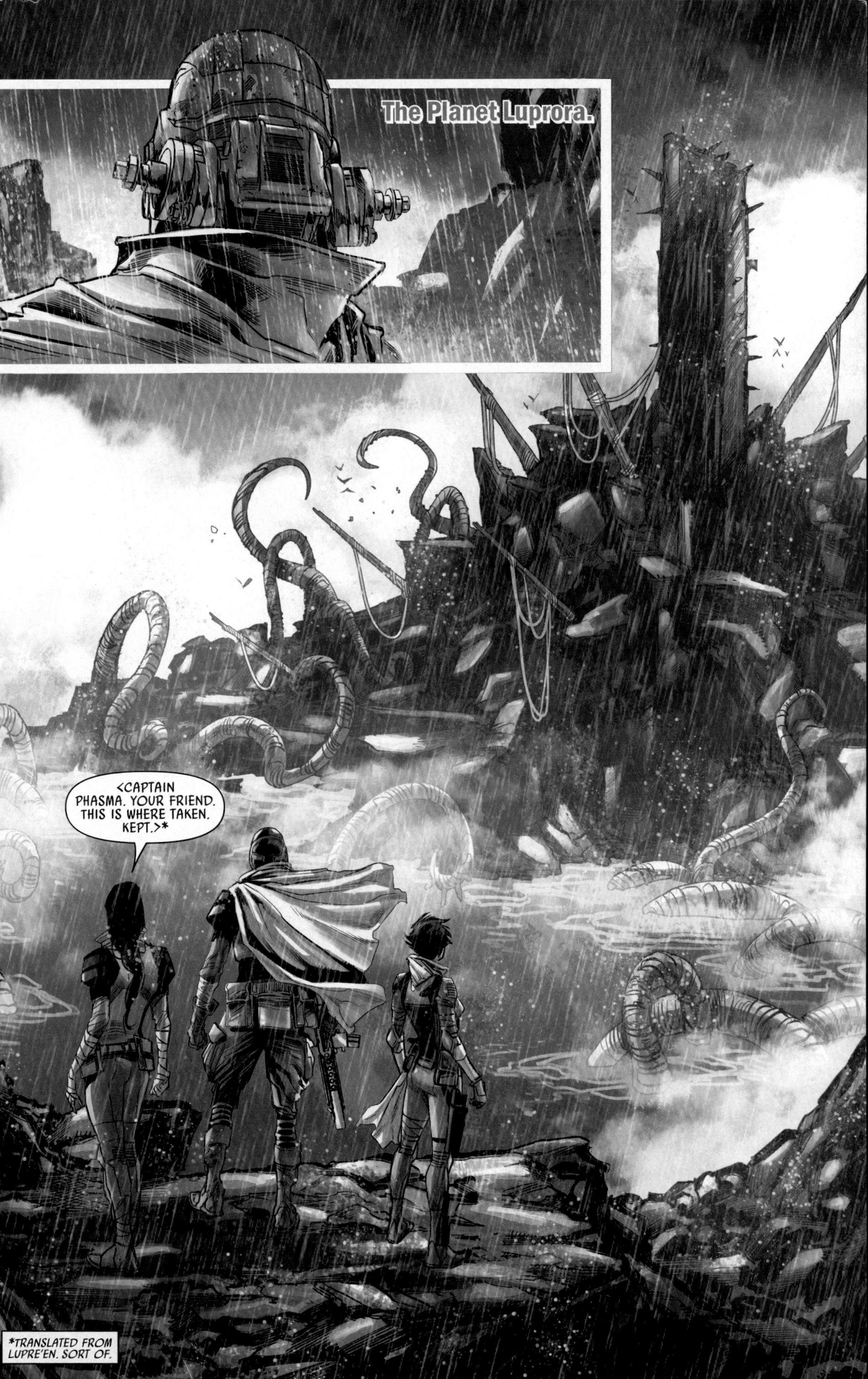
The Planet Luprora.
<CAPTAIN PHASMA. YOUR FRIEND. THIS IS WHERE TAKEN. KEPT.>*
*TRANSLATED FROM LUPRE'EN. SORT OF.

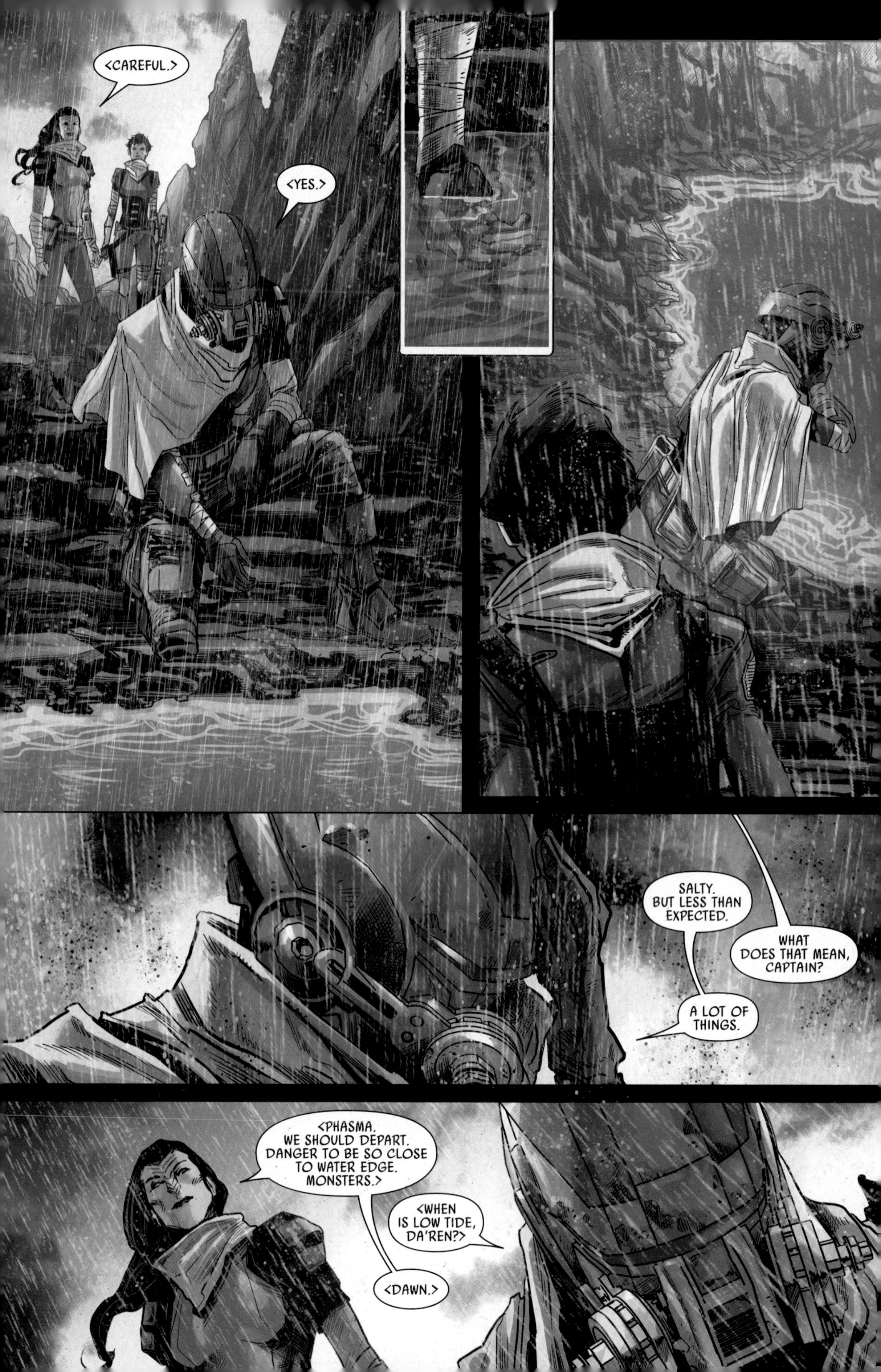
<CAREFUL.>
<YES.>
SALTY. BUT LESS THAN EXPECTED.
WHAT DOES THAT MEAN, CAPTAIN?
A LOT OF THINGS.
<PHASMA. WE SHOULD DEPART. DANGER TO BE SO CLOSE TO WATER EDGE. MONSTERS.>
<WHEN IS LOW TIDE, DA'REN?>
<DAWN.>

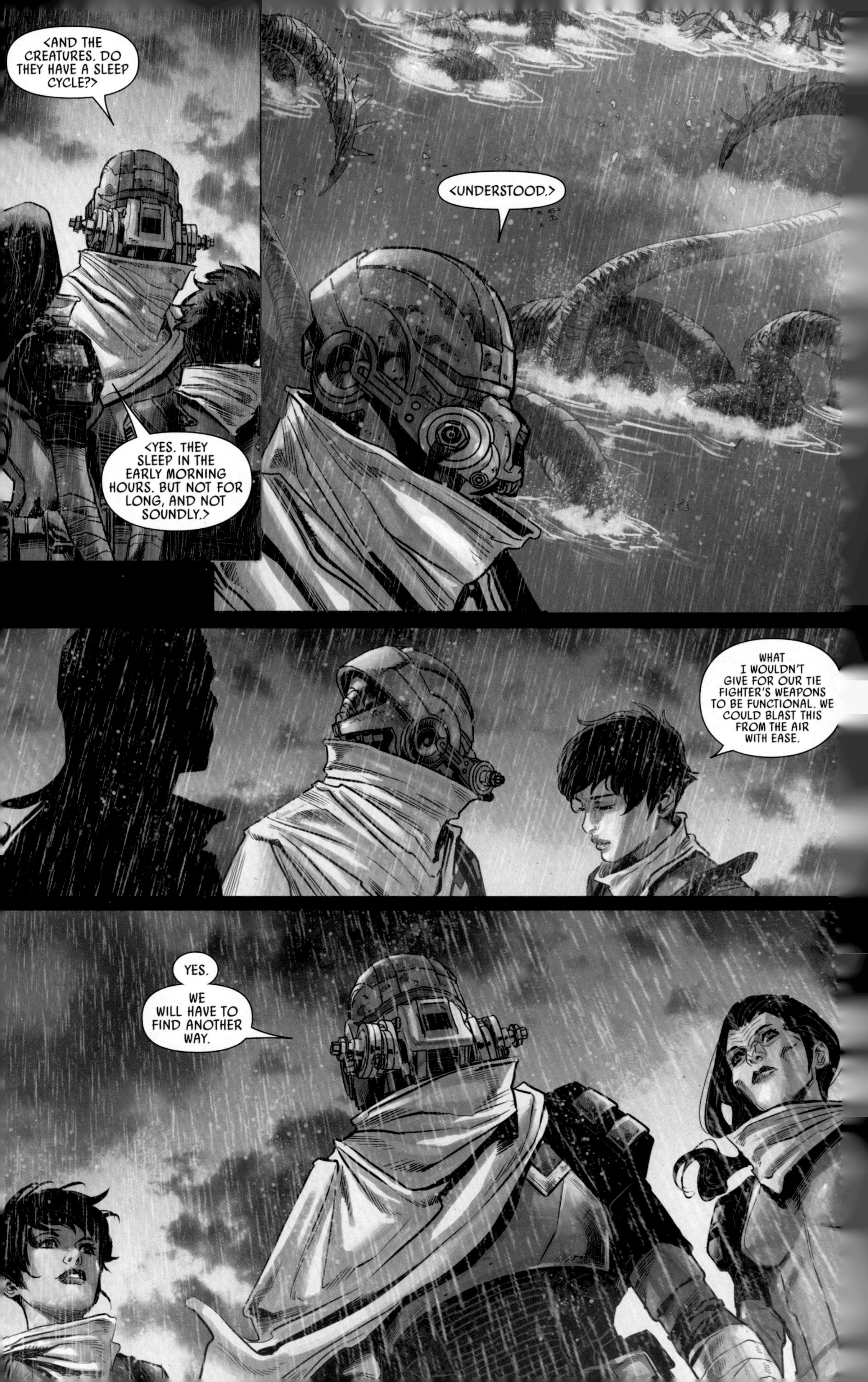

<AND THE CREATURES. DO THEY HAVE A SLEEP CYCLE?>
<YES. THEY SLEEP IN THE EARLY MORNING HOURS. BUT NOT FOR LONG, AND NOT SOUNDLY.>
<UNDERSTOOD.>
WHAT I WOULDN'T GIVE FOR OUR TIE FIGHTER'S WEAPONS TO BE FUNCTIONAL. WE COULD BLAST THIS FROM THE AIR WITH EASE.
YES.
WE WILL HAVE TO FIND ANOTHER WAY.

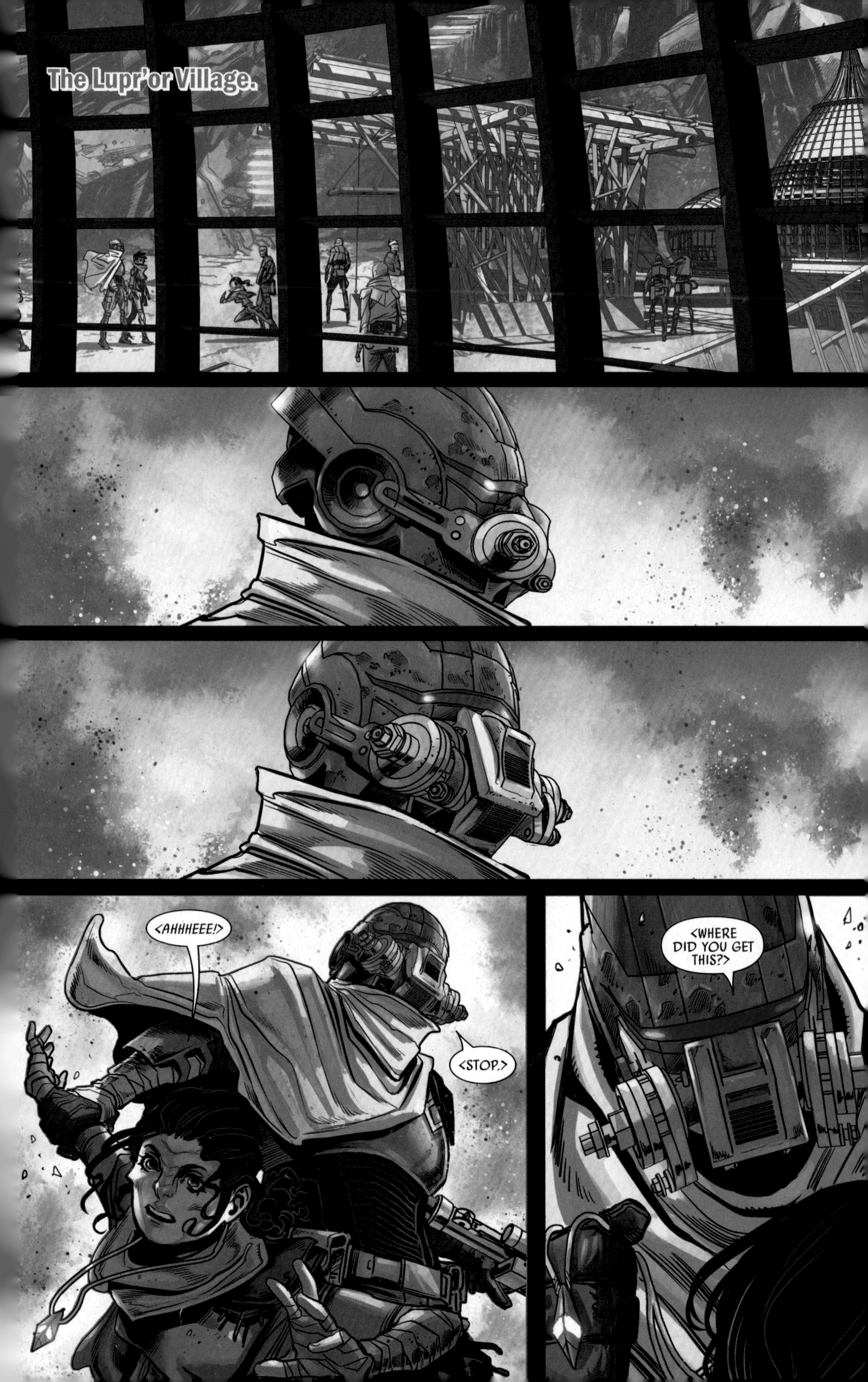
The Lupr'or Village.
<AHHHEEE!>
<STOP.>
<WHERE DID YOU GET THIS?>

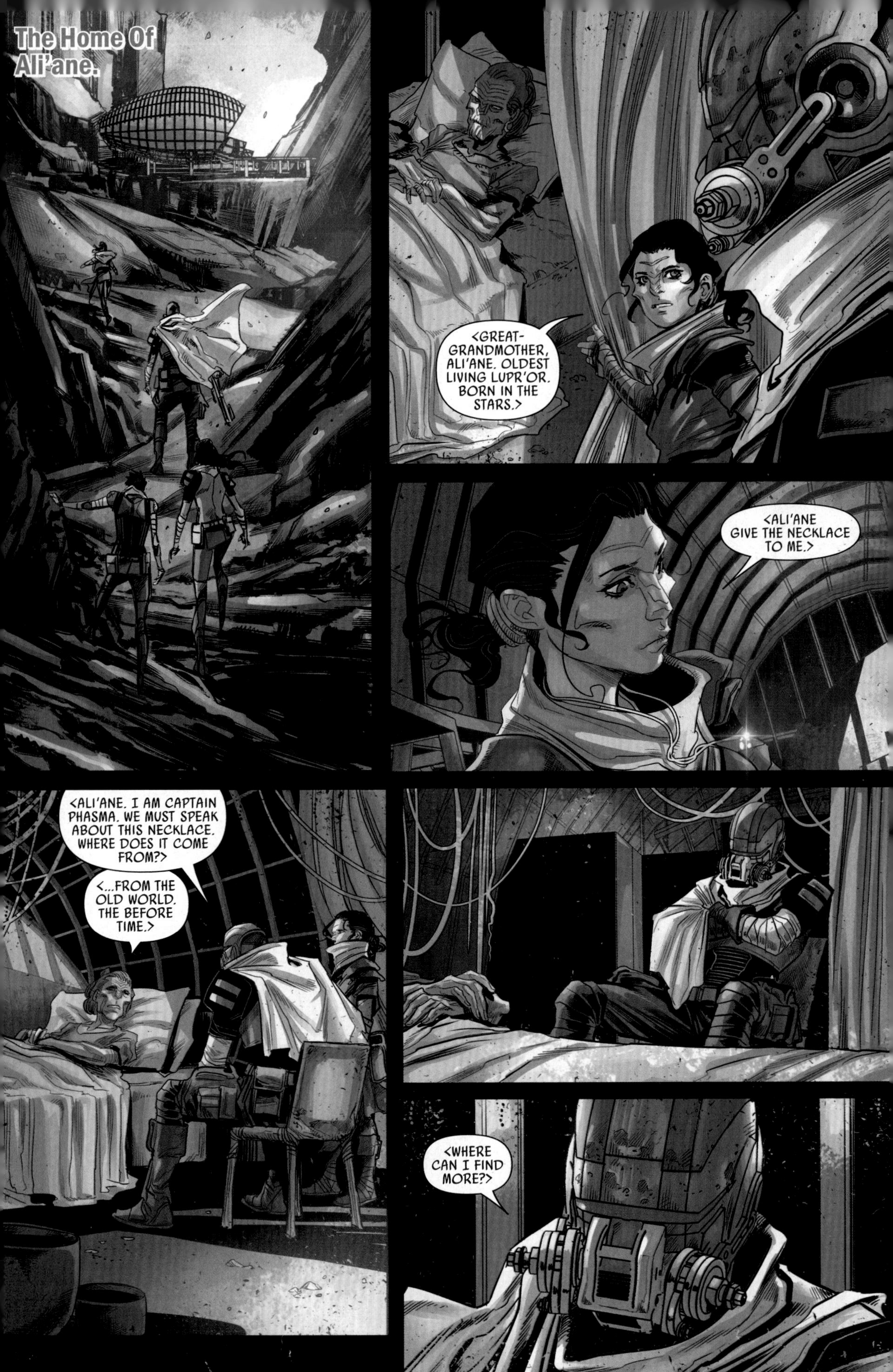
The Home Of Ali'ane.
<GREAT-GRANDMOTHER, ALI'ANE. OLDEST LIVING LUPR'OR. BORN IN THE STARS.>
<ALI'ANE GIVE THE NECKLACE TO ME.>
<ALI'ANE. I AM CAPTAIN PHASMA. WE MUST SPEAK ABOUT THIS NECKLACE. WHERE DOES IT COME FROM?>
<...FROM THE OLD WORLD. THE BEFORE TIME.>
<WHERE CAN I FIND MORE?>

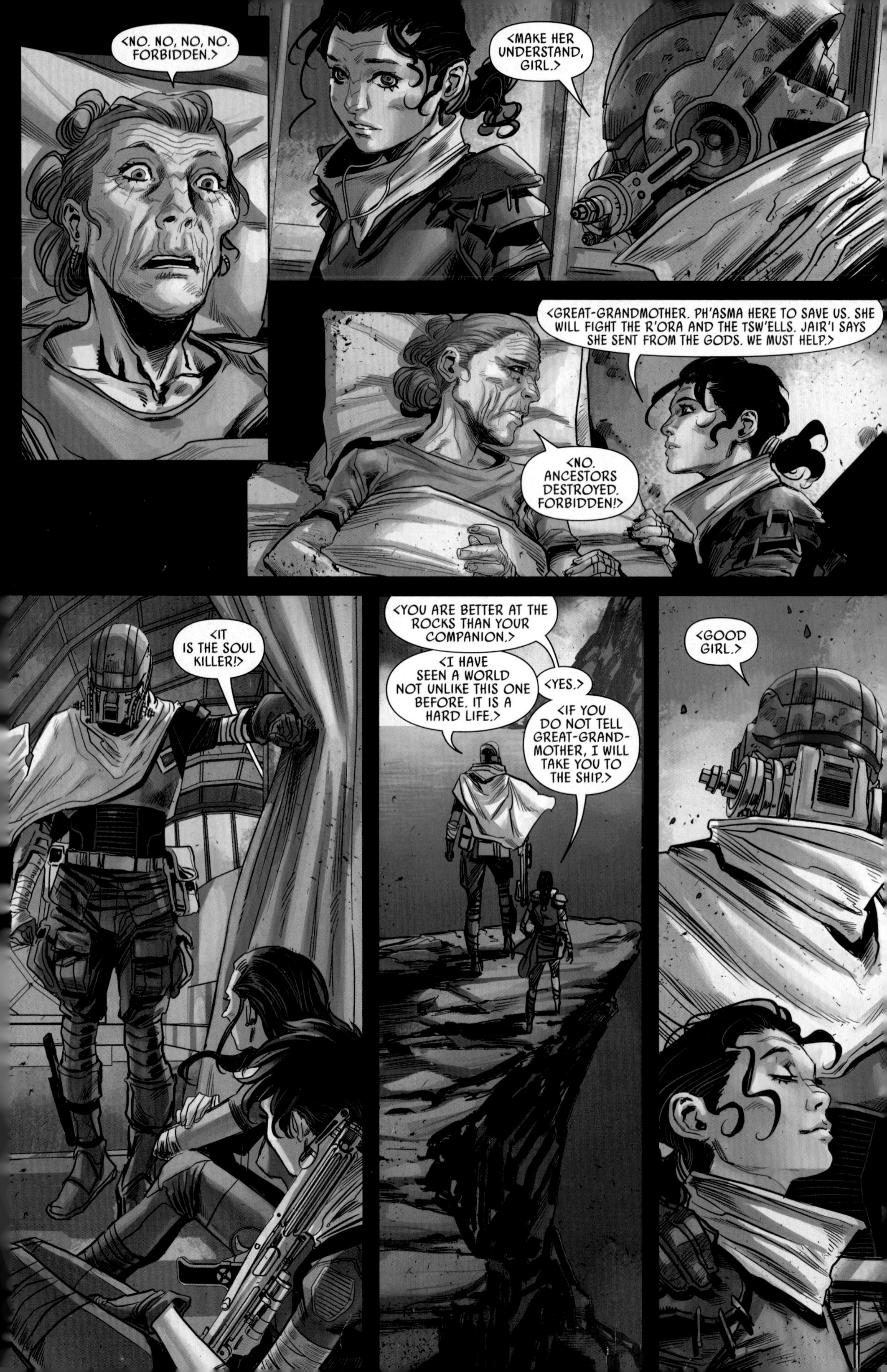
<NO. NO, NO, NO. FORBIDDEN.>
<MAKE HER UNDERSTAND, GIRL.>
<GREAT-GRANDMOTHER. PH'ASMA HERE TO SAVE US. SHE WILL FIGHT THE R'ORA AND THE TSW'ELLS. JAIR'I SAYS SHE SENT FROM THE GODS. WE MUST HELP.>
<NO. ANCESTORS DESTROYED. FORBIDDEN!>
<IT IS THE SOUL KILLER!>
<YOU ARE BETTER AT THE ROCKS THAN YOUR COMPANION.>
<I HAVE SEEN A WORLD NOT UNLIKE THIS ONE BEFORE. IT IS A HARD LIFE.>
<YES.>
<IF YOU DO NOT TELL GREAT-GRAND-MOTHER, I WILL TAKE YOU TO THE SHIP.>
<GOOD GIRL.>

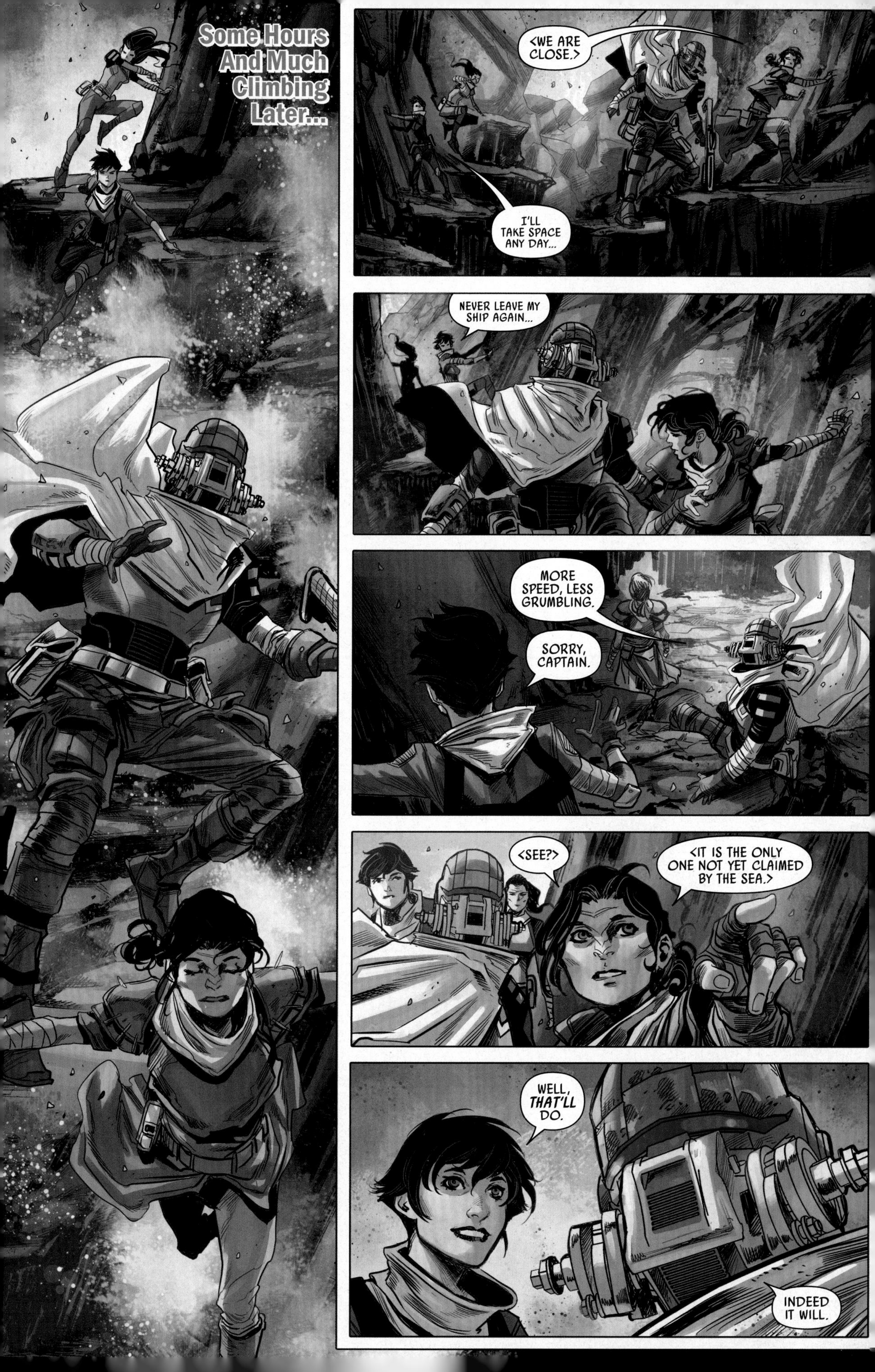
Some Hours And Much Climbing Later...
<WE ARE CLOSE.>
I'LL TAKE SPACE ANY DAY...
NEVER LEAVE MY SHIP AGAIN...
MORE SPEED, LESS GRUMBLING.
SORRY, CAPTAIN.
<SEE?>
<IT IS THE ONLY ONE NOT YET CLAIMED BY THE SEA.>
WELL, *THAT'LL* DO.
INDEED IT WILL.

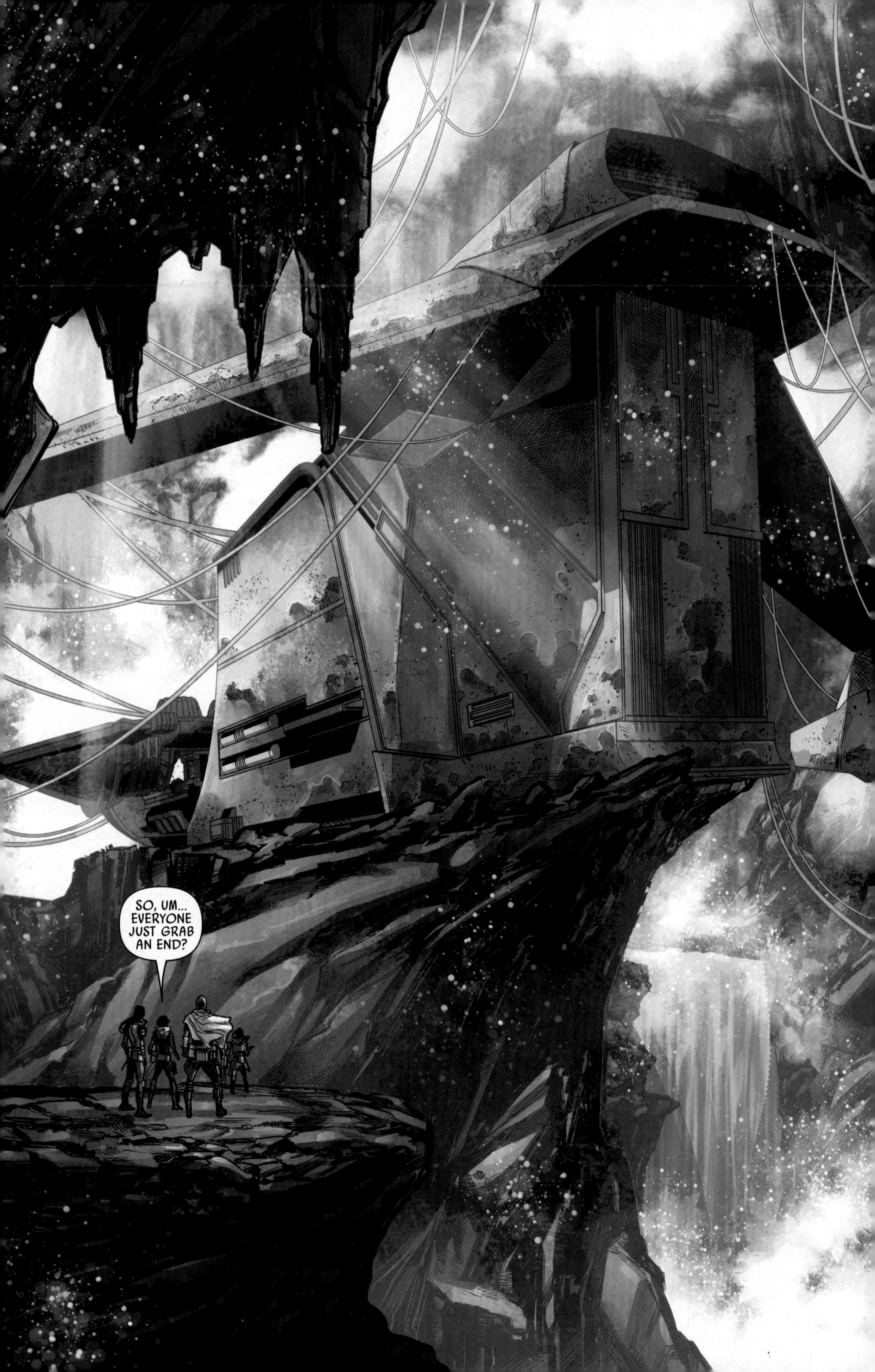
SO, UM... EVERYONE JUST GRAB AN END?

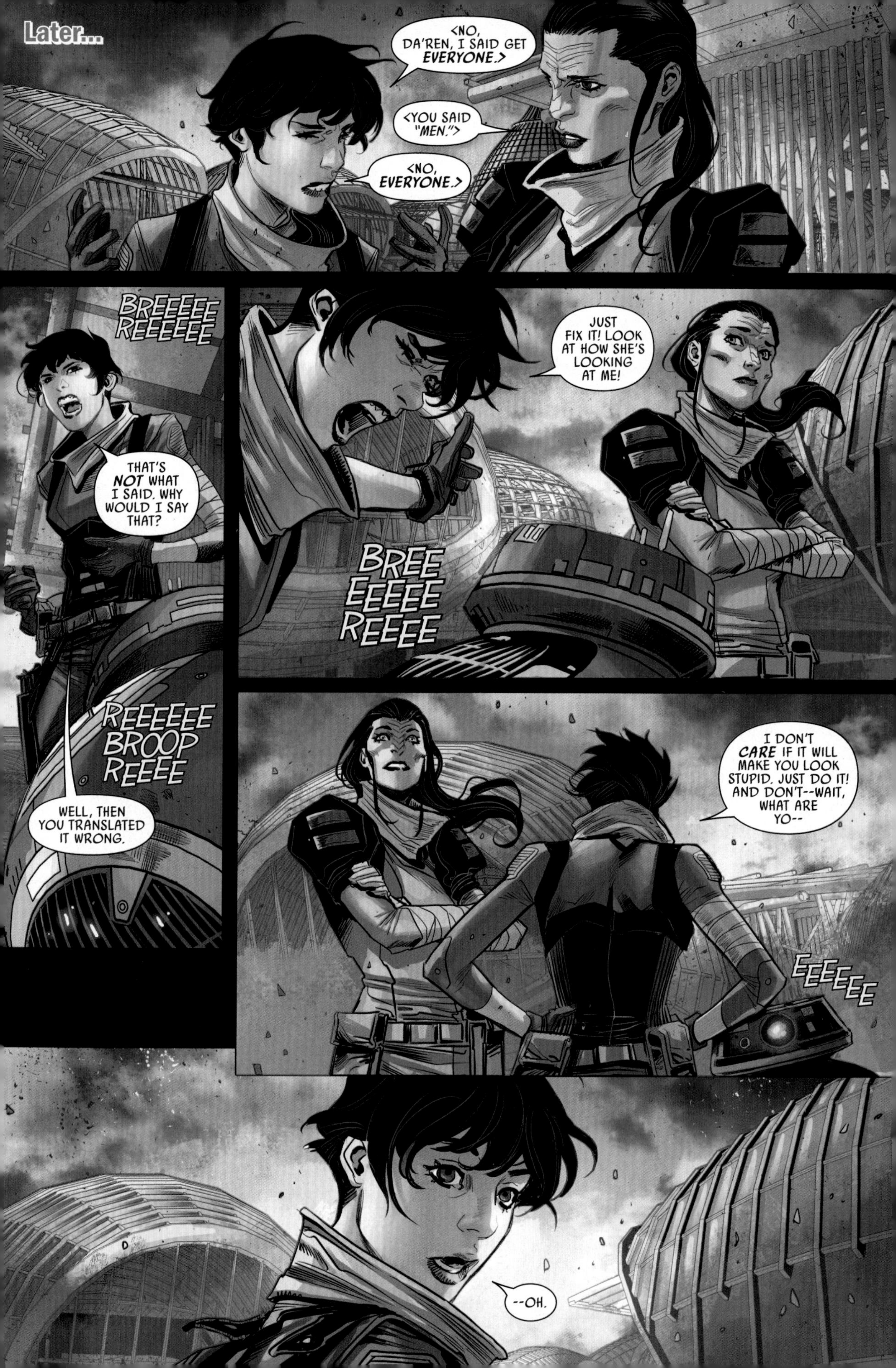
Later...
<NO, DA'REN, I SAID GET EVERYONE.>
<YOU SAID "MEN.">
<NO, EVERYONE.>
BREEEEEE REEEEEE
THAT'S NOT WHAT I SAID. WHY WOULD I SAY THAT?
REEEEEE BROOP REEEE
WELL, THEN YOU TRANSLATED IT WRONG.
JUST FIX IT! LOOK AT HOW SHE'S LOOKING AT ME!
BREE EEEEE REEEE
I DON'T CARE IF IT WILL MAKE YOU LOOK STUPID. JUST DO IT! AND DON'T--WAIT, WHAT ARE YO--
EEEEEE
--OH.

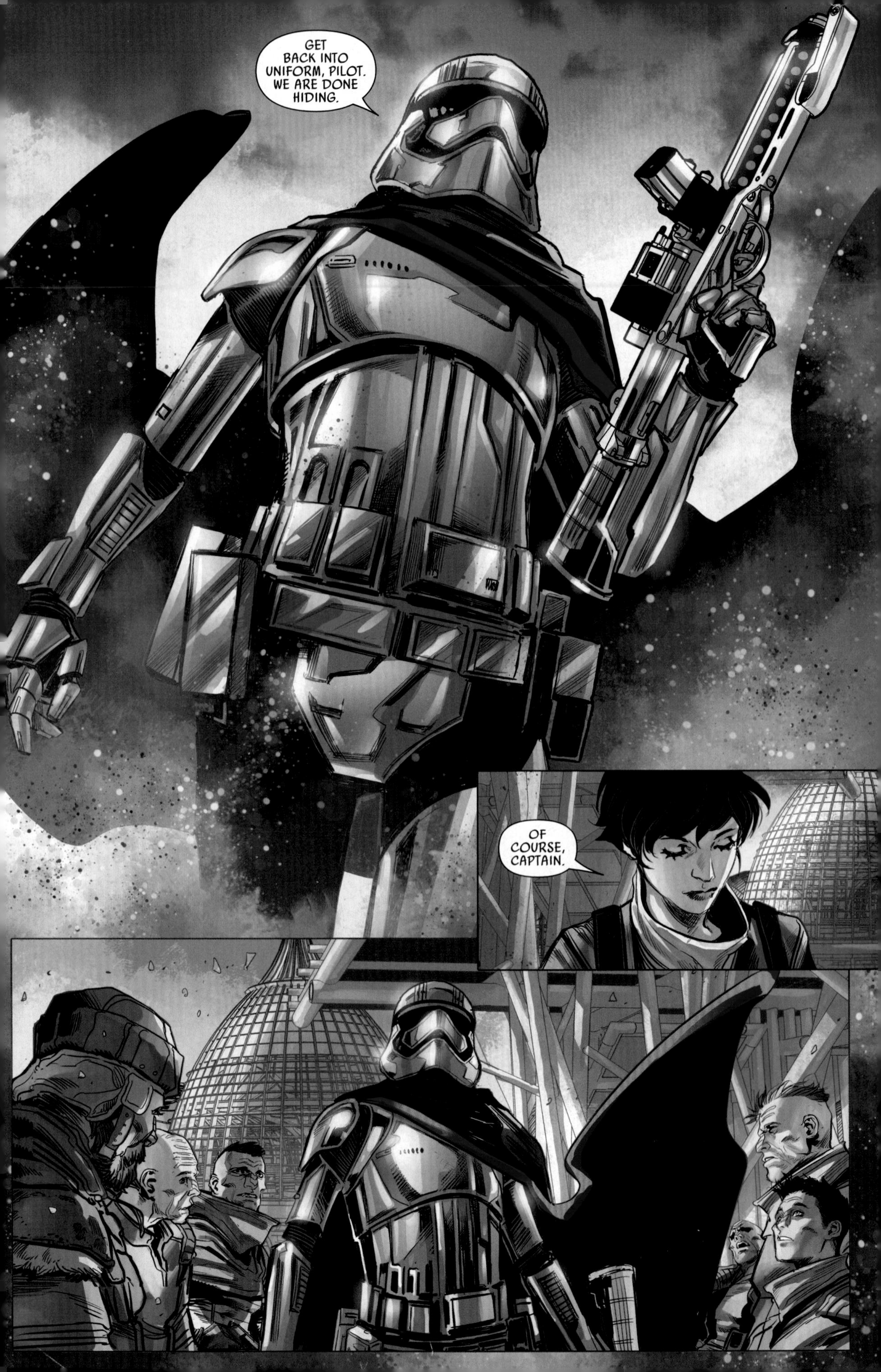
GET BACK INTO UNIFORM, PILOT. WE ARE DONE HIDING.
OF COURSE, CAPTAIN.

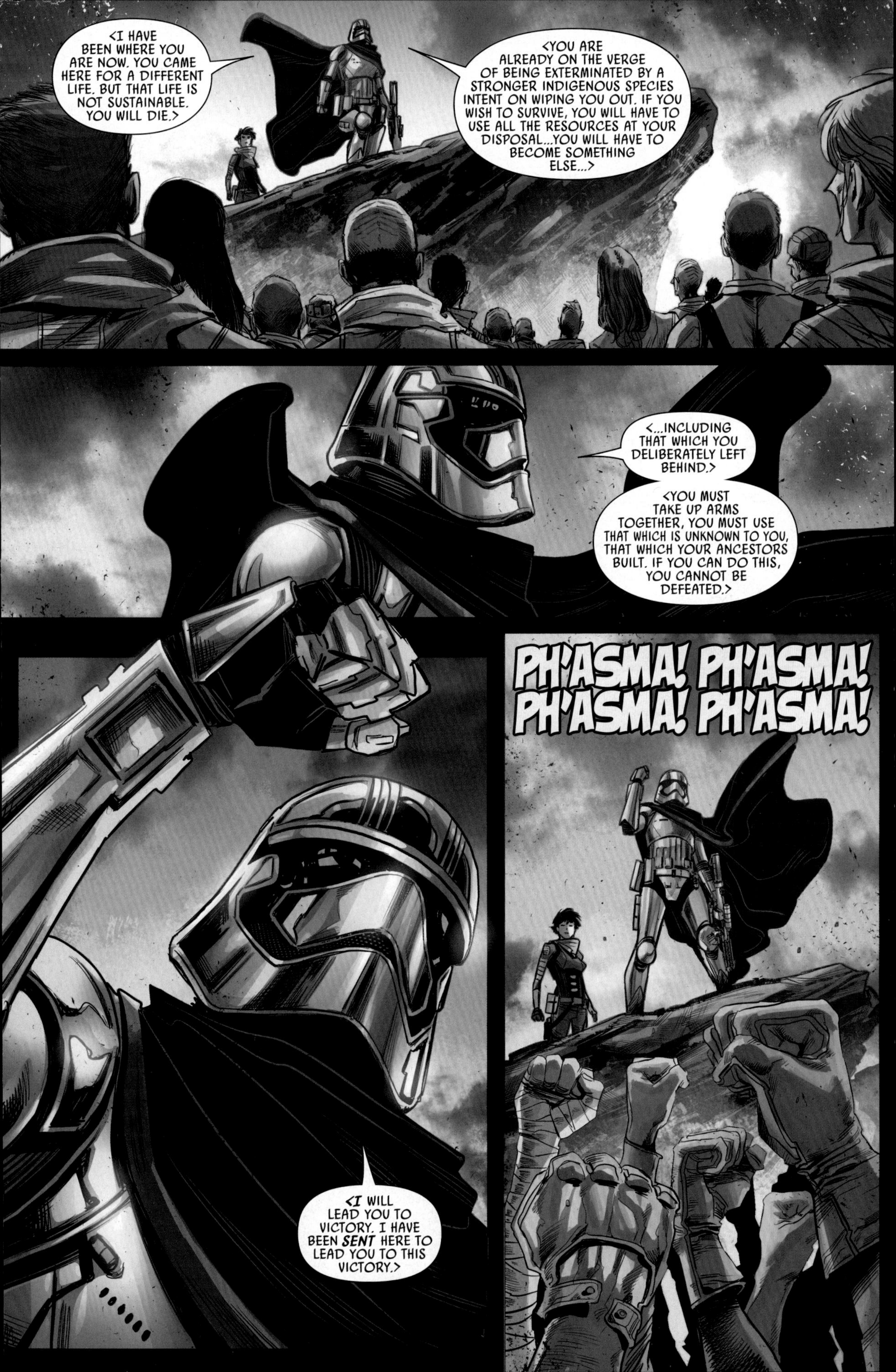
<I HAVE BEEN WHERE YOU ARE NOW. YOU CAME HERE FOR A DIFFERENT LIFE. BUT THAT LIFE IS NOT SUSTAINABLE. YOU WILL DIE.>
<YOU ARE ALREADY ON THE VERGE OF BEING EXTERMINATED BY A STRONGER INDIGENOUS SPECIES INTENT ON WIPING YOU OUT. IF YOU WISH TO SURVIVE, YOU WILL HAVE TO USE ALL THE RESOURCES AT YOUR DISPOSAL...YOU WILL HAVE TO BECOME SOMETHING ELSE...>
<...INCLUDING THAT WHICH YOU DELIBERATELY LEFT BEHIND.>
<YOU MUST TAKE UP ARMS TOGETHER, YOU MUST USE THAT WHICH IS UNKNOWN TO YOU, THAT WHICH YOUR ANCESTORS BUILT. IF YOU CAN DO THIS, YOU CANNOT BE DEFEATED.>
<*I* WILL LEAD YOU TO VICTORY. I HAVE BEEN ***SENT*** HERE TO LEAD YOU TO THIS VICTORY.>
PH'ASMA! PH'ASMA! PH'ASMA! PH'ASMA!

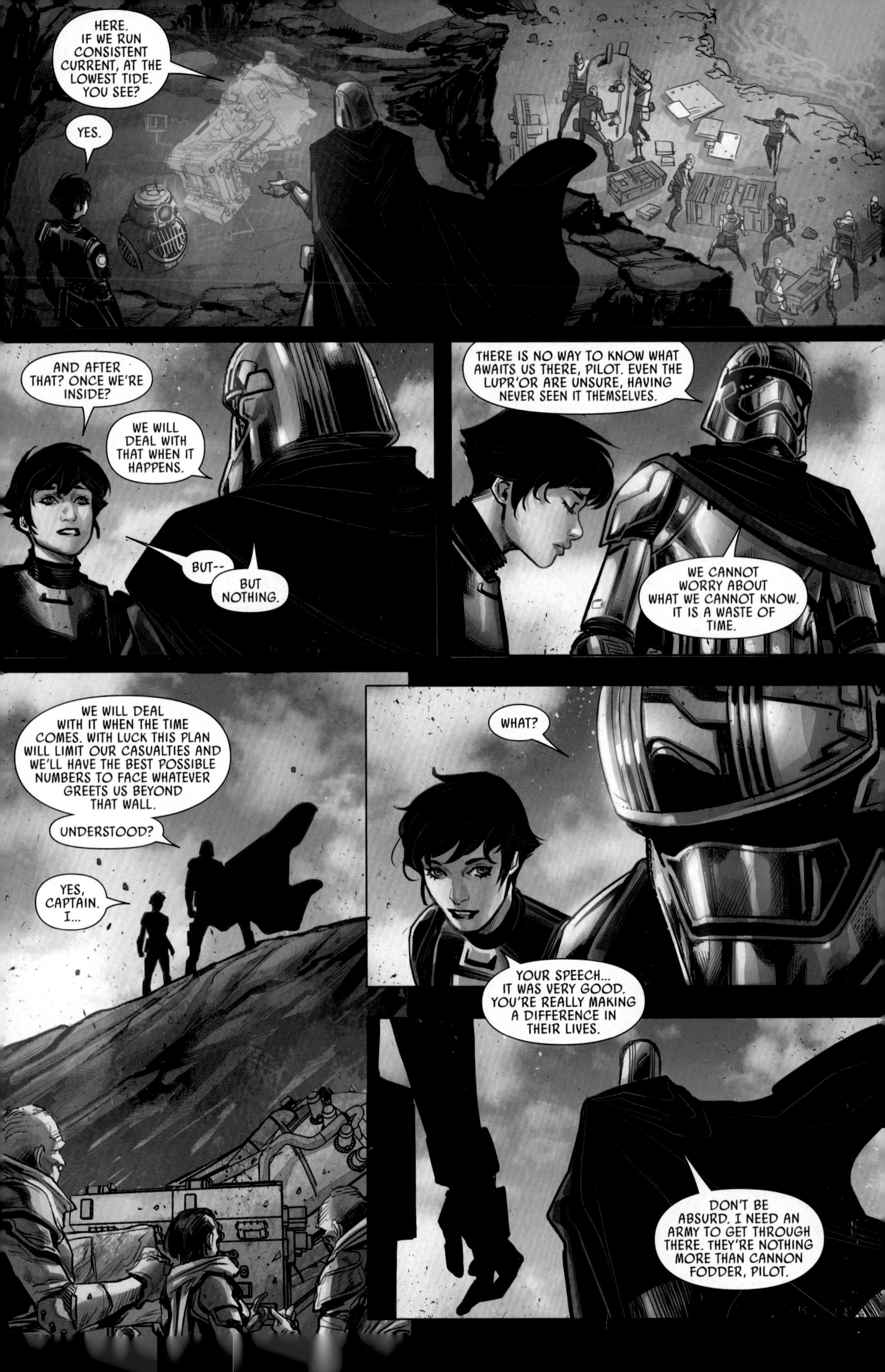
HERE. IF WE RUN CONSISTENT CURRENT, AT THE LOWEST TIDE. YOU SEE?
YES.
AND AFTER THAT? ONCE WE'RE INSIDE?
WE WILL DEAL WITH THAT WHEN IT HAPPENS.
BUT--
BUT NOTHING.
THERE IS NO WAY TO KNOW WHAT AWAITS US THERE, PILOT. EVEN THE LUPR'OR ARE UNSURE, HAVING NEVER SEEN IT THEMSELVES.
WE CANNOT WORRY ABOUT WHAT WE CANNOT KNOW. IT IS A WASTE OF TIME.
WE WILL DEAL WITH IT WHEN THE TIME COMES. WITH LUCK THIS PLAN WILL LIMIT OUR CASUALTIES AND WE'LL HAVE THE BEST POSSIBLE NUMBERS TO FACE WHATEVER GREETS US BEYOND THAT WALL.
UNDERSTOOD?
YES, CAPTAIN. I...
WHAT?
YOUR SPEECH... IT WAS VERY GOOD. YOU'RE REALLY MAKING A DIFFERENCE IN THEIR LIVES.
DON'T BE ABSURD. I NEED AN ARMY TO GET THROUGH THERE. THEY'RE NOTHING MORE THAN CANNON FODDER, PILOT.

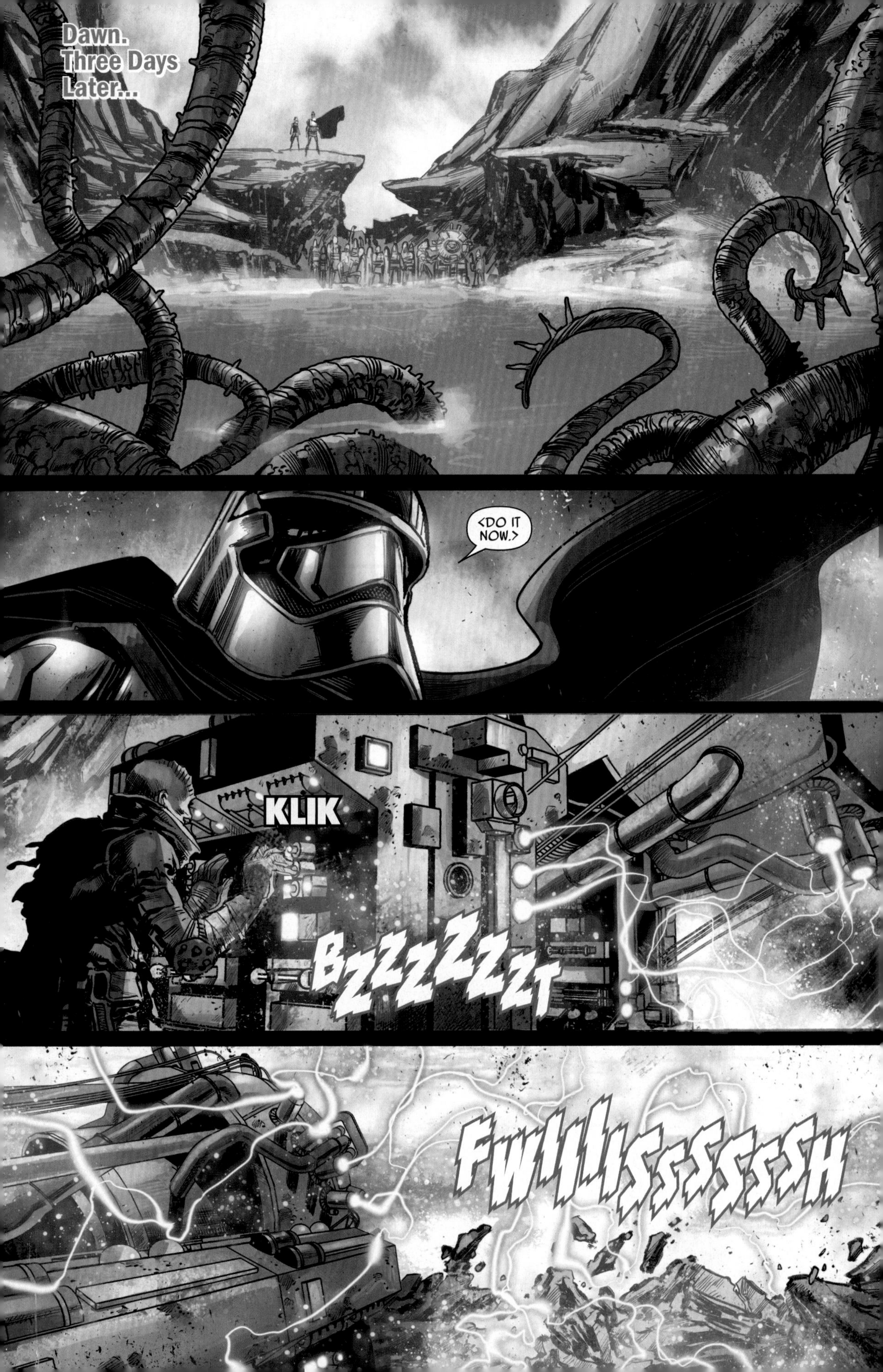

Dawn. Three Days Later...
<DO IT NOW.>
KLIK
BZZZZZZZT
FWHHISSSSSSH

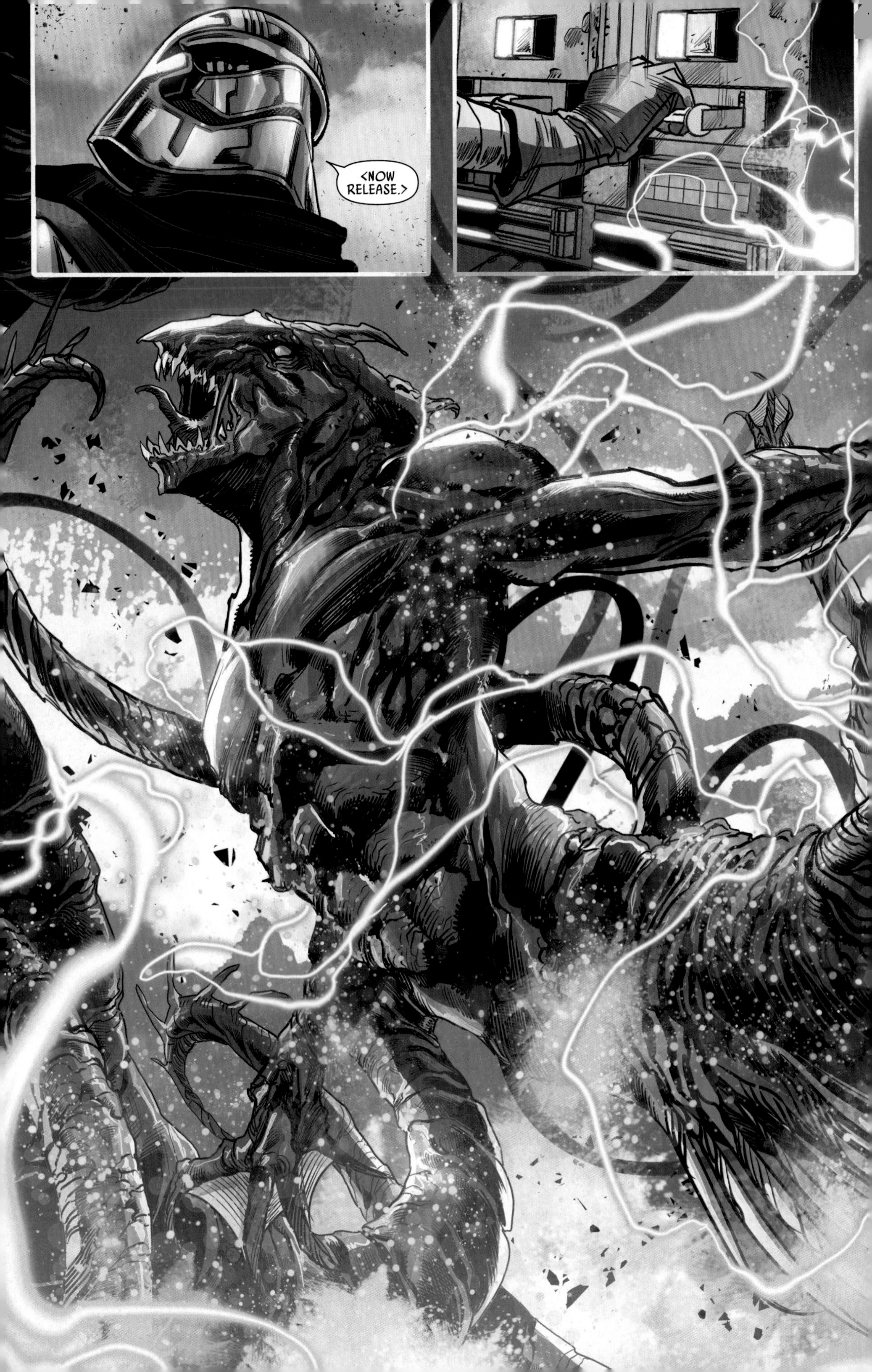
<NOW RELEASE.>

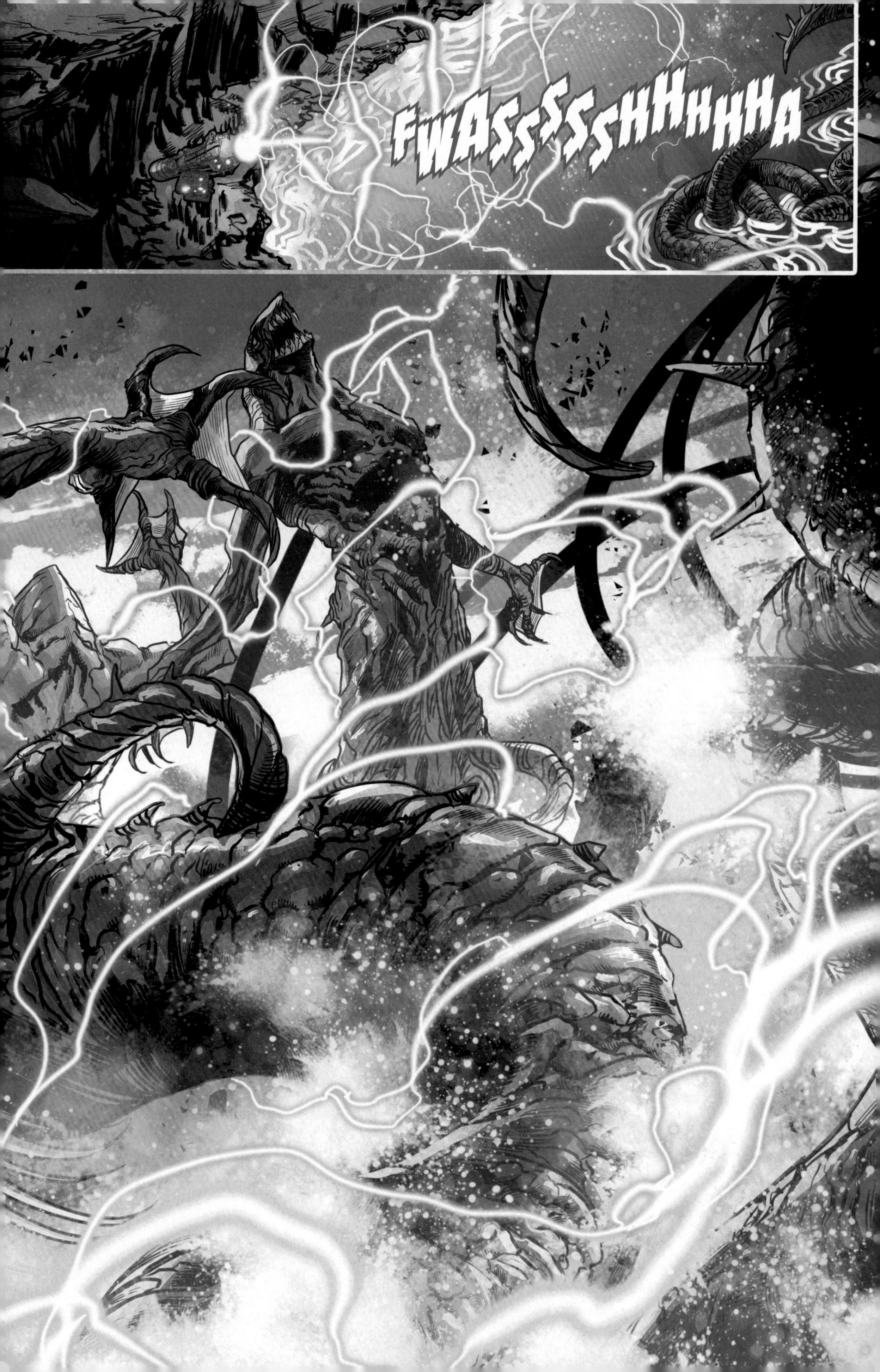
FWASSSSHHHHHA

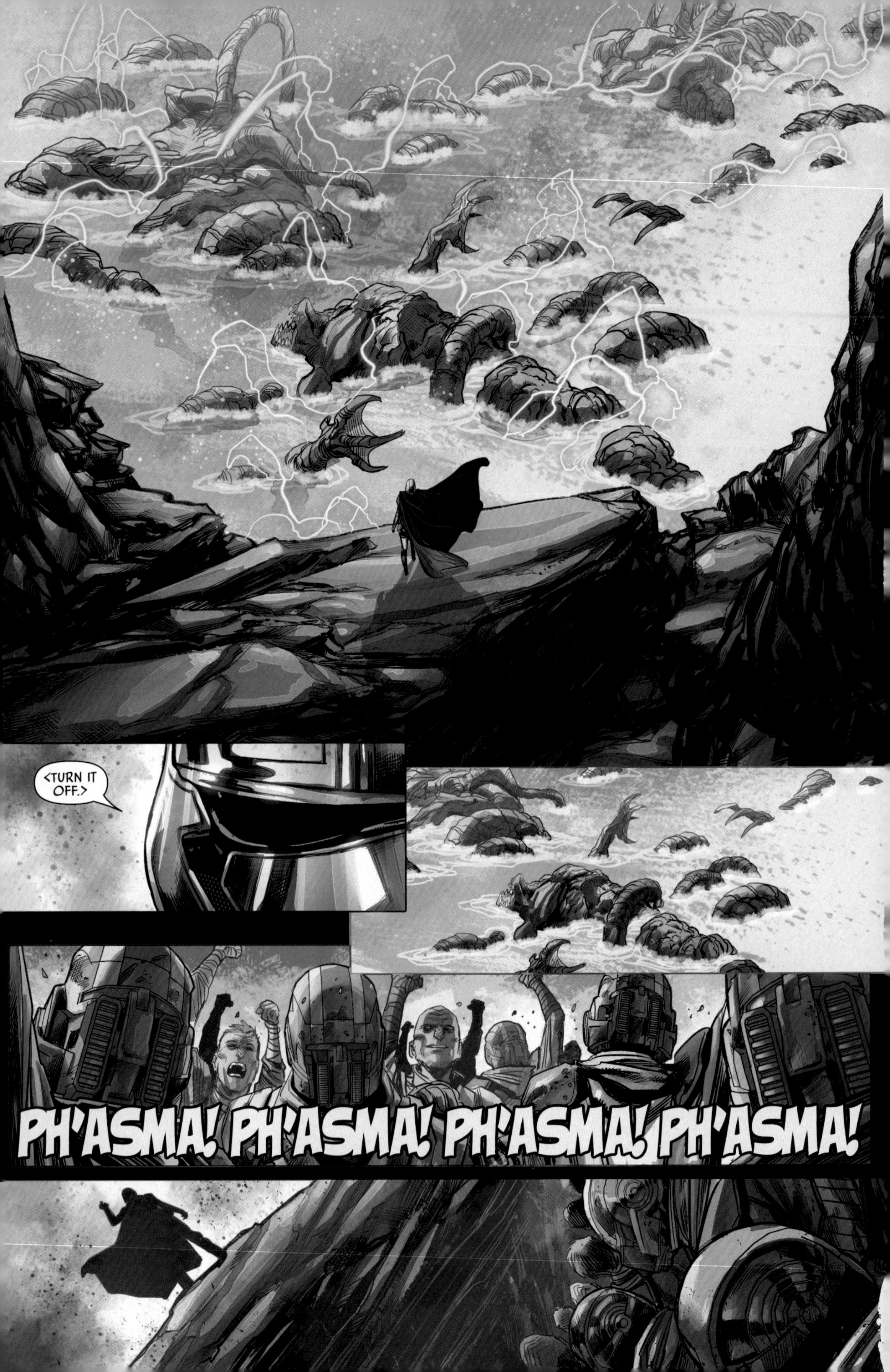
<TURN IT OFF.>
PH'ASMA! PH'ASMA! PH'ASMA! PH'ASMA!

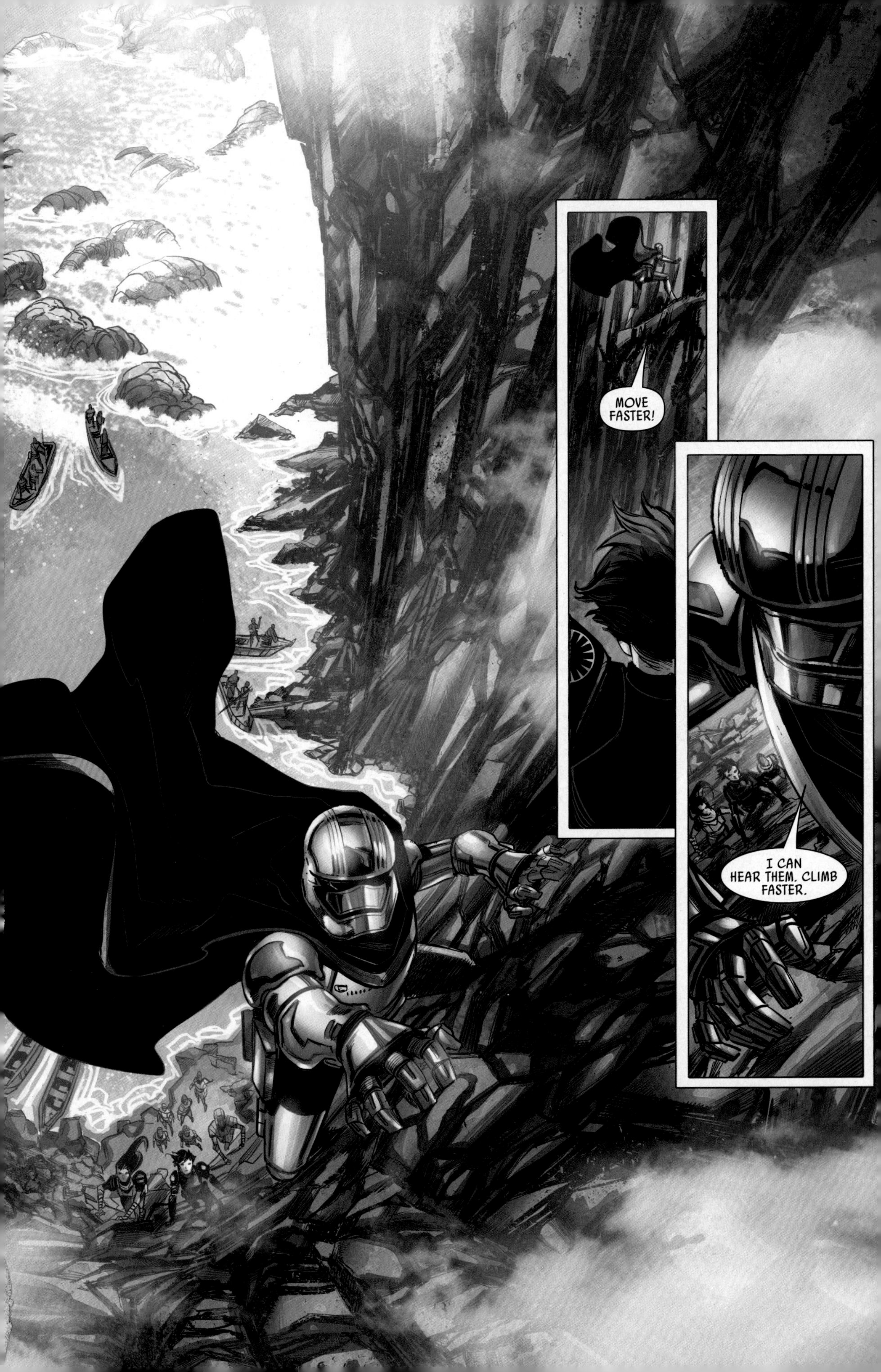
MOVE FASTER!
I CAN HEAR THEM. CLIMB FASTER.

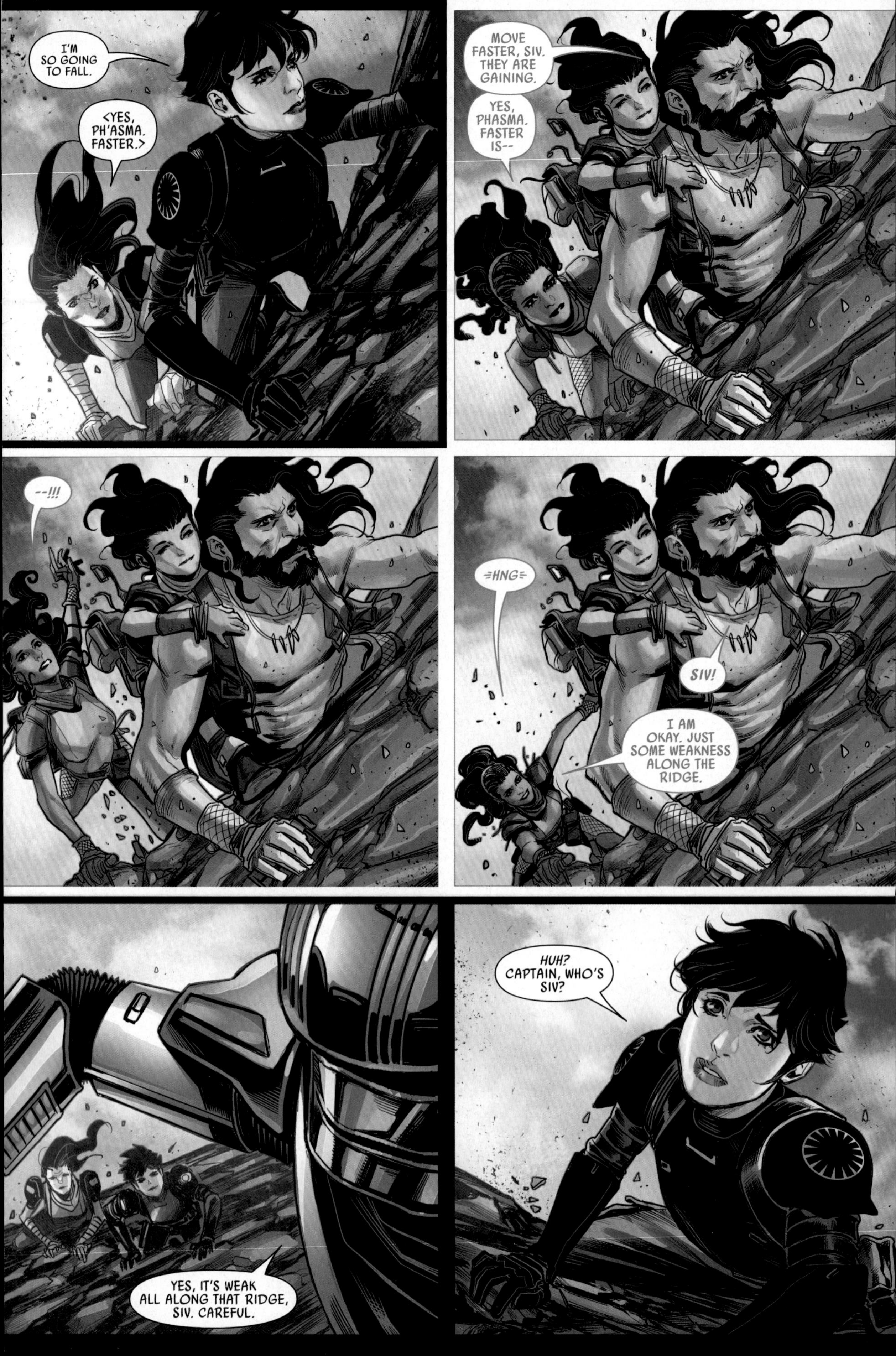
I'M SO GOING TO FALL.
<YES, PH'ASMA. FASTER.>
MOVE FASTER, SIV. THEY ARE GAINING.
YES, PHASMA. FASTER IS--
--!!!
HNG
SIV!
I AM OKAY. JUST SOME WEAKNESS ALONG THE RIDGE.
YES, IT'S WEAK ALL ALONG THAT RIDGE, SIV. CAREFUL.
HUH? CAPTAIN, WHO'S SIV?

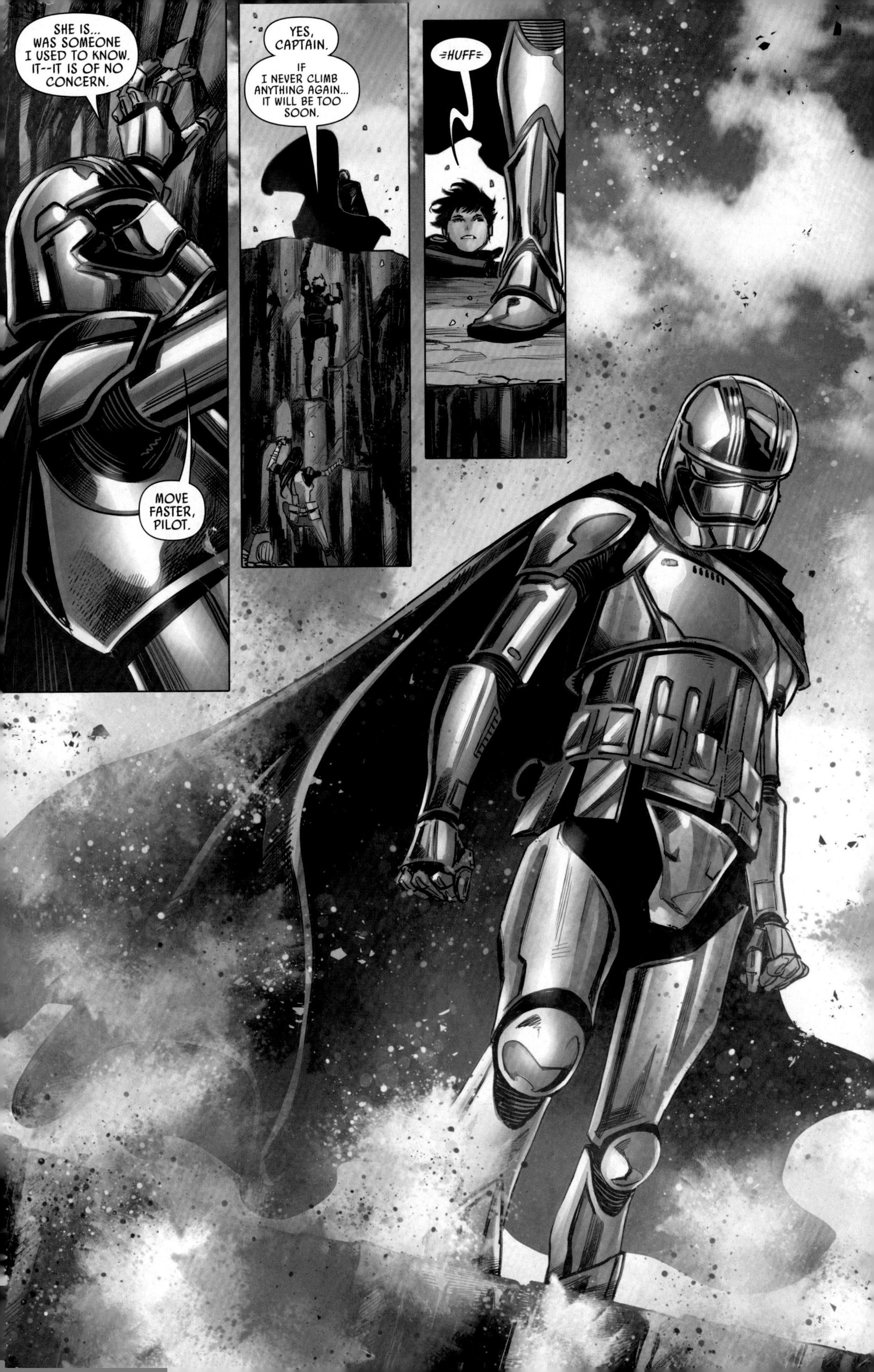
SHE IS... WAS SOMEONE I USED TO KNOW. IT--IT IS OF NO CONCERN.
MOVE FASTER, PILOT.
YES, CAPTAIN.
IF I NEVER CLIMB ANYTHING AGAIN... IT WILL BE TOO SOON.
=HUFF=

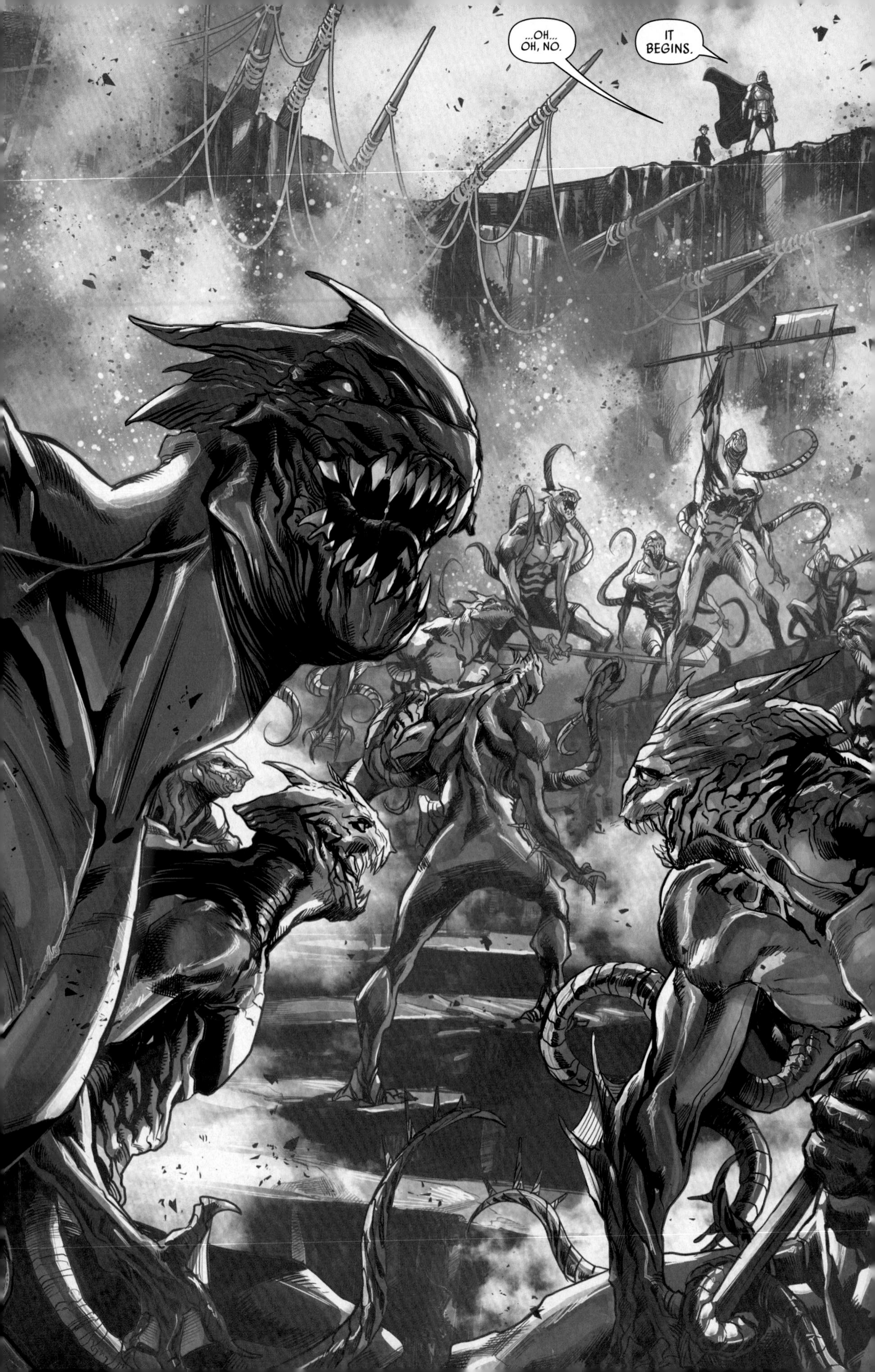
...OH...
OH, NO.
IT
BEGINS.

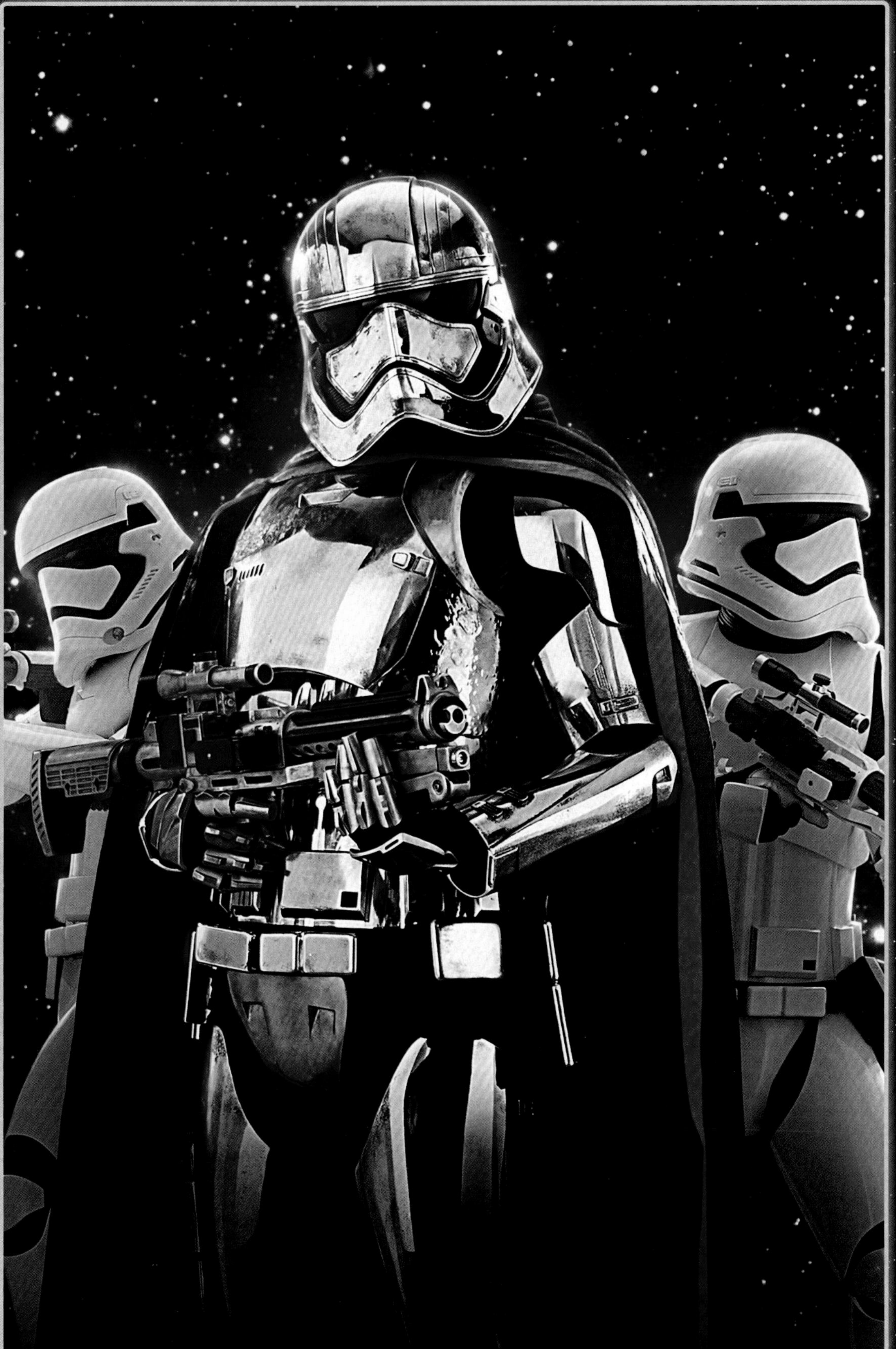

#4 Movie Variant

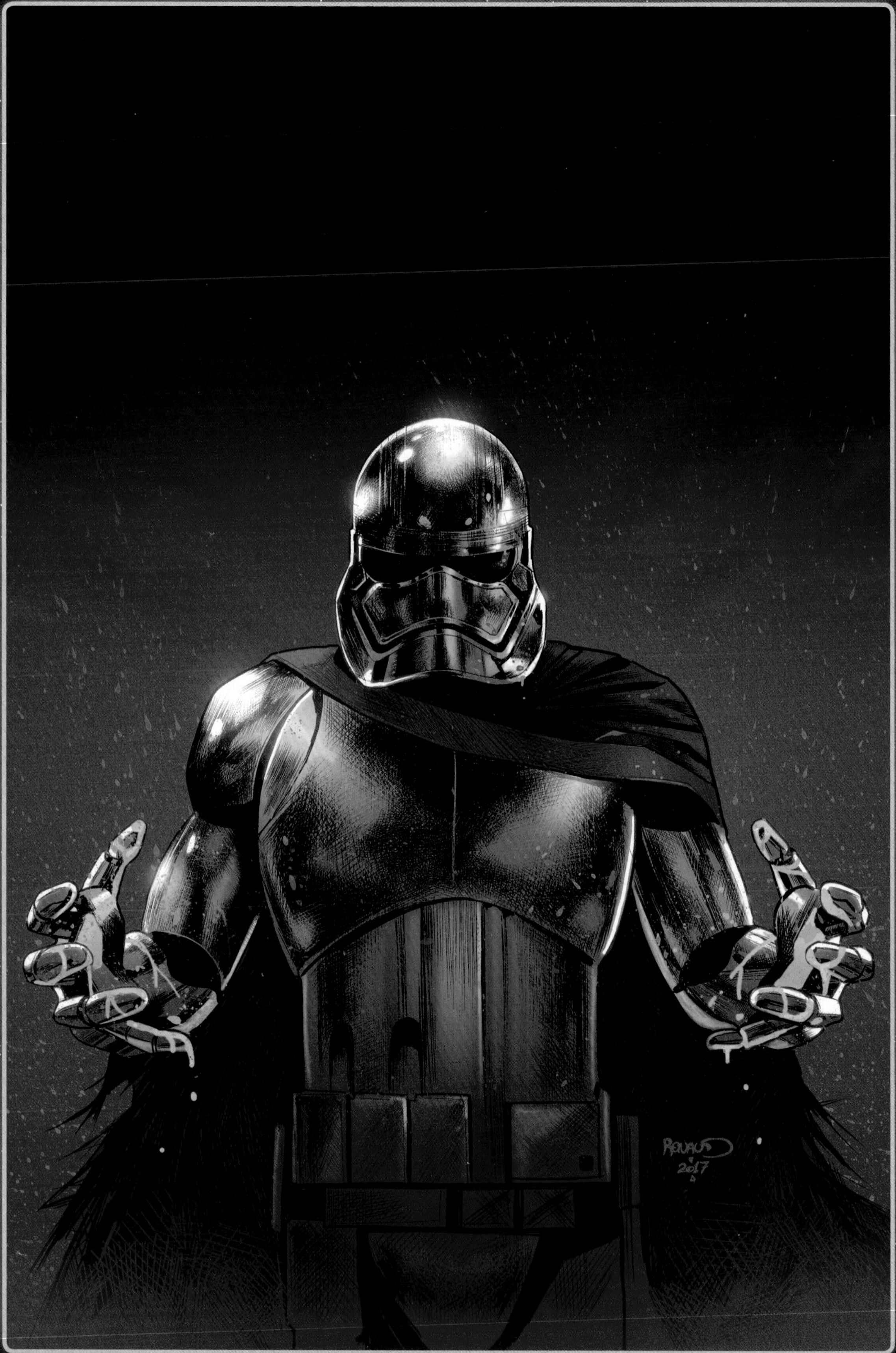

4

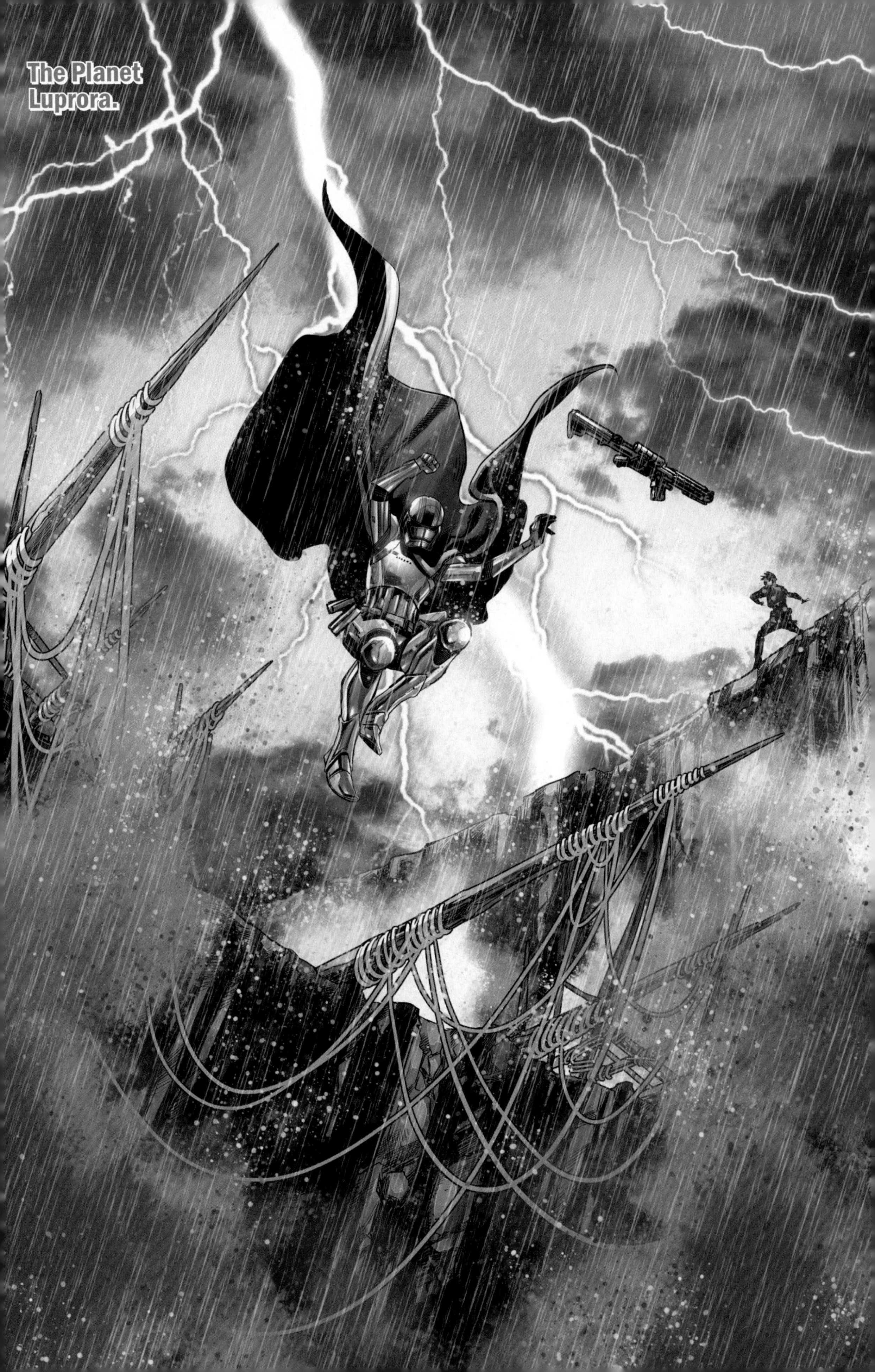
The Planet Luprora.

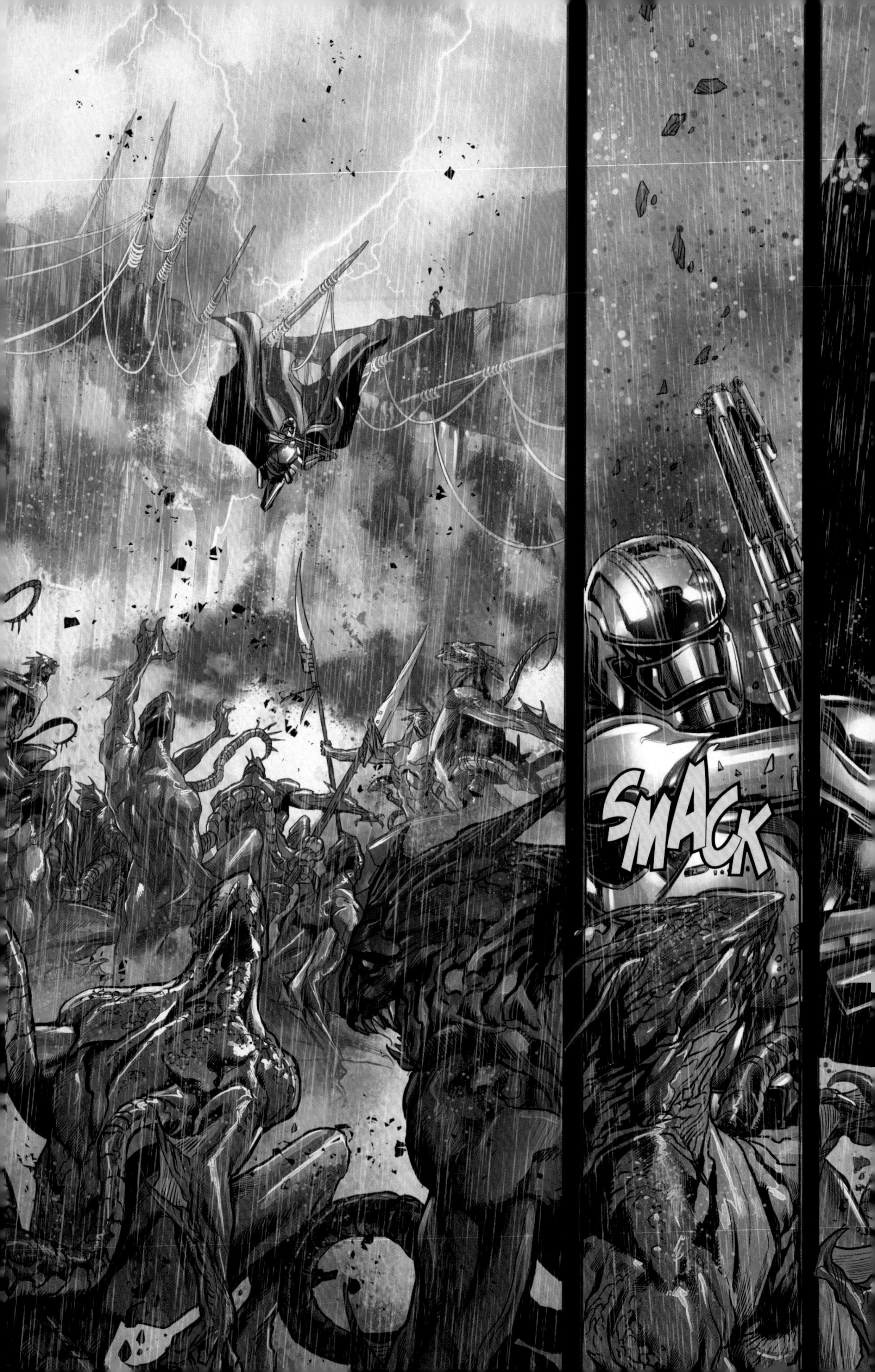
SMACK

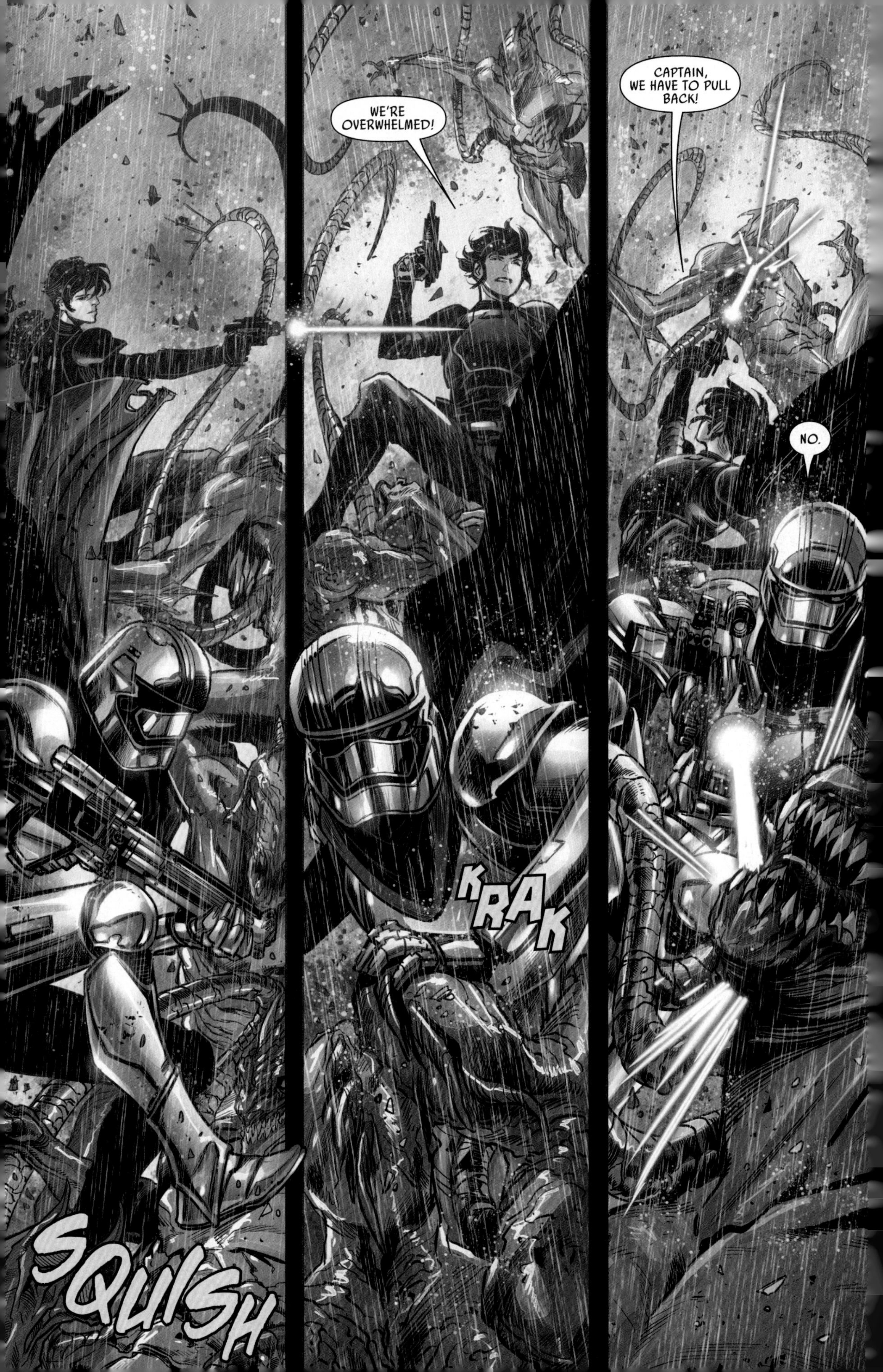
SQUISH
WE'RE OVERWHELMED!
KRAK
CAPTAIN, WE HAVE TO PULL BACK!
NO.

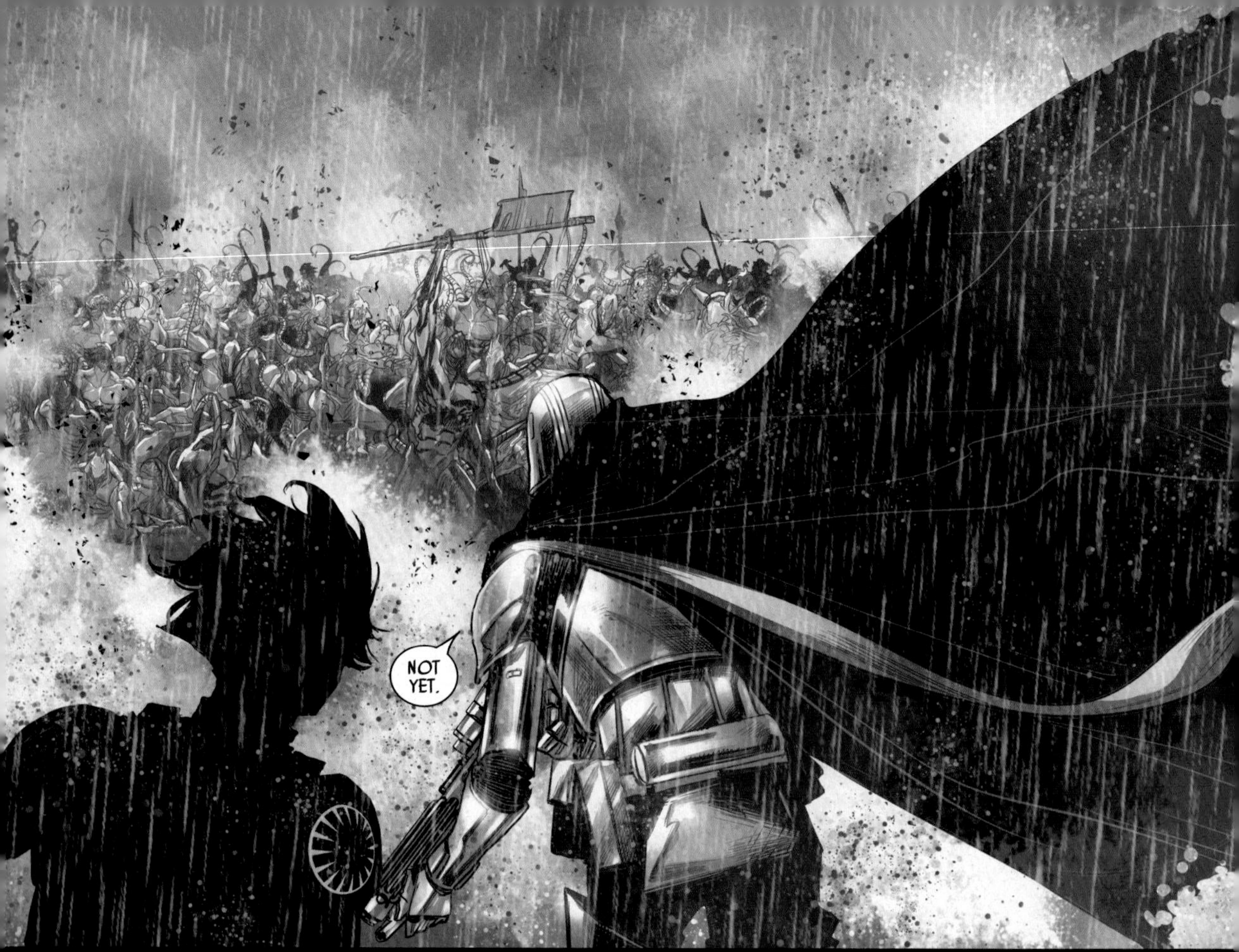
NOT YET.

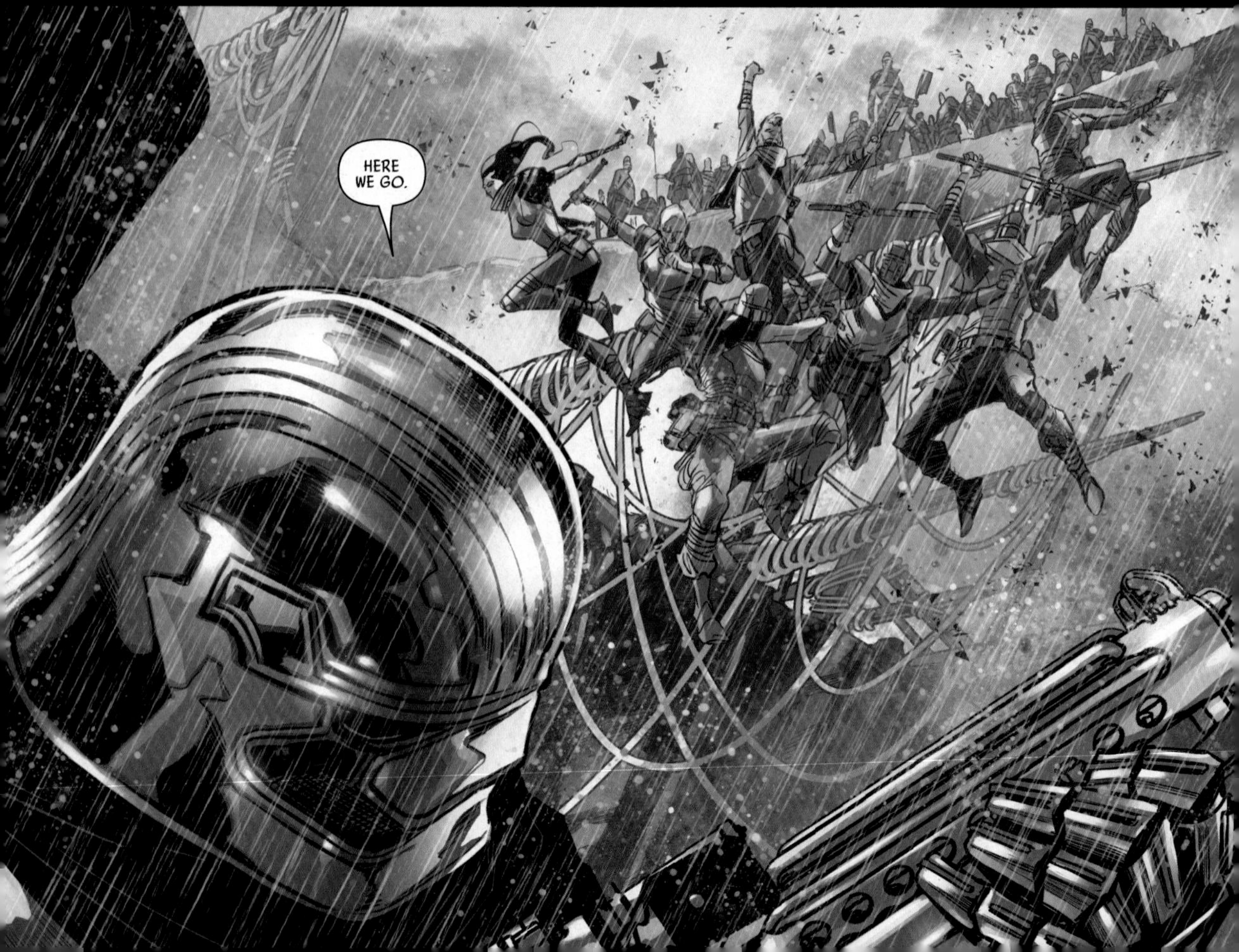
HERE WE GO.

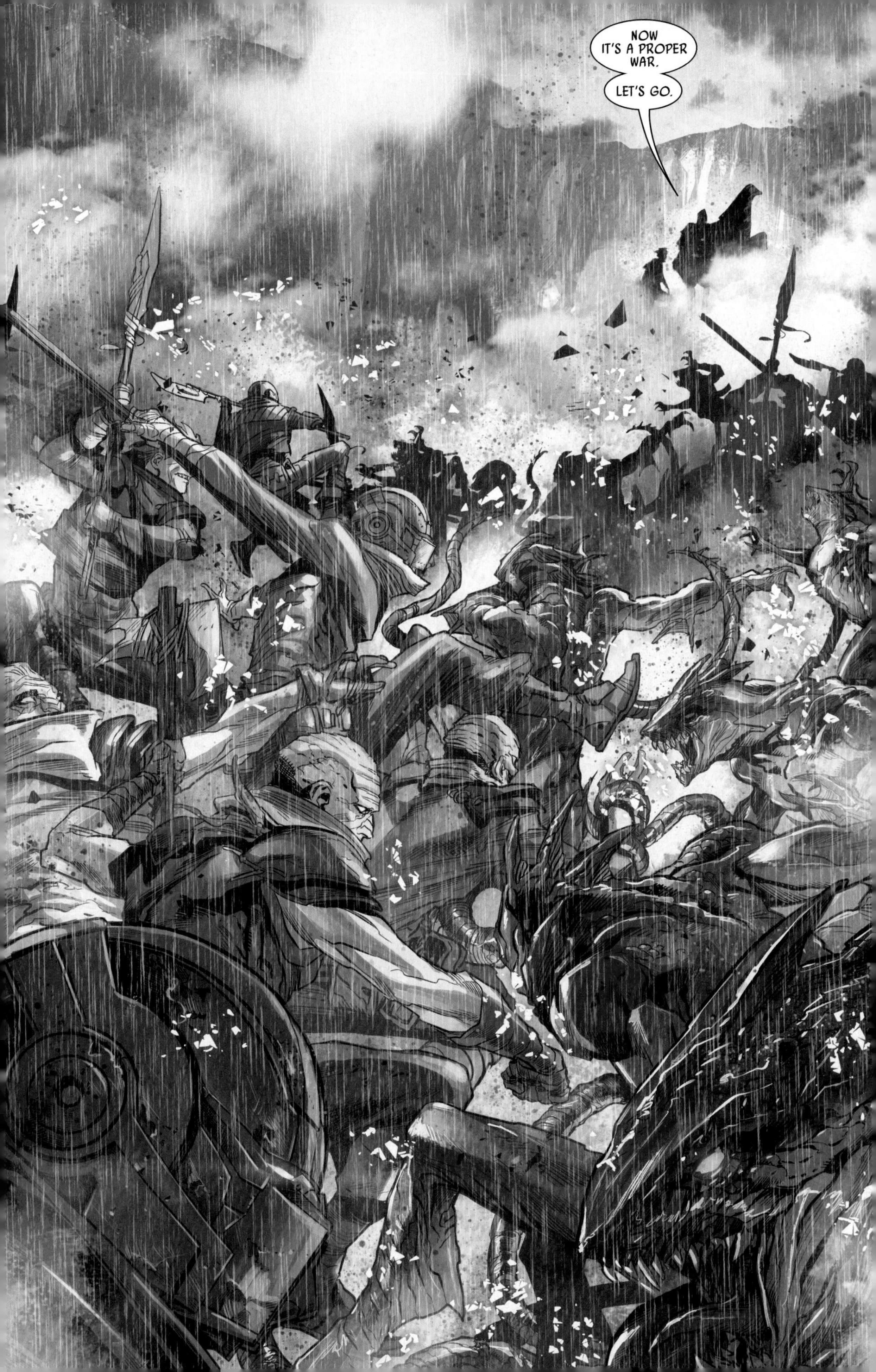
NOW IT'S A PROPER WAR.
LET'S GO.

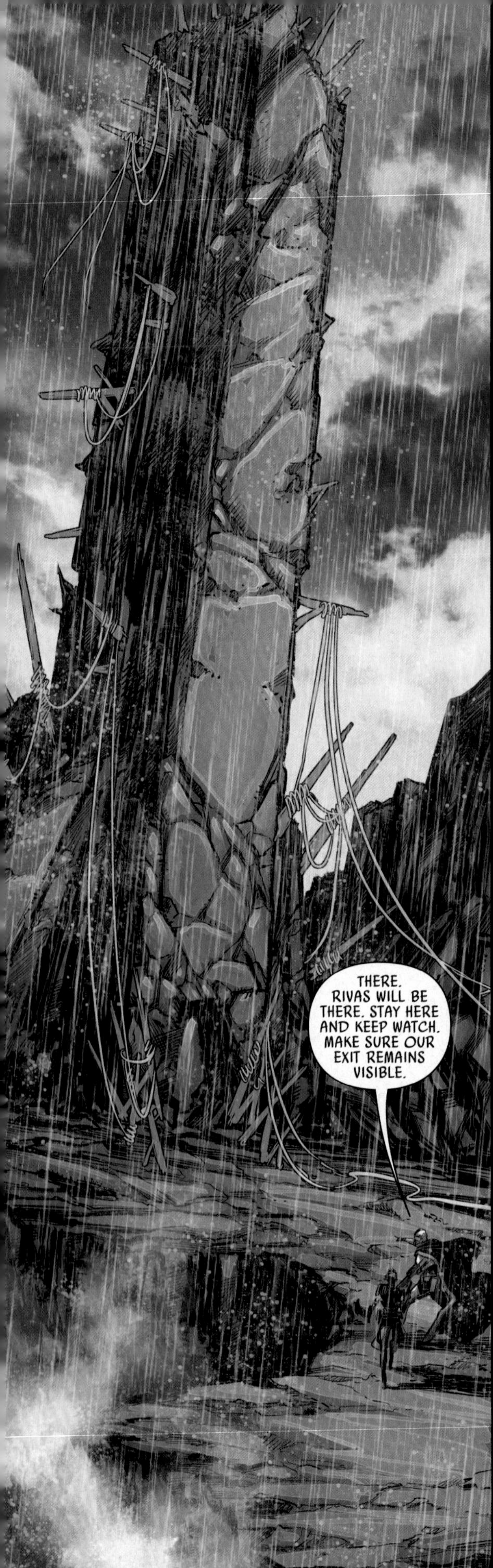
THERE. RIVAS WILL BE THERE. STAY HERE AND KEEP WATCH. MAKE SURE OUR EXIT REMAINS VISIBLE.
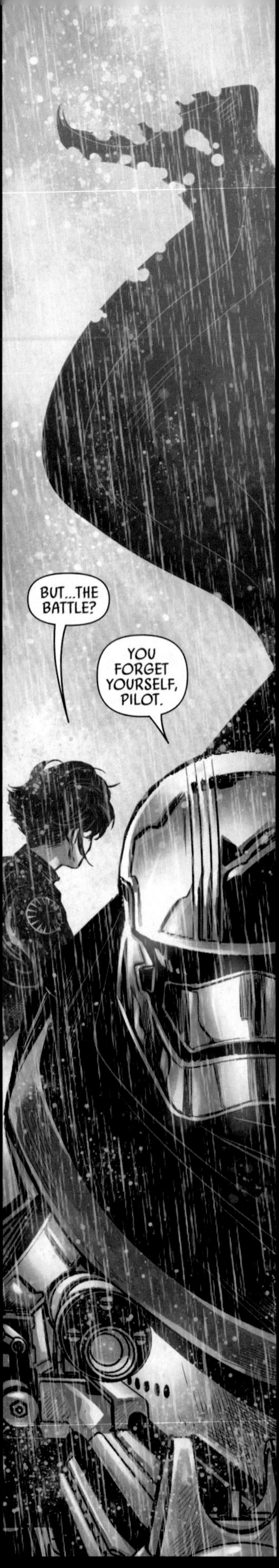
BUT...THE BATTLE?
YOU FORGET YOURSELF, PILOT.
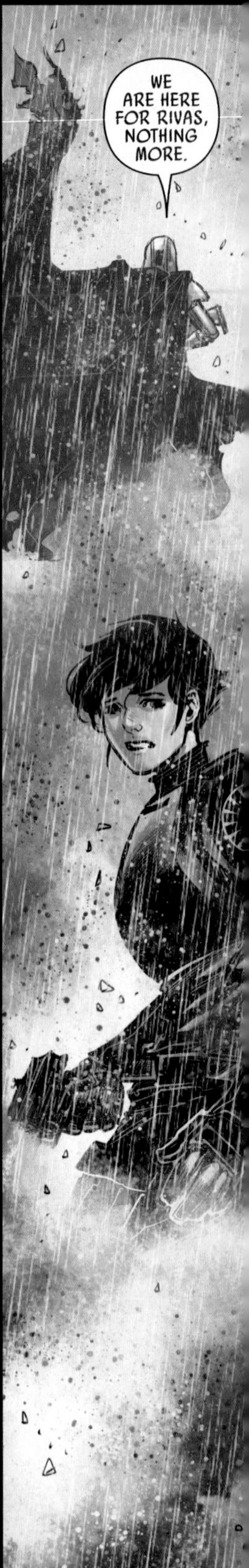
WE ARE HERE FOR RIVAS, NOTHING MORE.

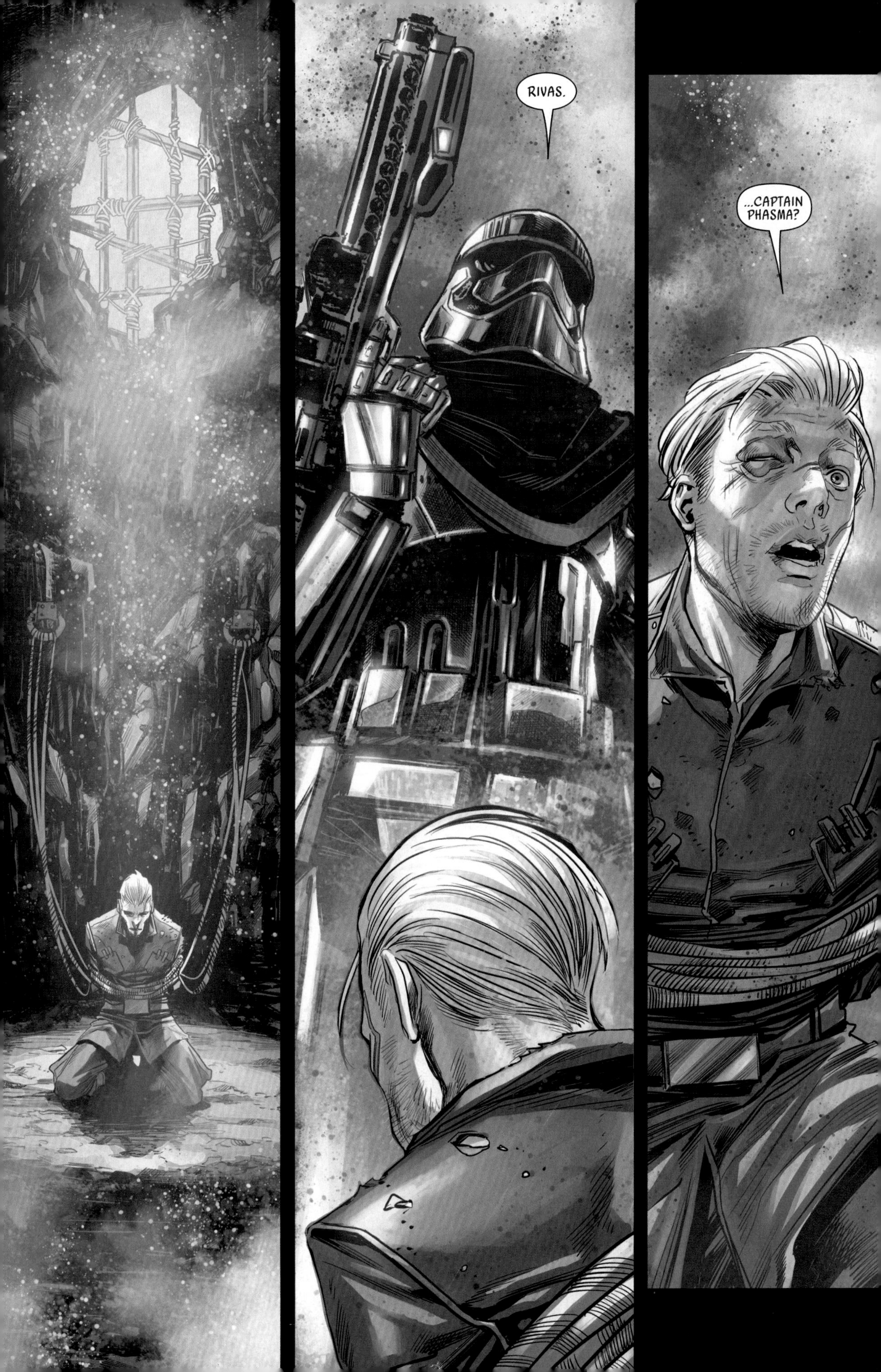
RIVAS.
...CAPTAIN PHASMA?

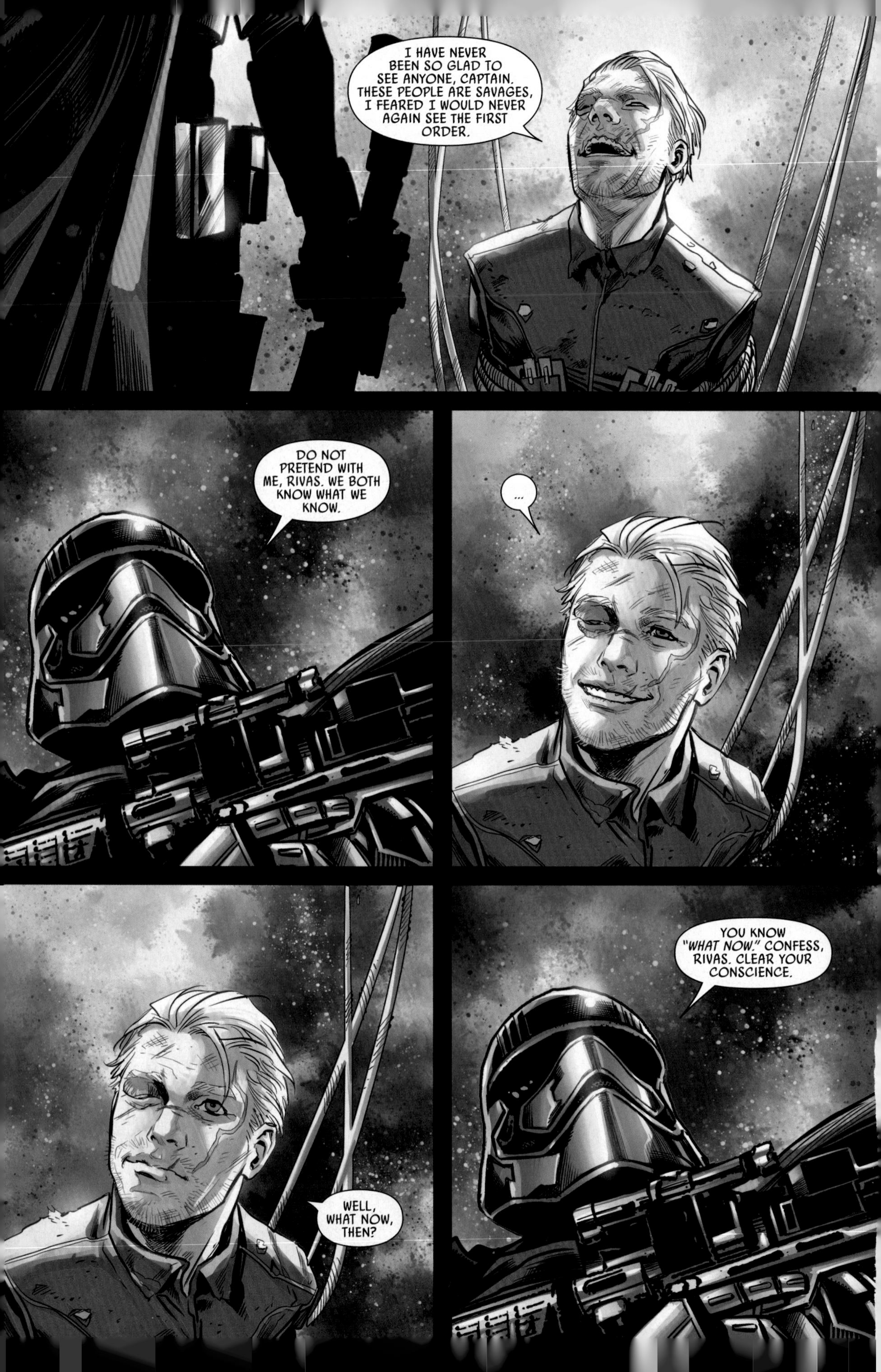
I HAVE NEVER BEEN SO GLAD TO SEE ANYONE, CAPTAIN. THESE PEOPLE ARE SAVAGES, I FEARED I WOULD NEVER AGAIN SEE THE FIRST ORDER.
DO NOT PRETEND WITH ME, RIVAS. WE BOTH KNOW WHAT WE KNOW.
...
WELL, WHAT NOW, THEN?
YOU KNOW "WHAT NOW." CONFESS, RIVAS. CLEAR YOUR CONSCIENCE.

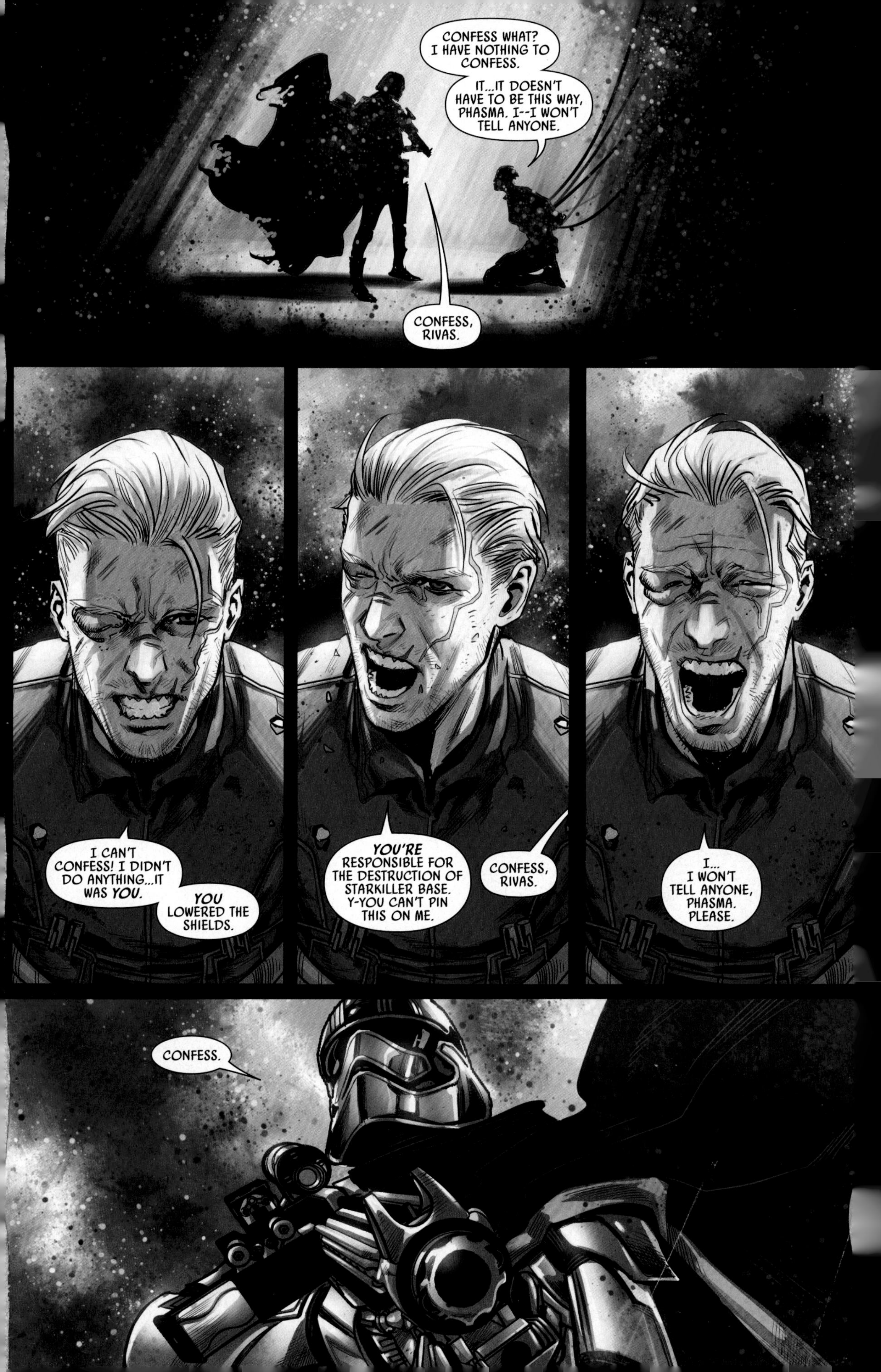
CONFESS WHAT? I HAVE NOTHING TO CONFESS.
IT...IT DOESN'T HAVE TO BE THIS WAY, PHASMA. I--I WON'T TELL ANYONE.
CONFESS, RIVAS.
I CAN'T CONFESS! I DIDN'T DO ANYTHING...IT WAS *YOU*.
YOU LOWERED THE SHIELDS.
YOU'RE RESPONSIBLE FOR THE DESTRUCTION OF STARKILLER BASE. Y-YOU CAN'T PIN THIS ON ME.
CONFESS, RIVAS.
I... I WON'T TELL ANYONE, PHASMA. PLEASE.
CONFESS.

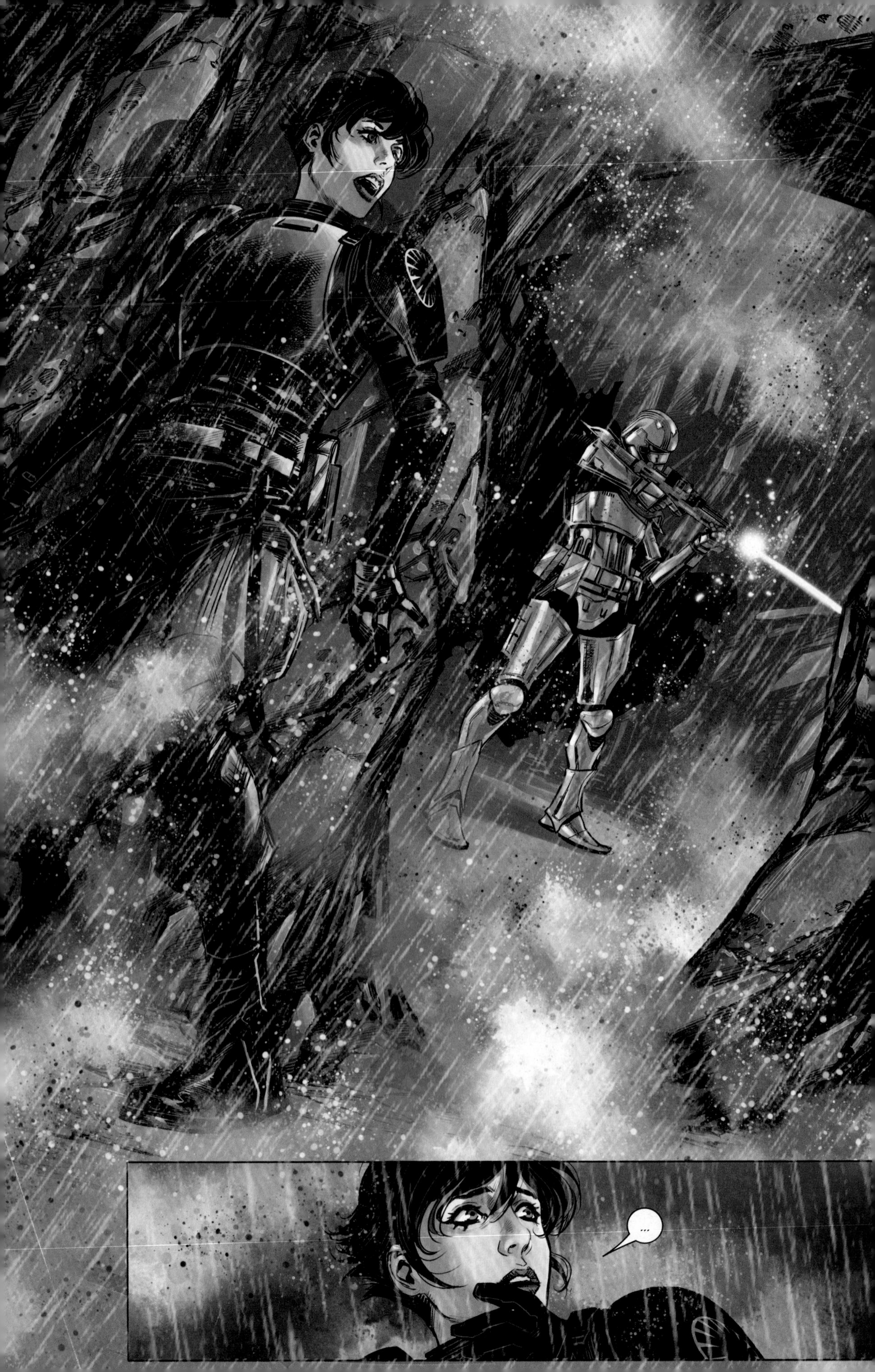
...

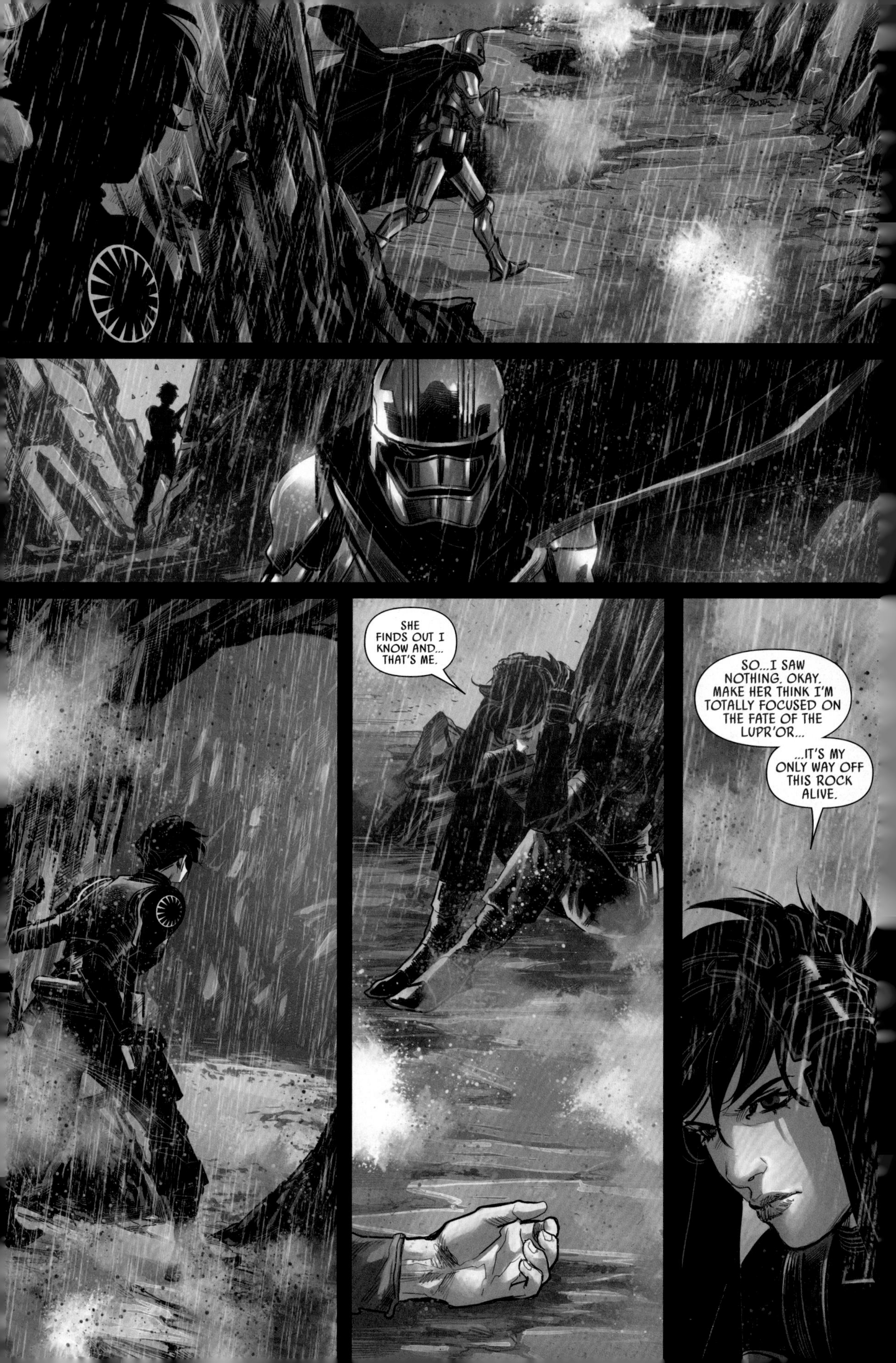
SHE FINDS OUT I KNOW AND... THAT'S ME.
SO...I SAW NOTHING. OKAY. MAKE HER THINK I'M TOTALLY FOCUSED ON THE FATE OF THE LUPR'OR...
...IT'S MY ONLY WAY OFF THIS ROCK ALIVE.

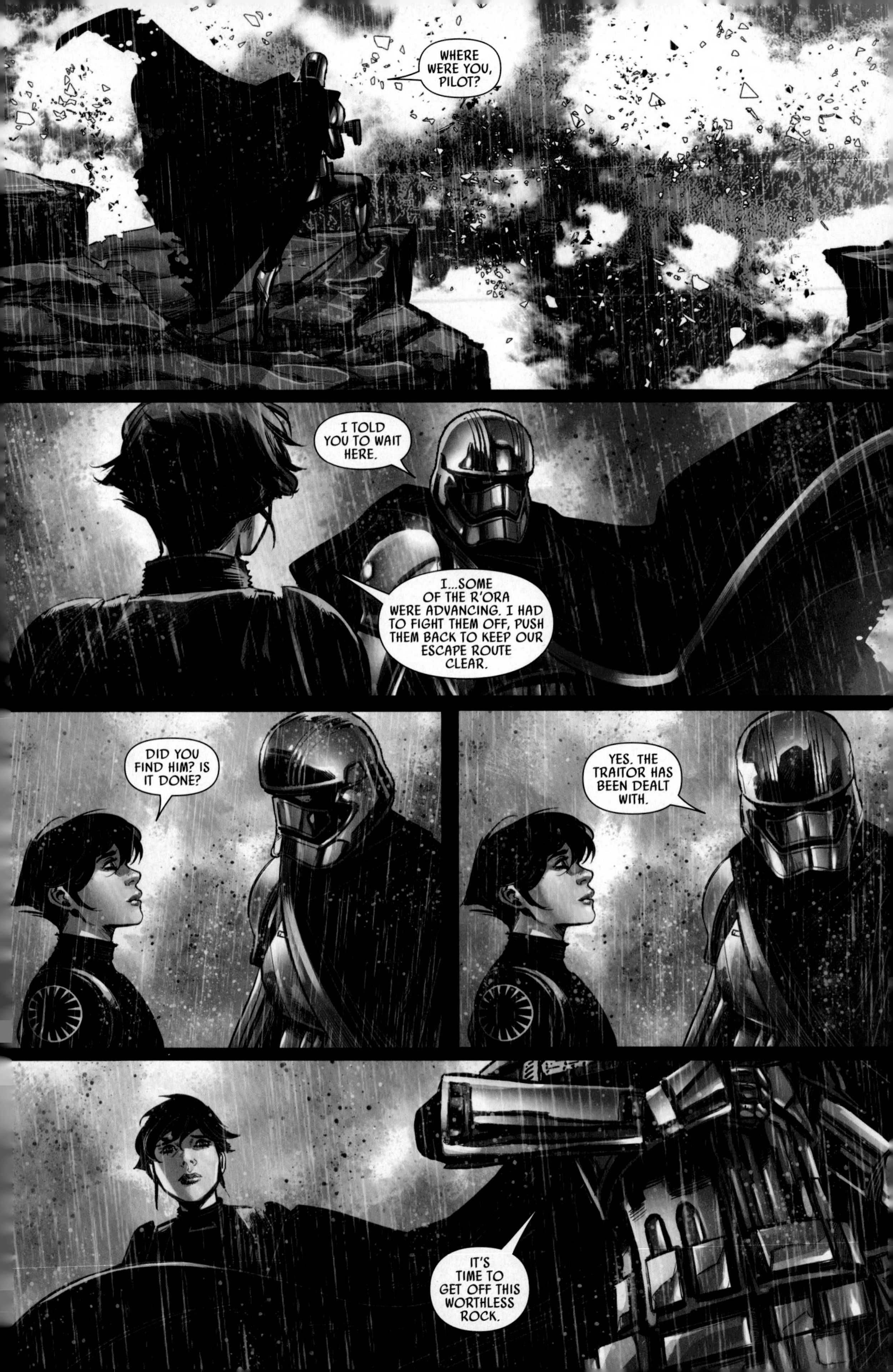
WHERE WERE YOU, PILOT?
I TOLD YOU TO WAIT HERE.
I...SOME OF THE R'ORA WERE ADVANCING. I HAD TO FIGHT THEM OFF, PUSH THEM BACK TO KEEP OUR ESCAPE ROUTE CLEAR.
DID YOU FIND HIM? IS IT DONE?
YES. THE TRAITOR HAS BEEN DEALT WITH.
IT'S TIME TO GET OFF THIS WORTHLESS ROCK.

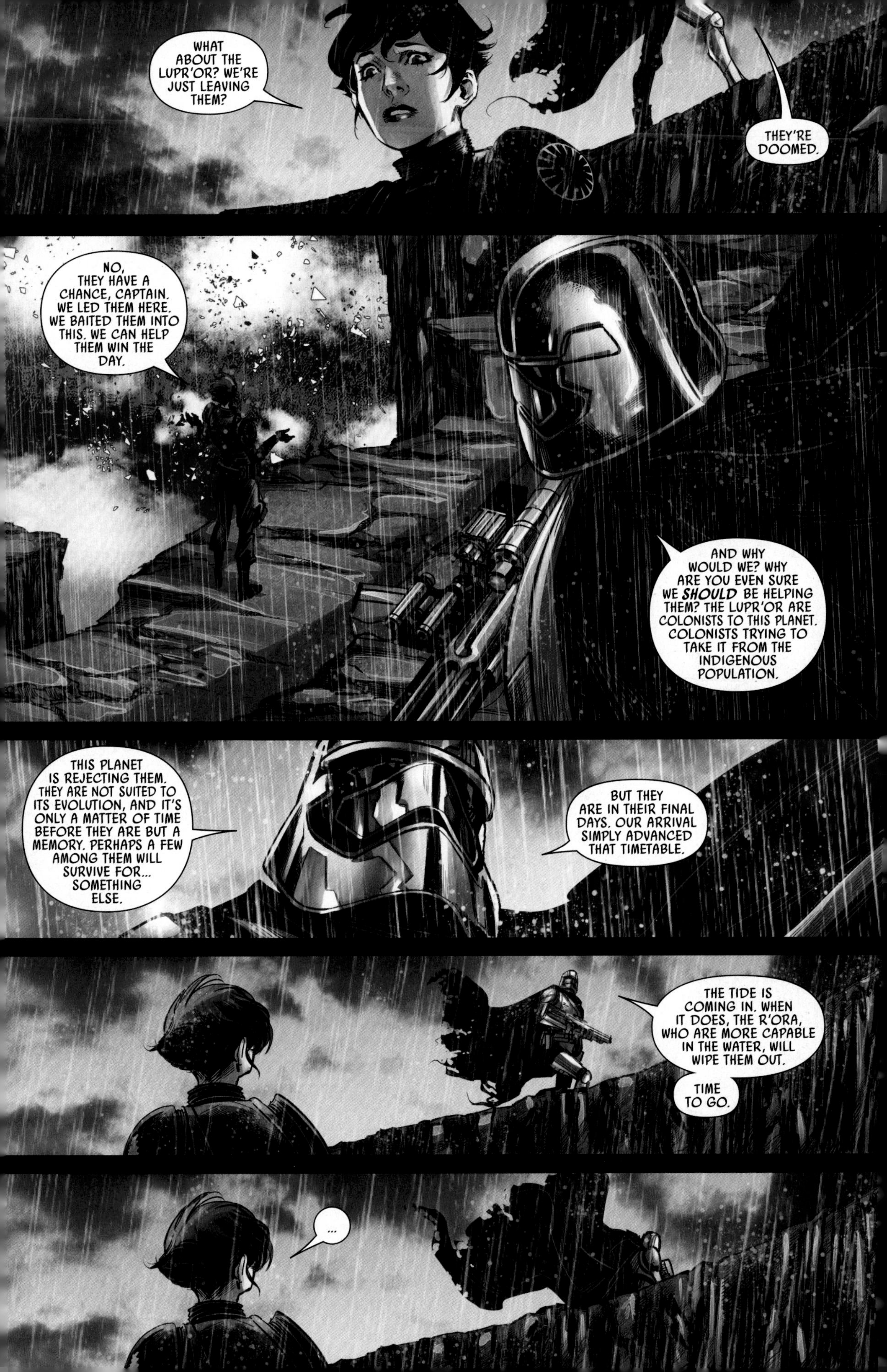
WHAT ABOUT THE LUPR'OR? WE'RE JUST LEAVING THEM?
THEY'RE DOOMED.
NO, THEY HAVE A CHANCE, CAPTAIN. WE LED THEM HERE. WE BAITED THEM INTO THIS. WE CAN HELP THEM WIN THE DAY.
AND WHY WOULD WE? WHY ARE YOU EVEN SURE WE *SHOULD* BE HELPING THEM? THE LUPR'OR ARE COLONISTS TO THIS PLANET. COLONISTS TRYING TO TAKE IT FROM THE INDIGENOUS POPULATION.
THIS PLANET IS REJECTING THEM. THEY ARE NOT SUITED TO ITS EVOLUTION, AND IT'S ONLY A MATTER OF TIME BEFORE THEY ARE BUT A MEMORY. PERHAPS A FEW AMONG THEM WILL SURVIVE FOR... SOMETHING ELSE.
BUT THEY ARE IN THEIR FINAL DAYS. OUR ARRIVAL SIMPLY ADVANCED THAT TIMETABLE.
THE TIDE IS COMING IN. WHEN IT DOES, THE R'ORA, WHO ARE MORE CAPABLE IN THE WATER, WILL WIPE THEM OUT.
TIME TO GO.
...

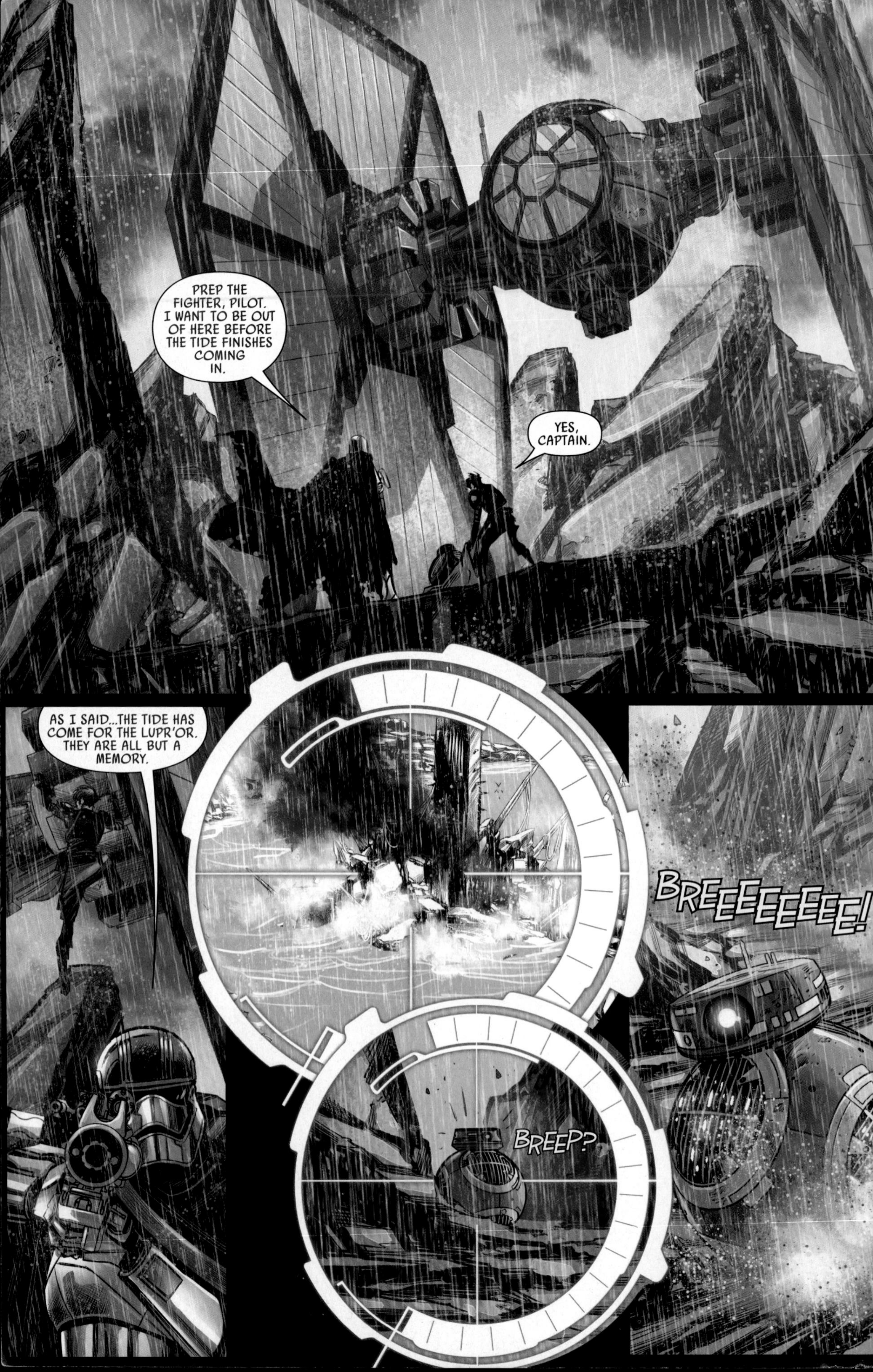
PREP THE FIGHTER, PILOT. I WANT TO BE OUT OF HERE BEFORE THE TIDE FINISHES COMING IN.
YES, CAPTAIN.
AS I SAID...THE TIDE HAS COME FOR THE LUPR'OR. THEY ARE ALL BUT A MEMORY.
BREEP?
BREEEEEEEEE!

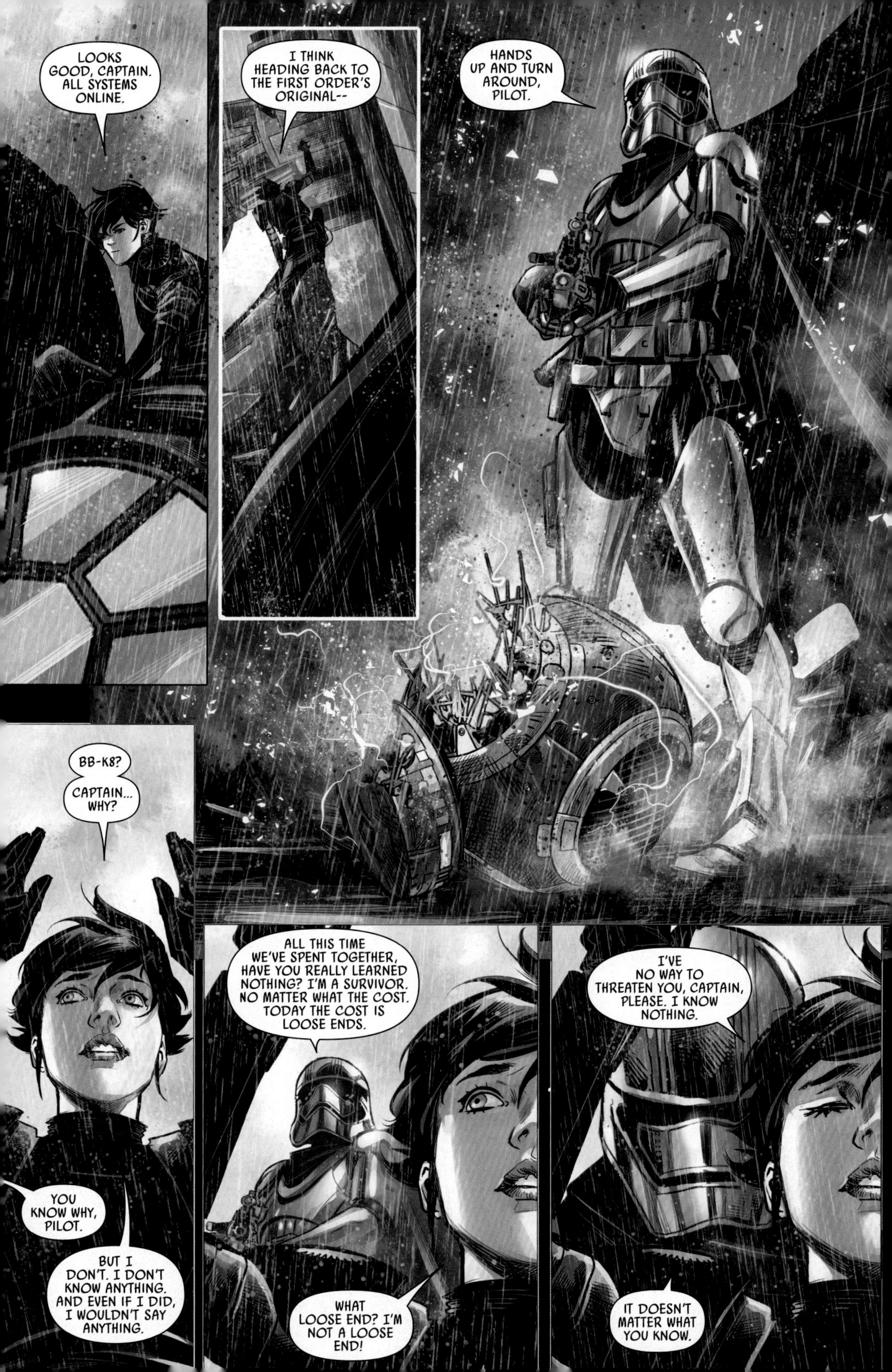
LOOKS GOOD, CAPTAIN. ALL SYSTEMS ONLINE.
I THINK HEADING BACK TO THE FIRST ORDER'S ORIGINAL--
HANDS UP AND TURN AROUND, PILOT.
BB-K8?
CAPTAIN... WHY?
YOU KNOW WHY, PILOT.
BUT I DON'T. I DON'T KNOW ANYTHING. AND EVEN IF I DID, I WOULDN'T SAY ANYTHING.
ALL THIS TIME WE'VE SPENT TOGETHER, HAVE YOU REALLY LEARNED NOTHING? I'M A SURVIVOR. NO MATTER WHAT THE COST. TODAY THE COST IS LOOSE ENDS.
WHAT LOOSE END? I'M NOT A LOOSE END!
I'VE NO WAY TO THREATEN YOU, CAPTAIN, PLEASE. I KNOW NOTHING.
IT DOESN'T MATTER WHAT YOU KNOW.

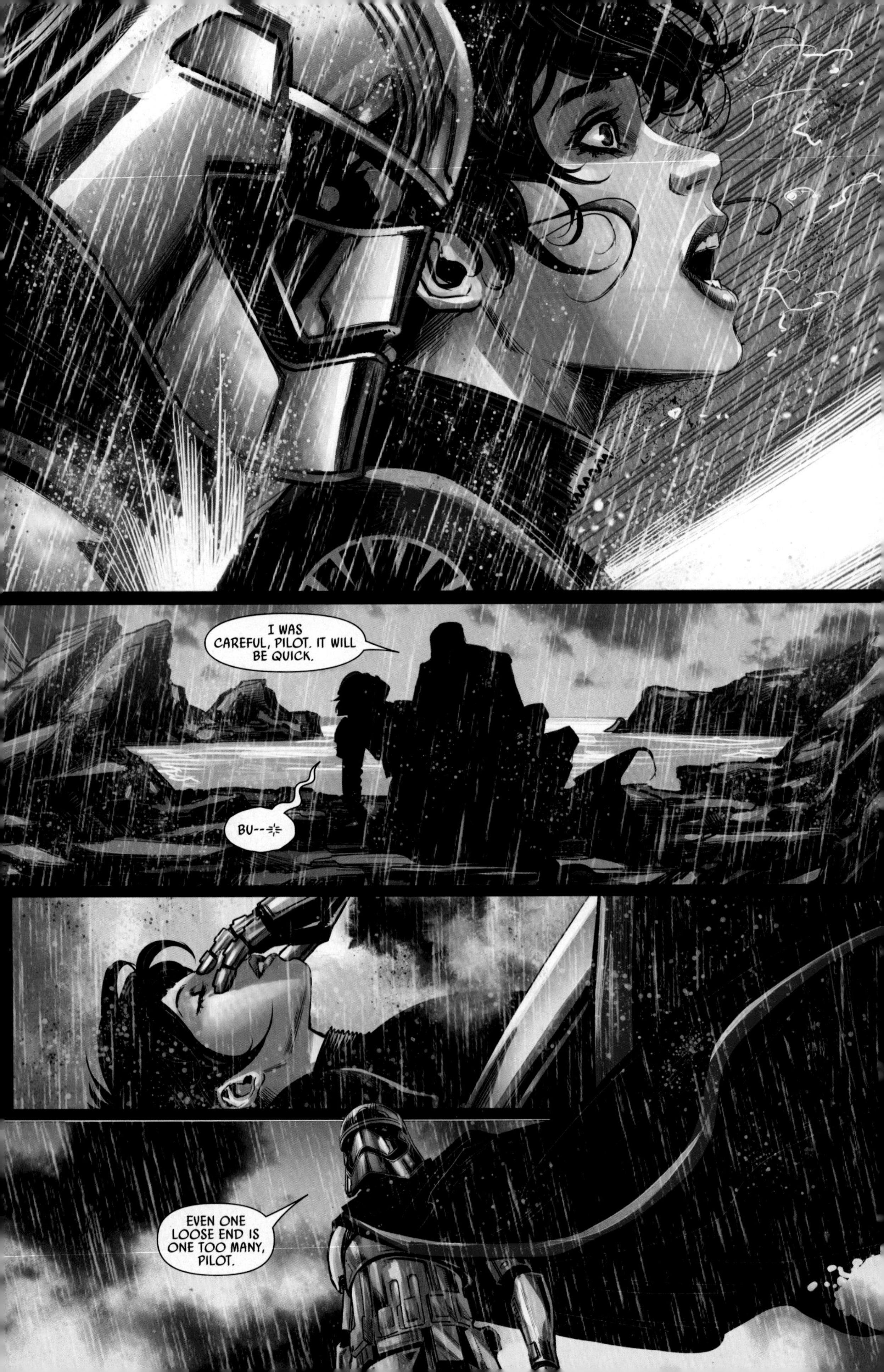
I WAS CAREFUL, PILOT. IT WILL BE QUICK.
BU--
EVEN ONE LOOSE END IS ONE TOO MANY, PILOT.

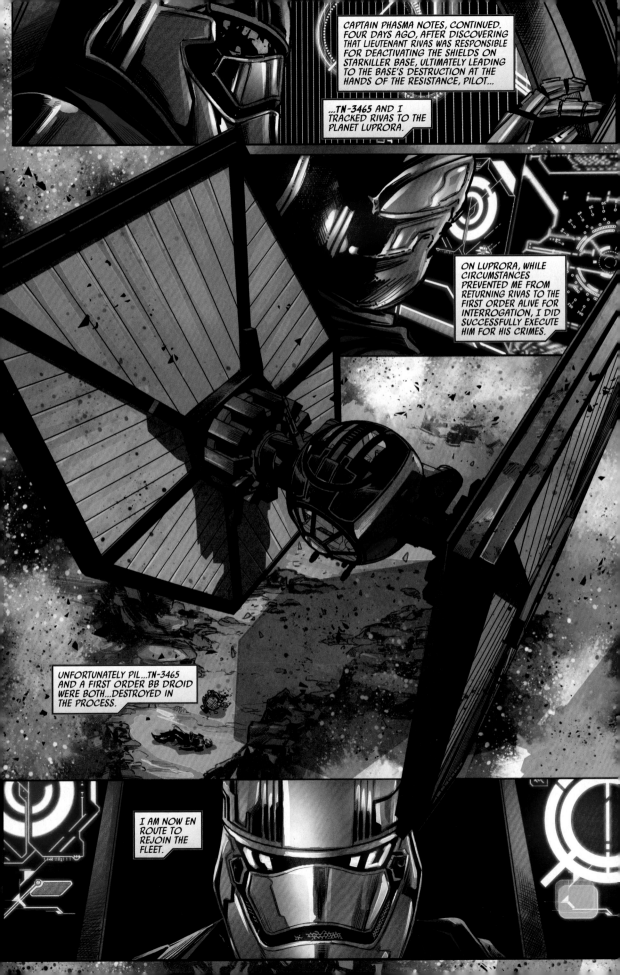

CAPTAIN PHASMA NOTES, CONTINUED. FOUR DAYS AGO, AFTER DISCOVERING THAT LIEUTENANT RIVAS WAS RESPONSIBLE FOR DEACTIVATING THE SHIELDS ON STARKILLER BASE, ULTIMATELY LEADING TO THE BASE'S DESTRUCTION AT THE HANDS OF THE RESISTANCE, PILOT...

...TN-3465 AND I TRACKED RIVAS TO THE PLANET LUPRORA.

ON LUPRORA, WHILE CIRCUMSTANCES PREVENTED ME FROM RETURNING RIVAS TO THE FIRST ORDER ALIVE FOR INTERROGATION, I DID SUCCESSFULLY EXECUTE HIM FOR HIS CRIMES.

UNFORTUNATELY PIL...TN-3465 AND A FIRST ORDER BB DROID WERE BOTH...DESTROYED IN THE PROCESS.

I AM NOW EN ROUTE TO REJOIN THE FLEET.

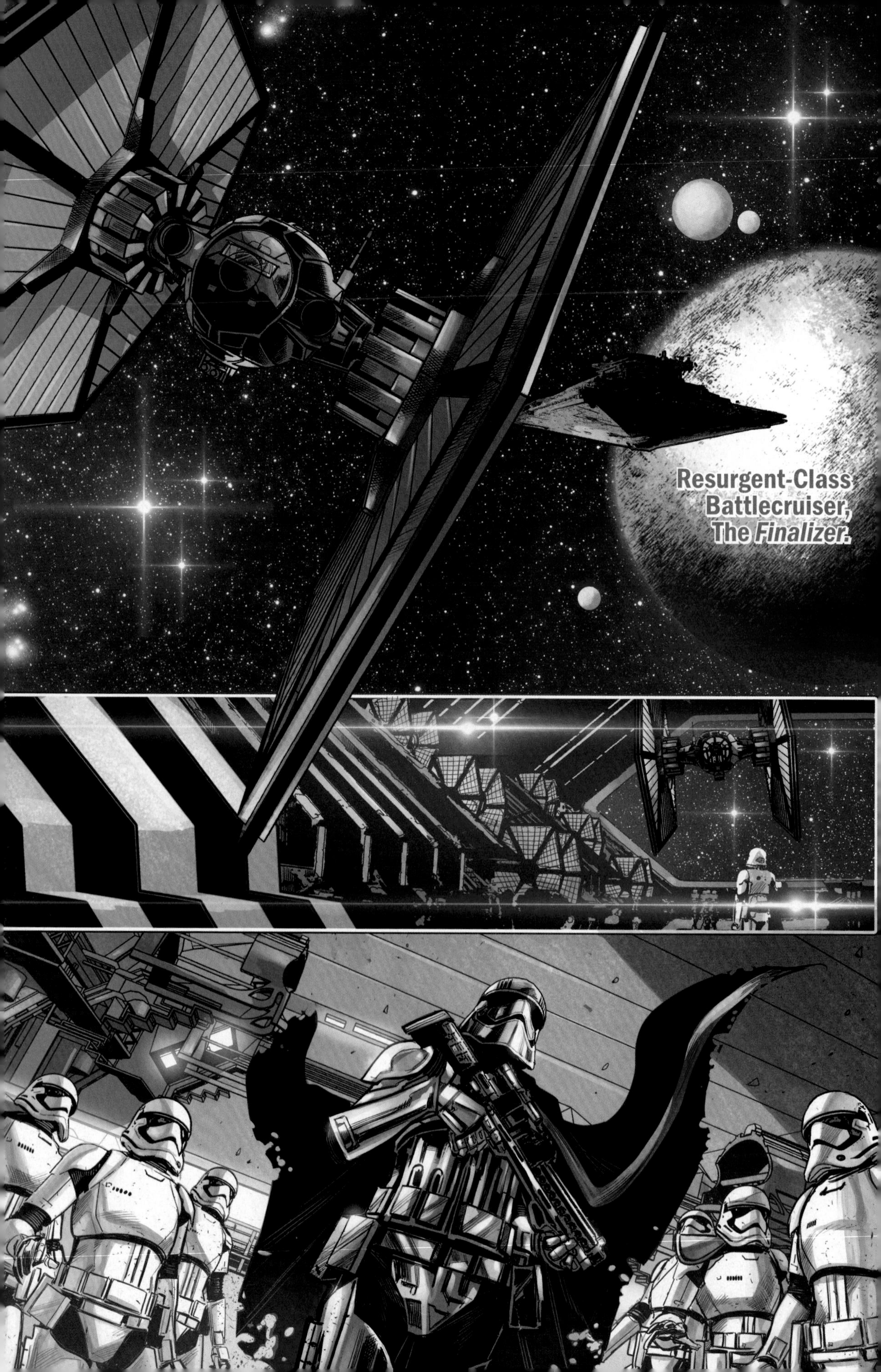
Resurgent-Class Battlecruiser, The *Finalizer.*

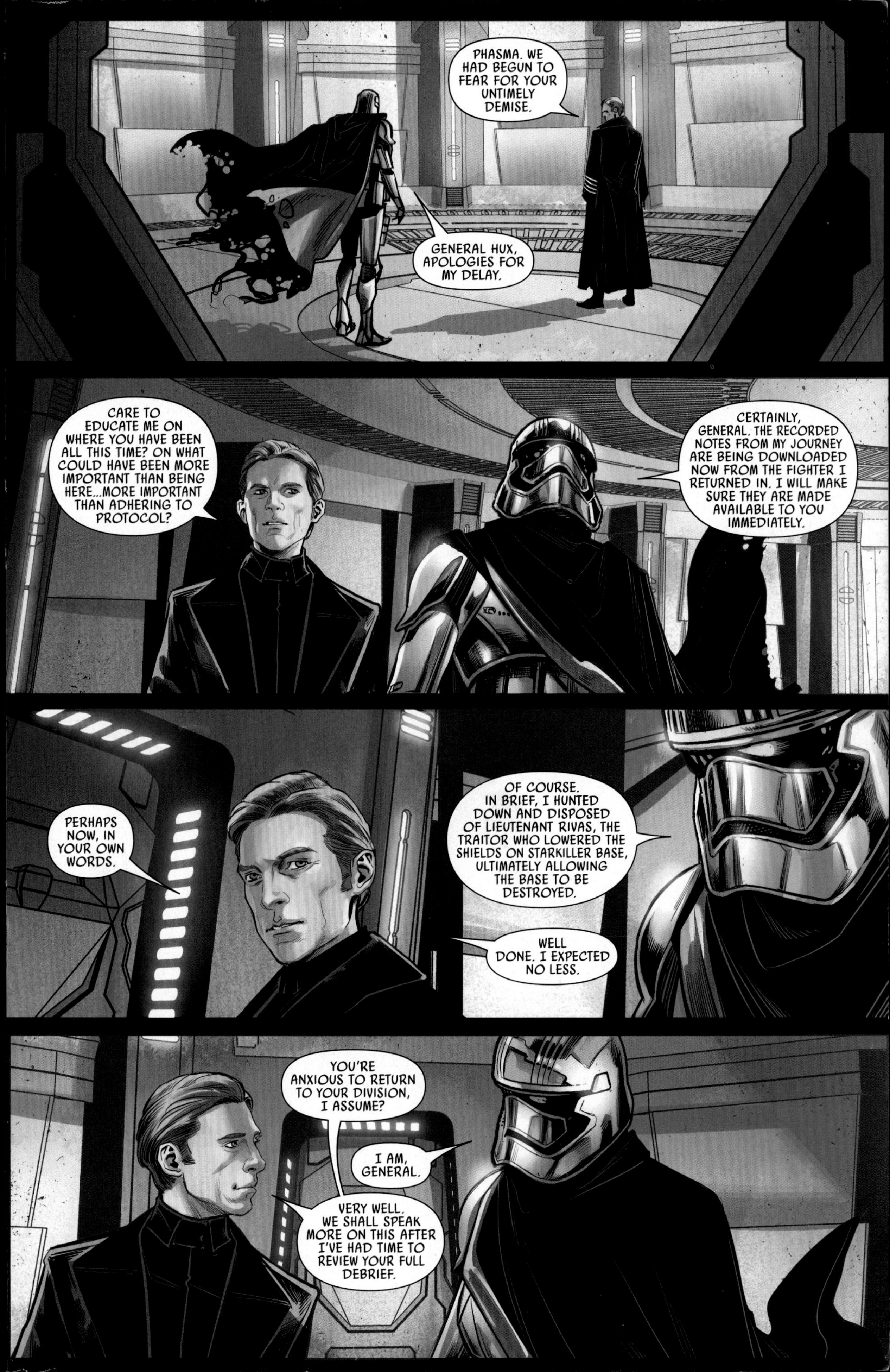
PHASMA. WE HAD BEGUN TO FEAR FOR YOUR UNTIMELY DEMISE.
GENERAL HUX, APOLOGIES FOR MY DELAY.
CARE TO EDUCATE ME ON WHERE YOU HAVE BEEN ALL THIS TIME? ON WHAT COULD HAVE BEEN MORE IMPORTANT THAN BEING HERE...MORE IMPORTANT THAN ADHERING TO PROTOCOL?
CERTAINLY, GENERAL. THE RECORDED NOTES FROM MY JOURNEY ARE BEING DOWNLOADED NOW FROM THE FIGHTER I RETURNED IN. I WILL MAKE SURE THEY ARE MADE AVAILABLE TO YOU IMMEDIATELY.
PERHAPS NOW, IN YOUR OWN WORDS.
OF COURSE. IN BRIEF, I HUNTED DOWN AND DISPOSED OF LIEUTENANT RIVAS, THE TRAITOR WHO LOWERED THE SHIELDS ON STARKILLER BASE, ULTIMATELY ALLOWING THE BASE TO BE DESTROYED.
WELL DONE. I EXPECTED NO LESS.
YOU'RE ANXIOUS TO RETURN TO YOUR DIVISION, I ASSUME?
I AM, GENERAL.
VERY WELL. WE SHALL SPEAK MORE ON THIS AFTER I'VE HAD TIME TO REVIEW YOUR FULL DEBRIEF.

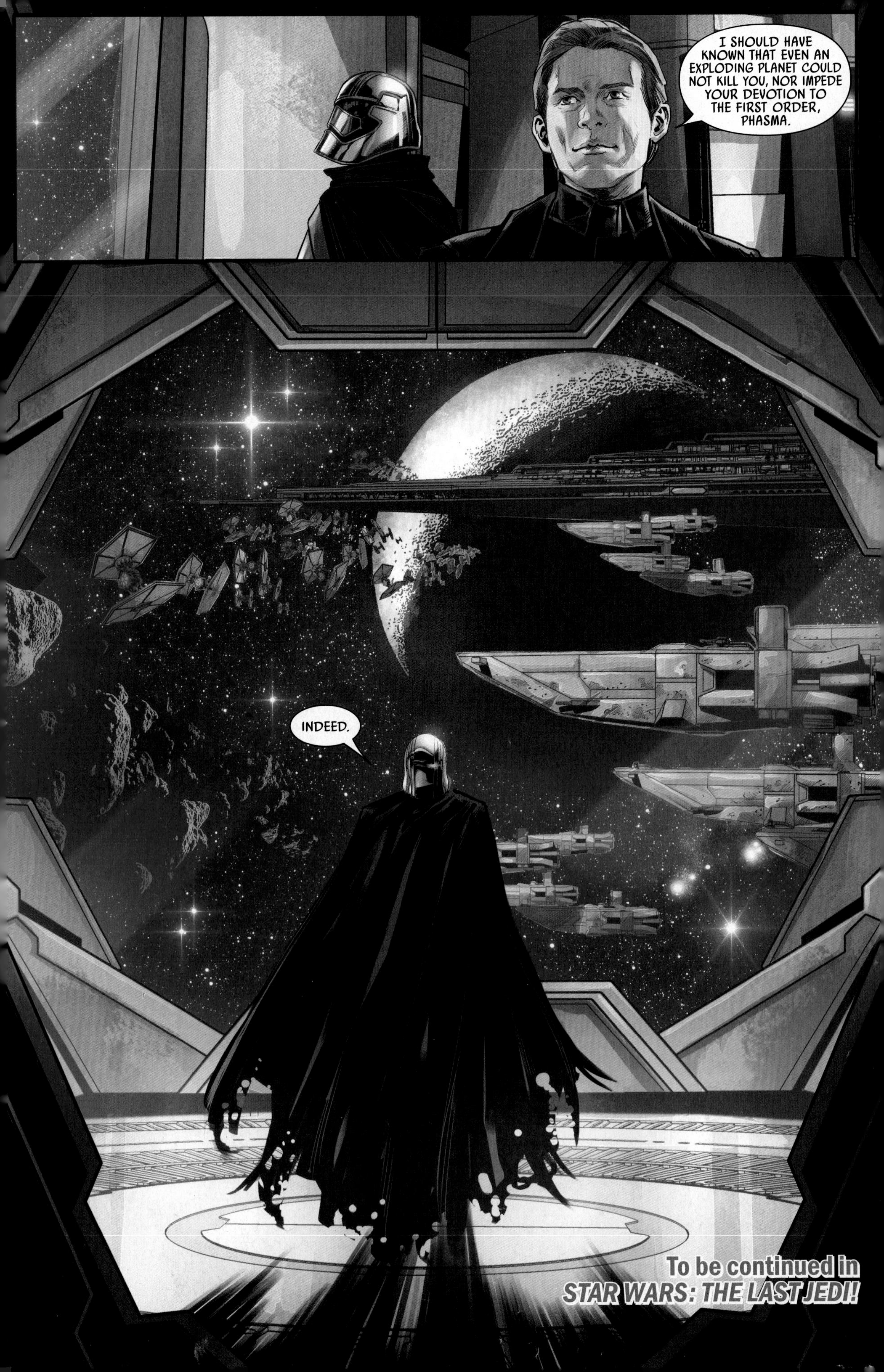
I SHOULD HAVE KNOWN THAT EVEN AN EXPLODING PLANET COULD NOT KILL YOU, NOR IMPEDE YOUR DEVOTION TO THE FIRST ORDER, PHASMA.
INDEED.
To be continued in STAR WARS: THE LAST JEDI!

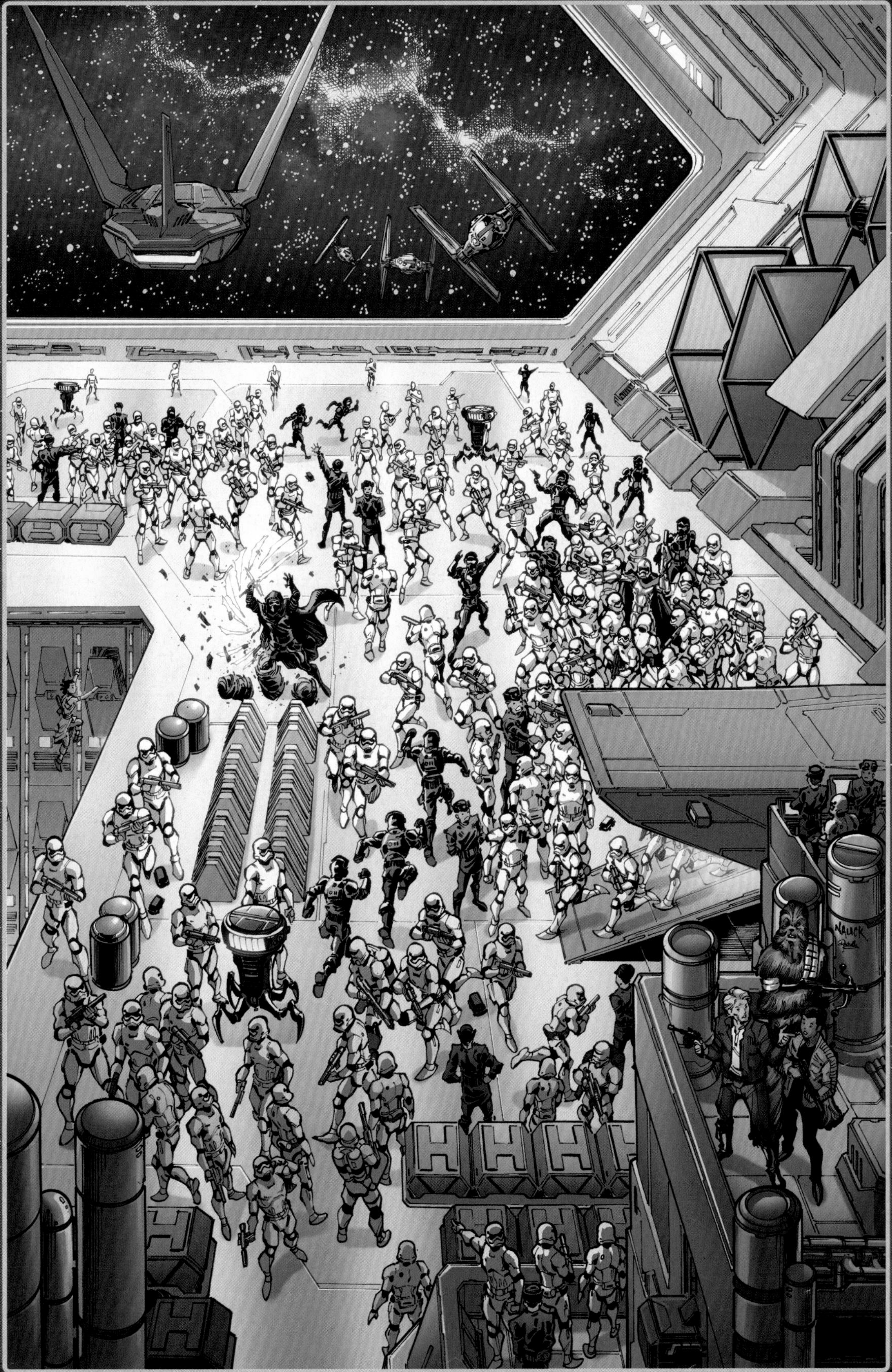

#1 Where's Phasma? Variant by TODD NAUCK & RACHELLE ROSENBERG

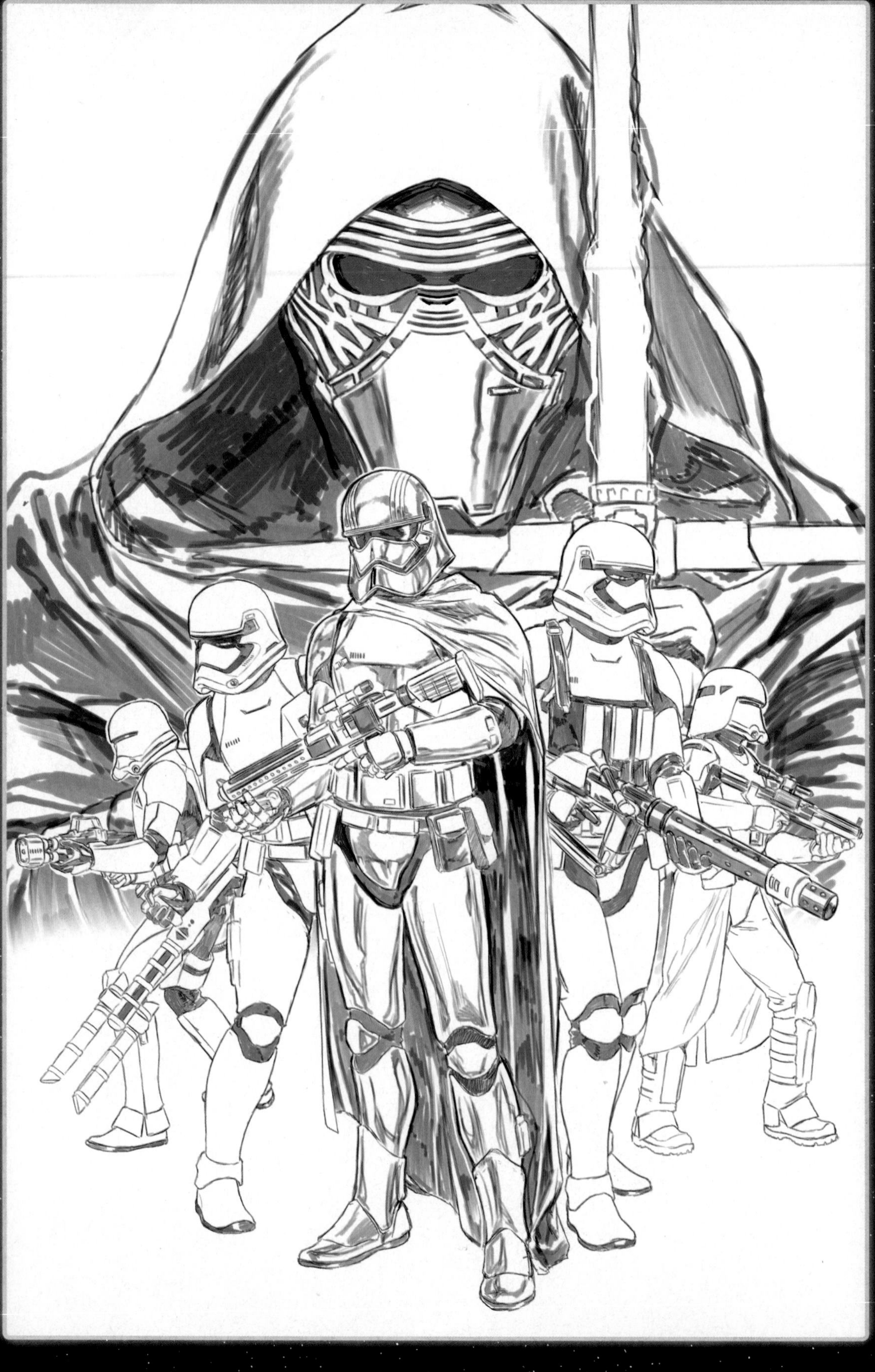

#1 Black and White Variant by MARK BROOKS

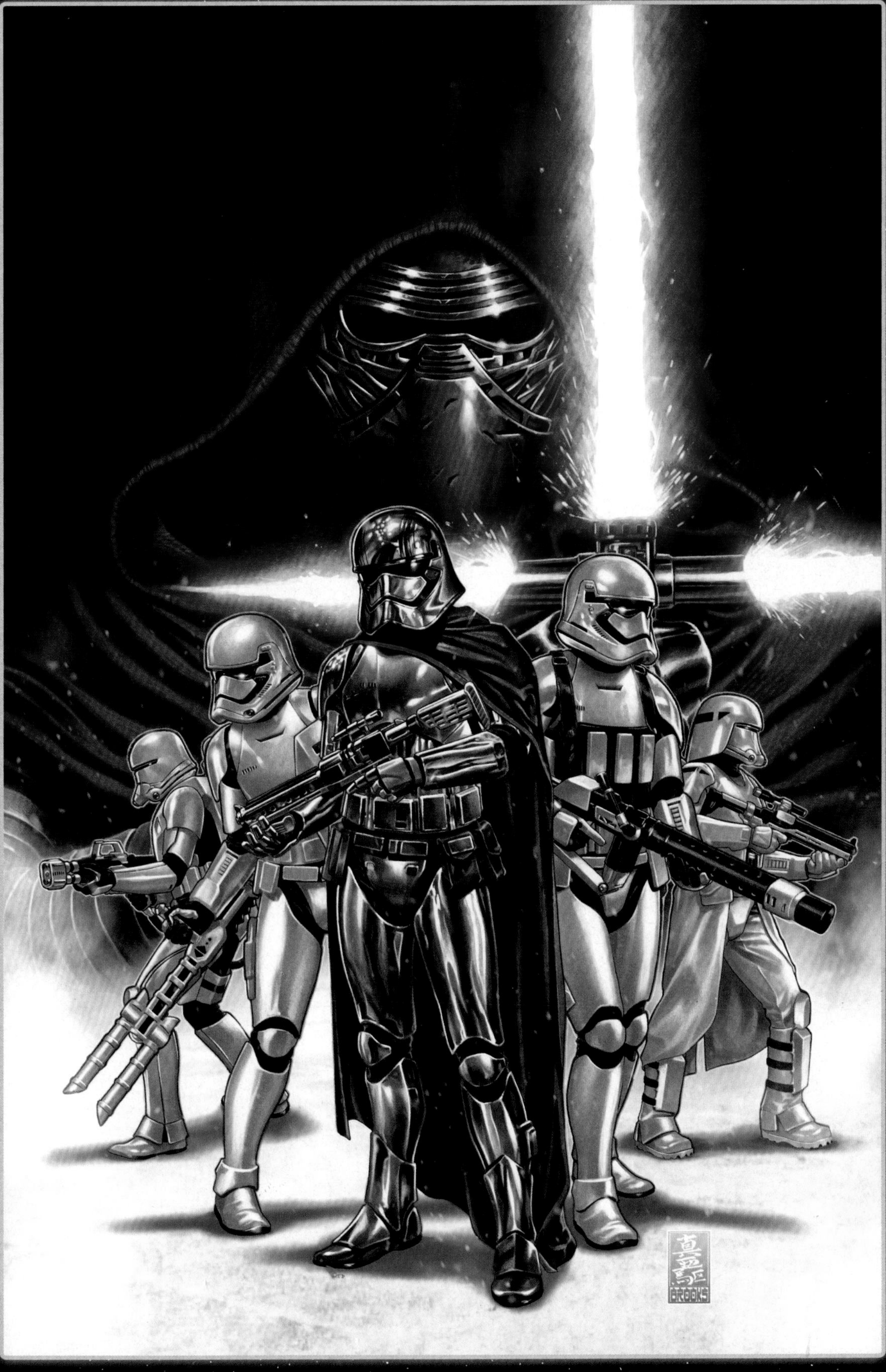
BROOKS

#1 Variant by MARK BROOKS

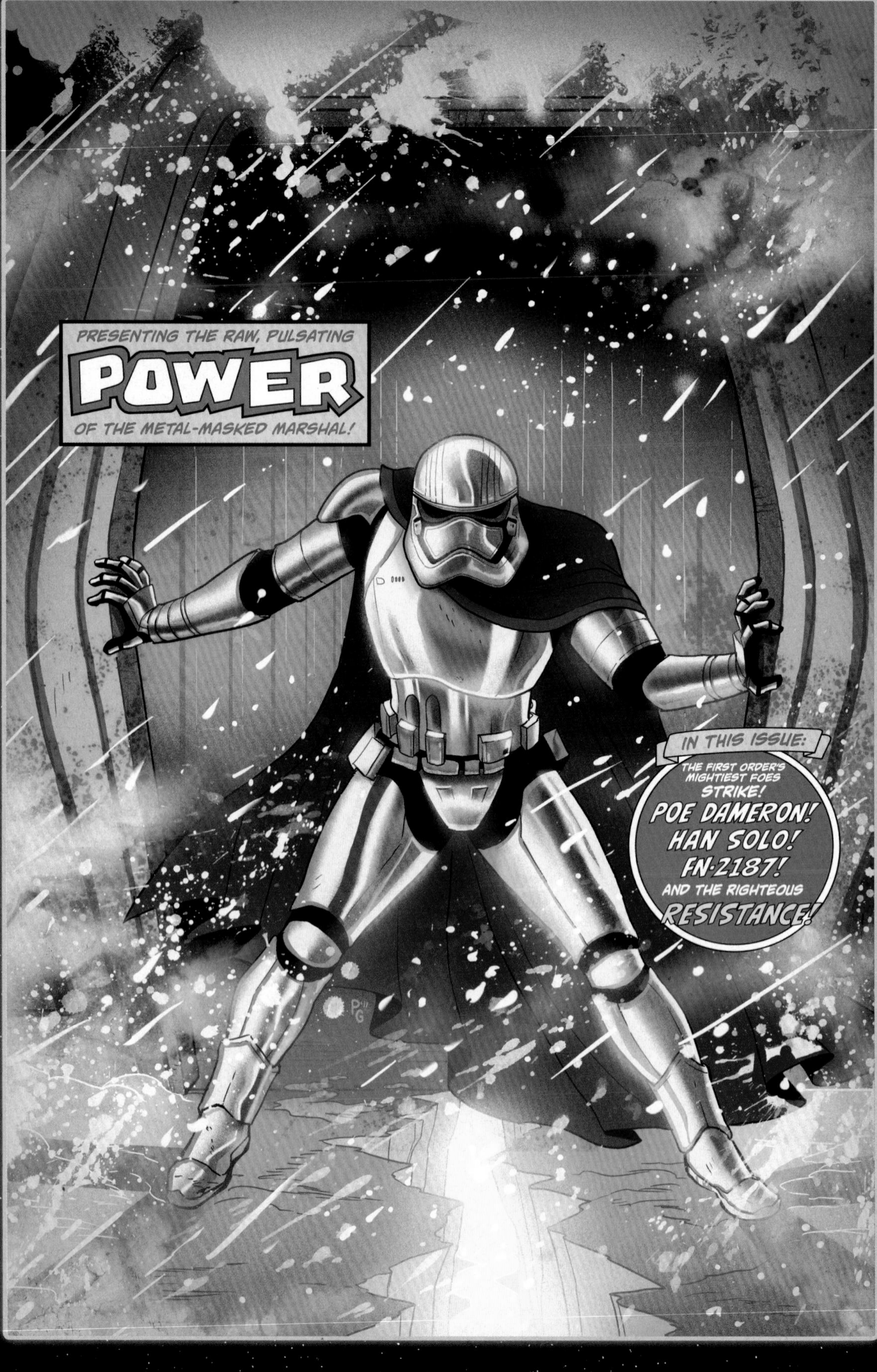
PRESENTING THE RAW, PULSATING
POWER
OF THE METAL-MASKED MARSHAL!
IN THIS ISSUE:
THE FIRST ORDER'S MIGHTIEST FOES STRIKE!
POE DAMERON!
HAN SOLO!
FN-2187!
AND THE RIGHTEOUS
RESISTANCE!

#1 Homage Variant by PAULINA GANUCHEAU

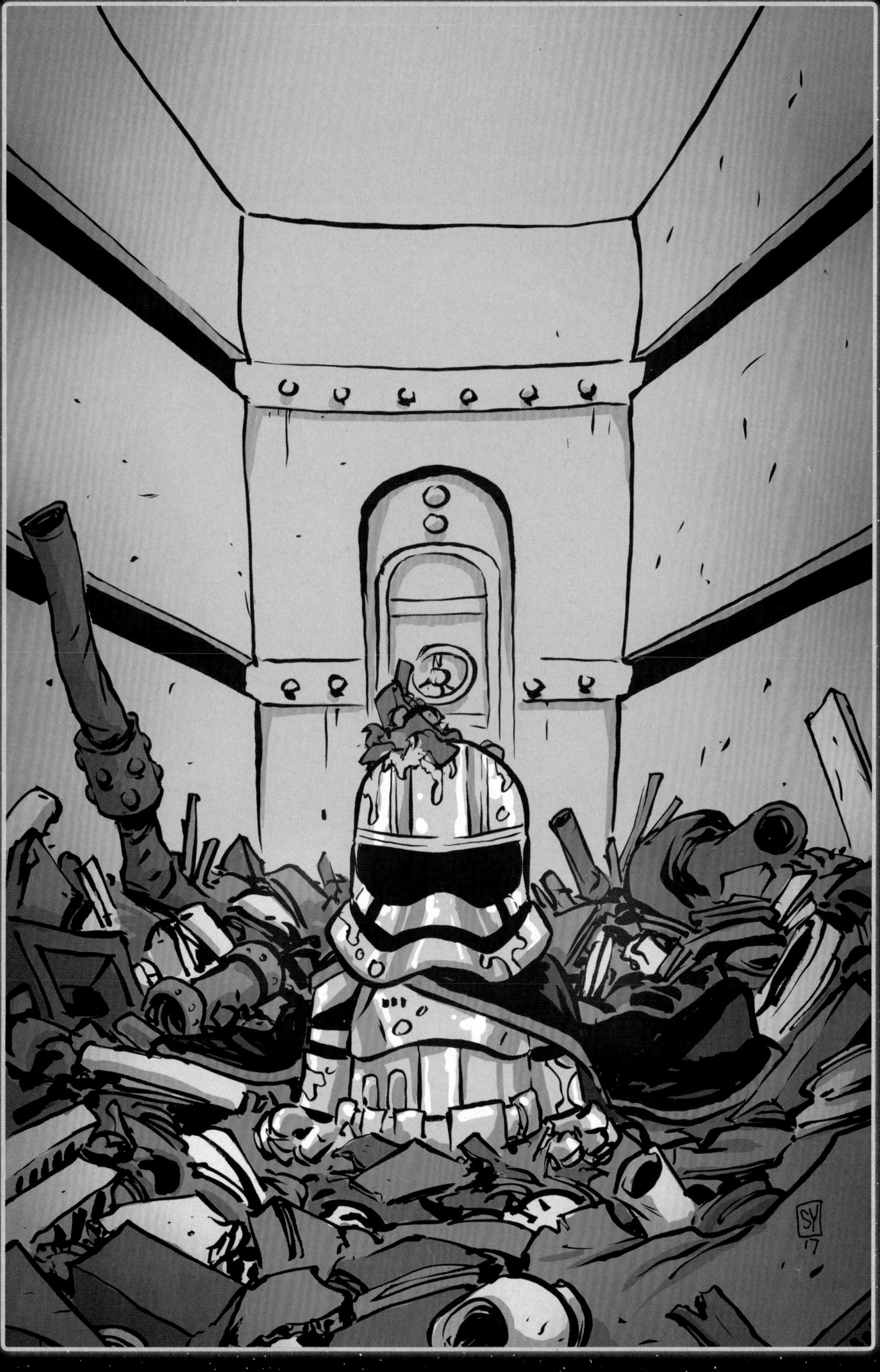
SY
'17

#1 Variant by SKOTTIE YOUNG

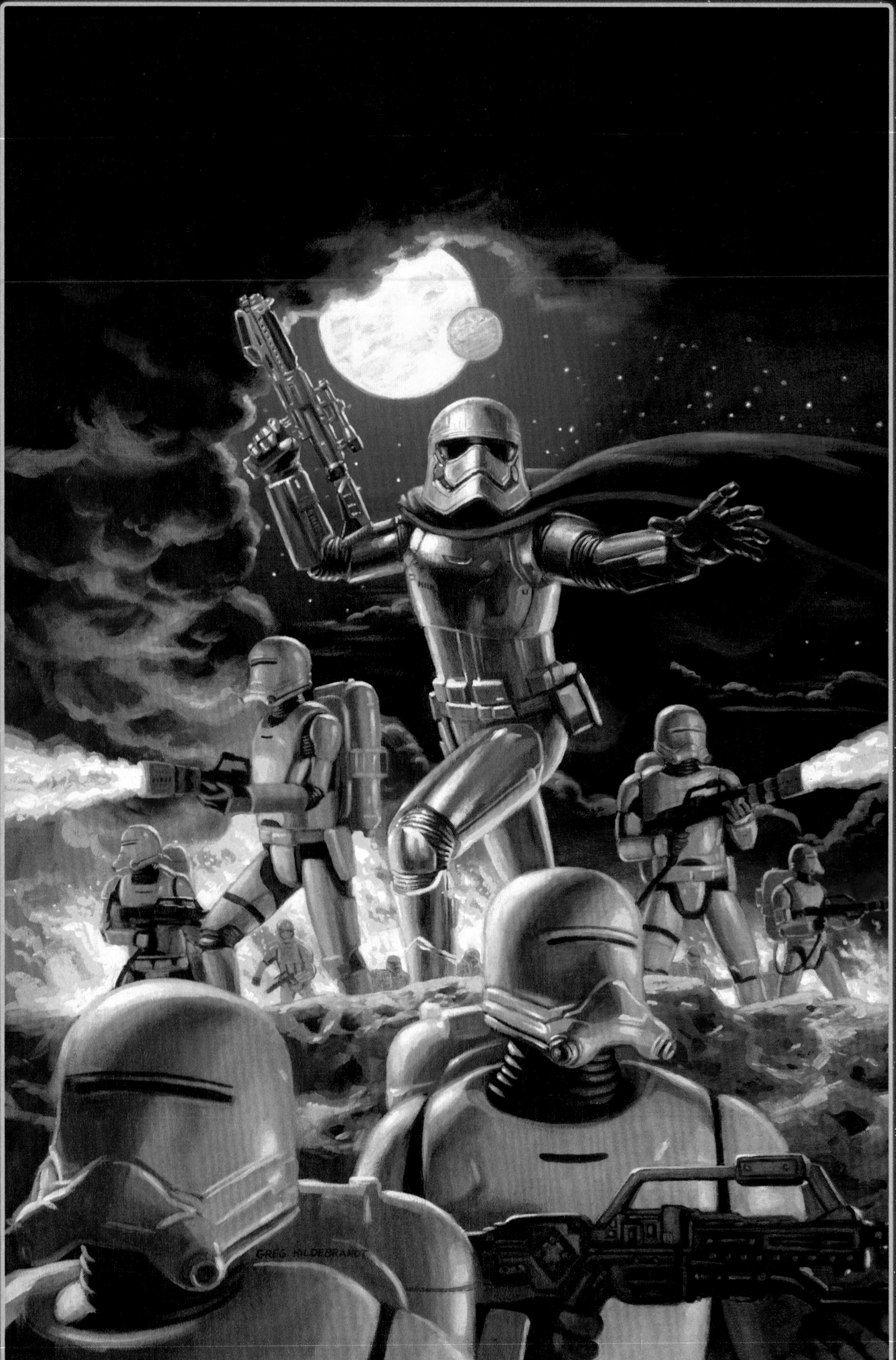
GREG HILDEBRANDT

#2 Variant by GREG HILDEBRANDT

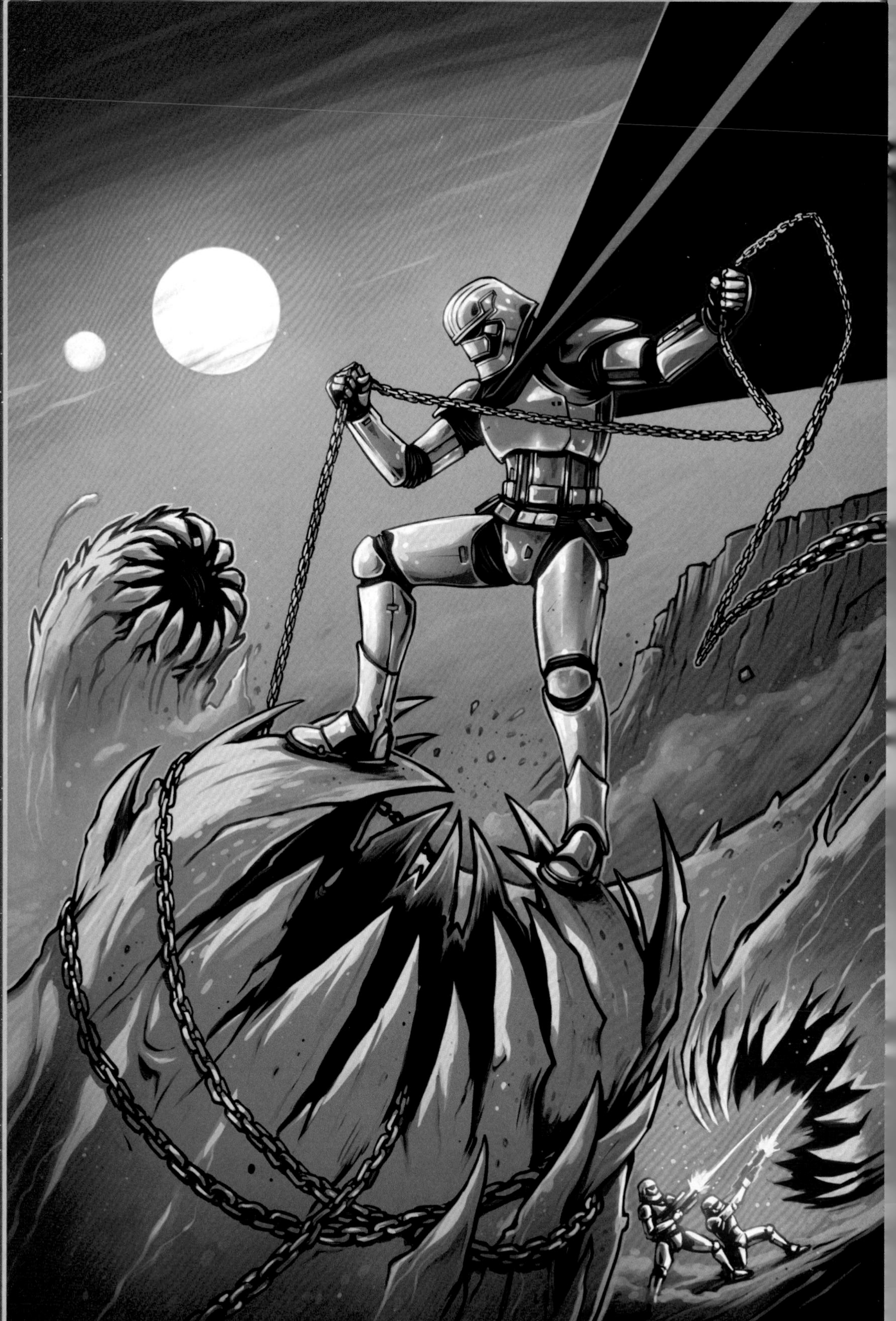

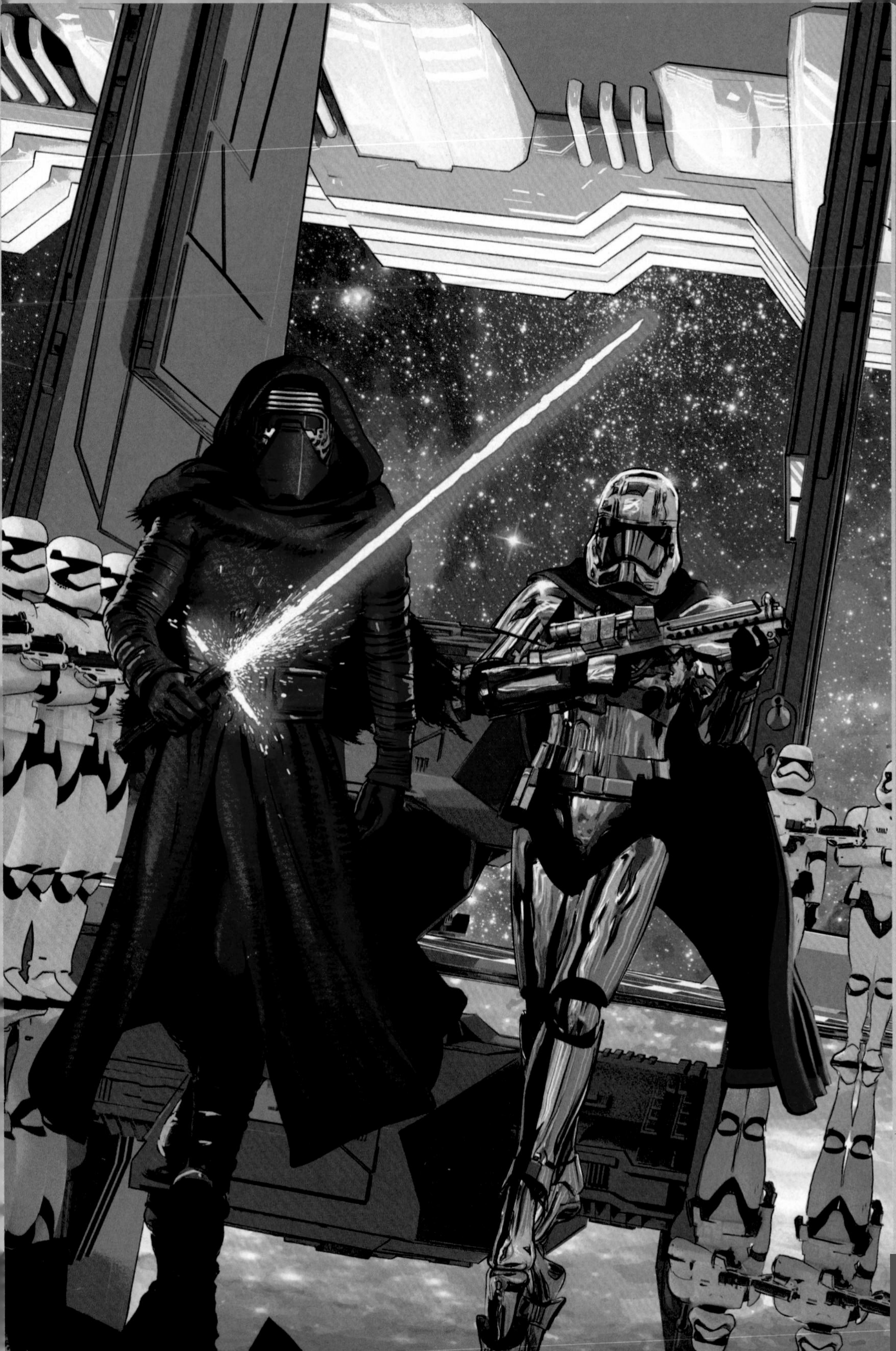

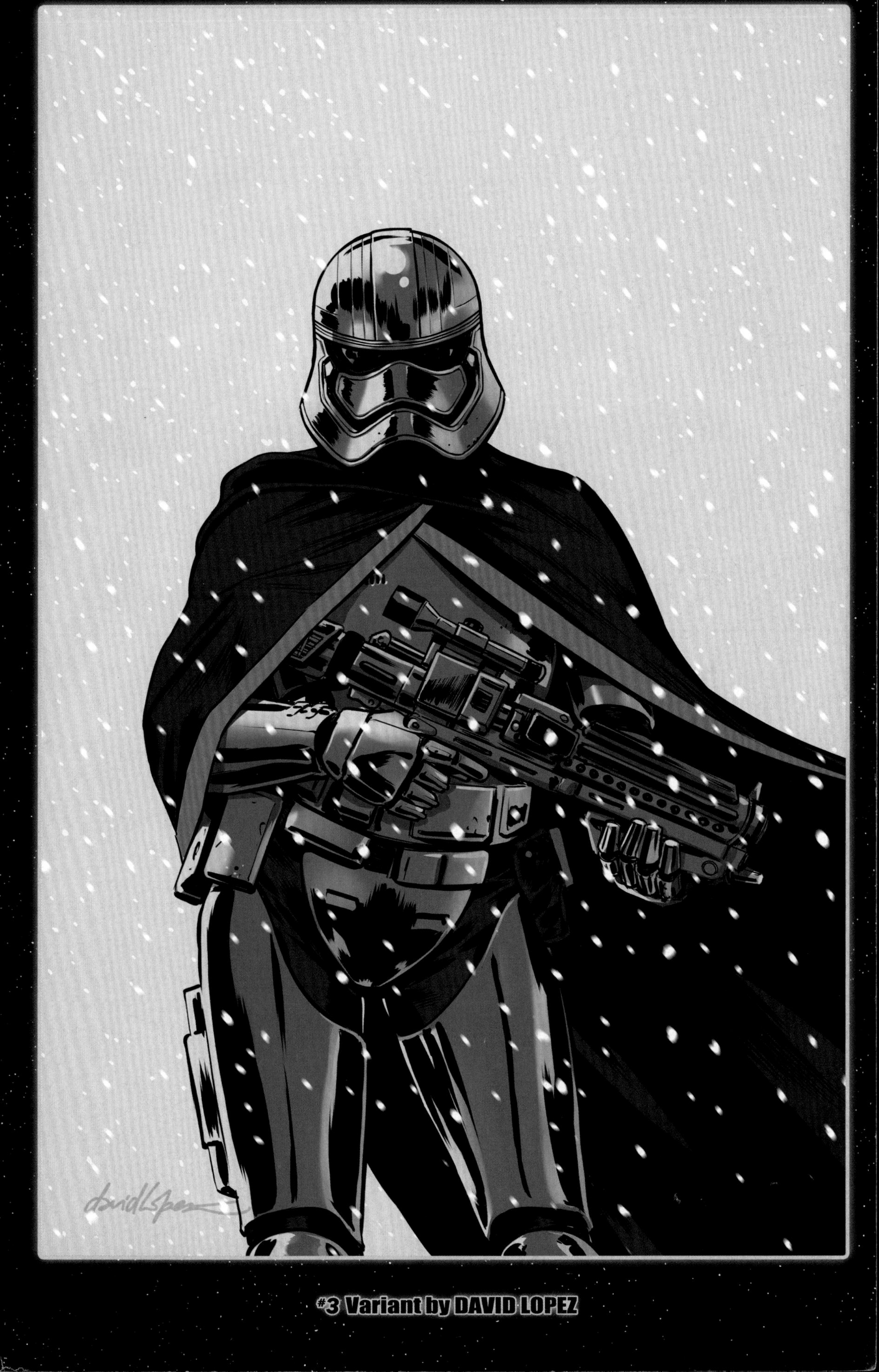

#3 Variant by DAVID LOPEZ

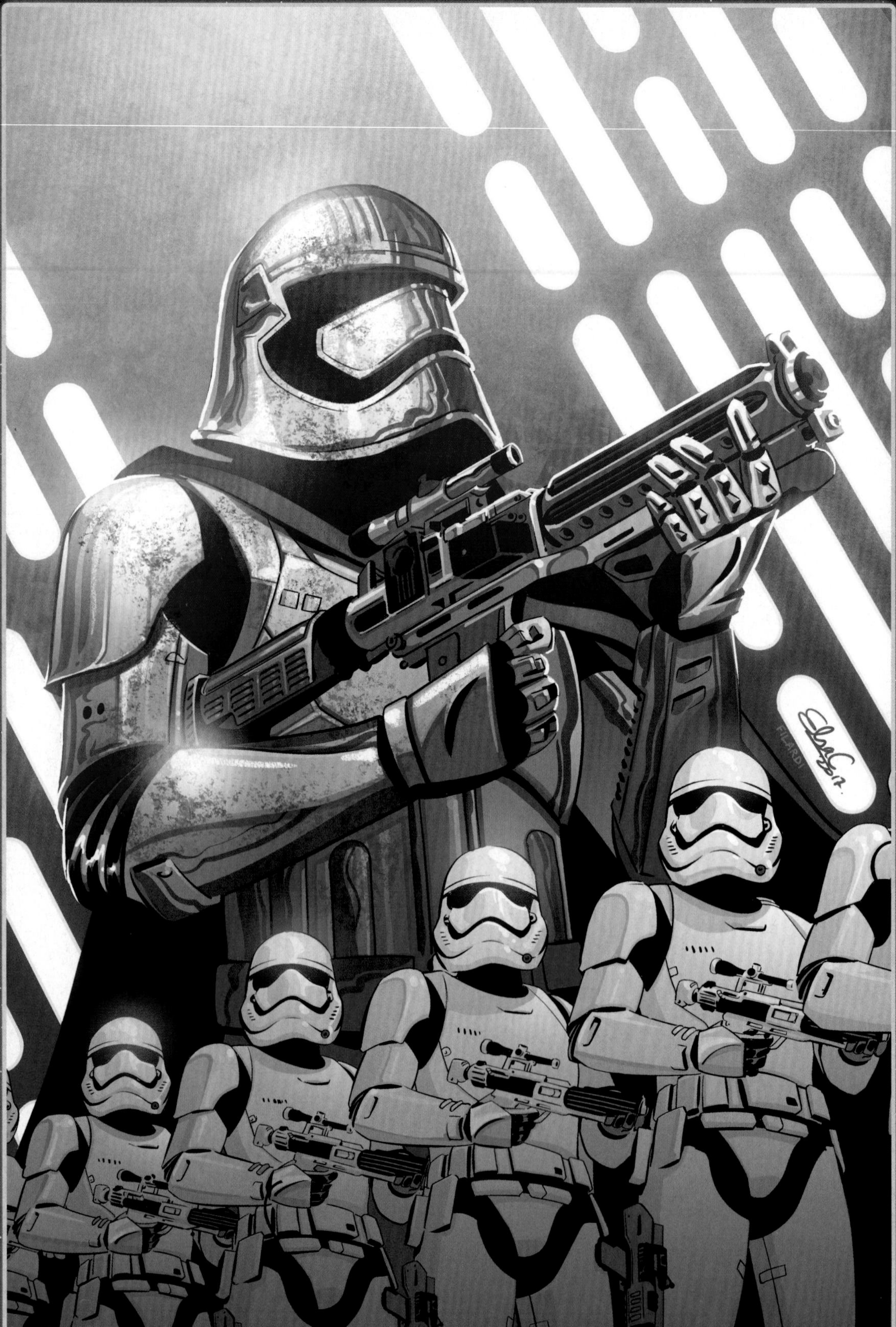
FILARDI

#4 Variant by ELSA CHARRETIER & NICK FILARDI

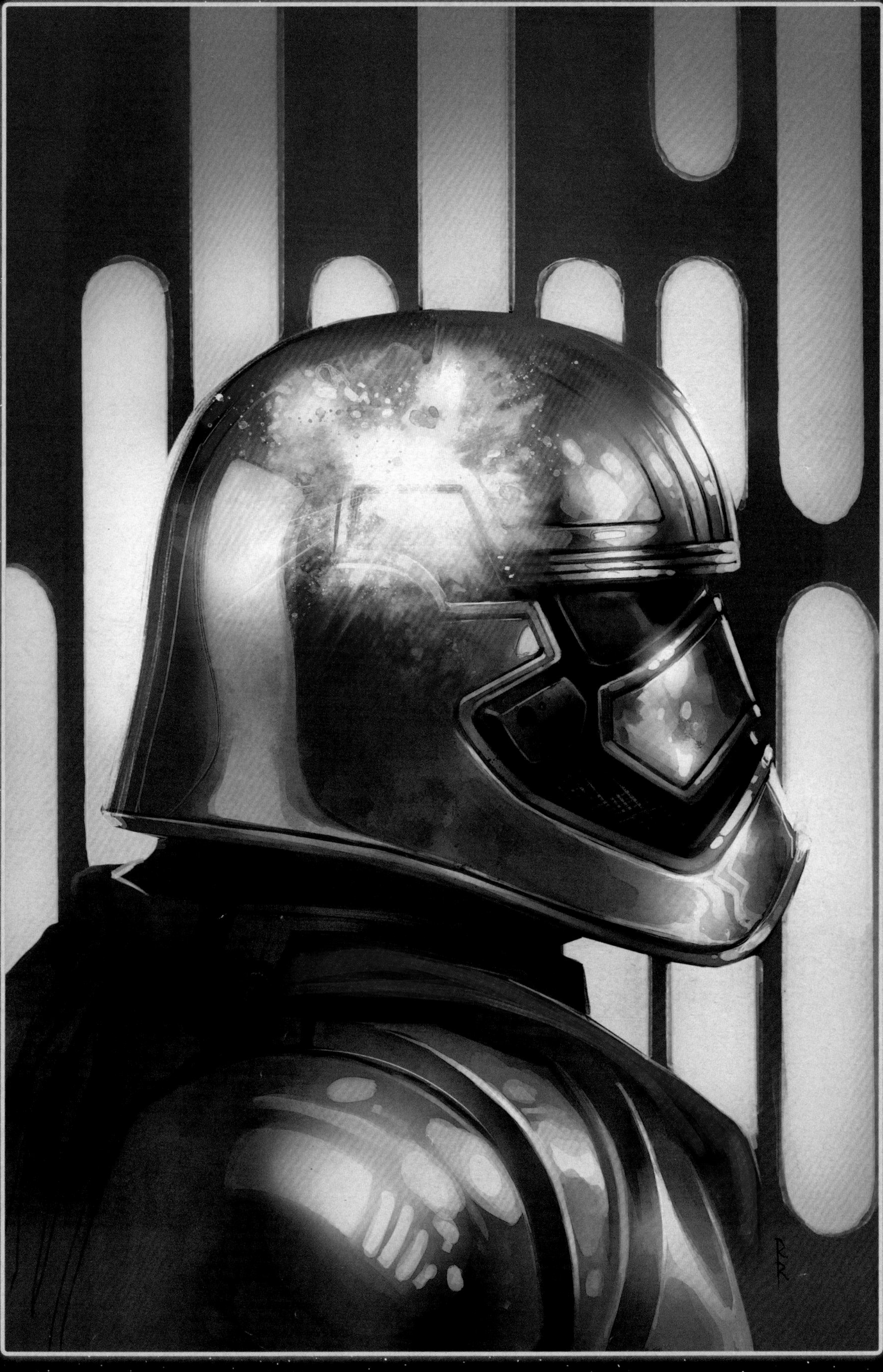

#4 Variant by ROD REIS

CAPTAIN PHASMA

Character designs by MARCO CHECCHETTO

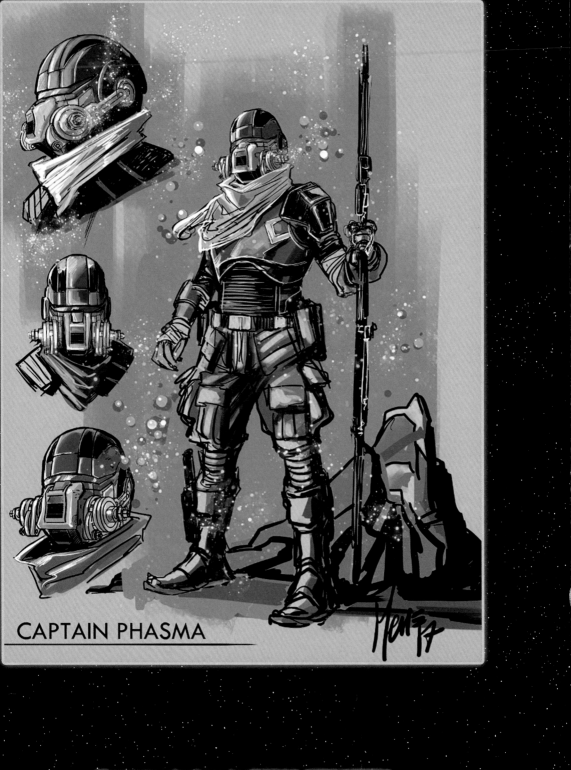

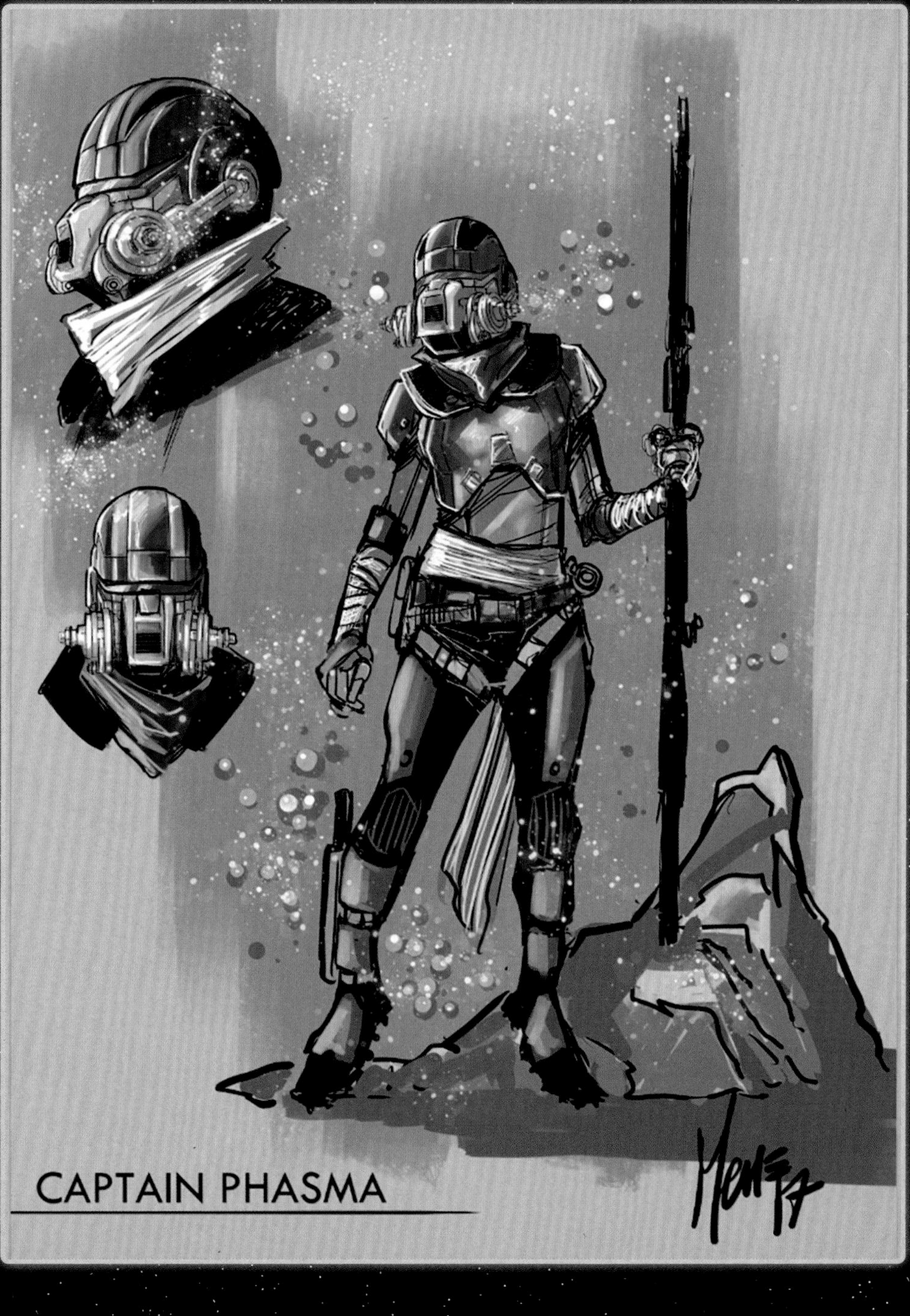

CAPTAIN PHASMA

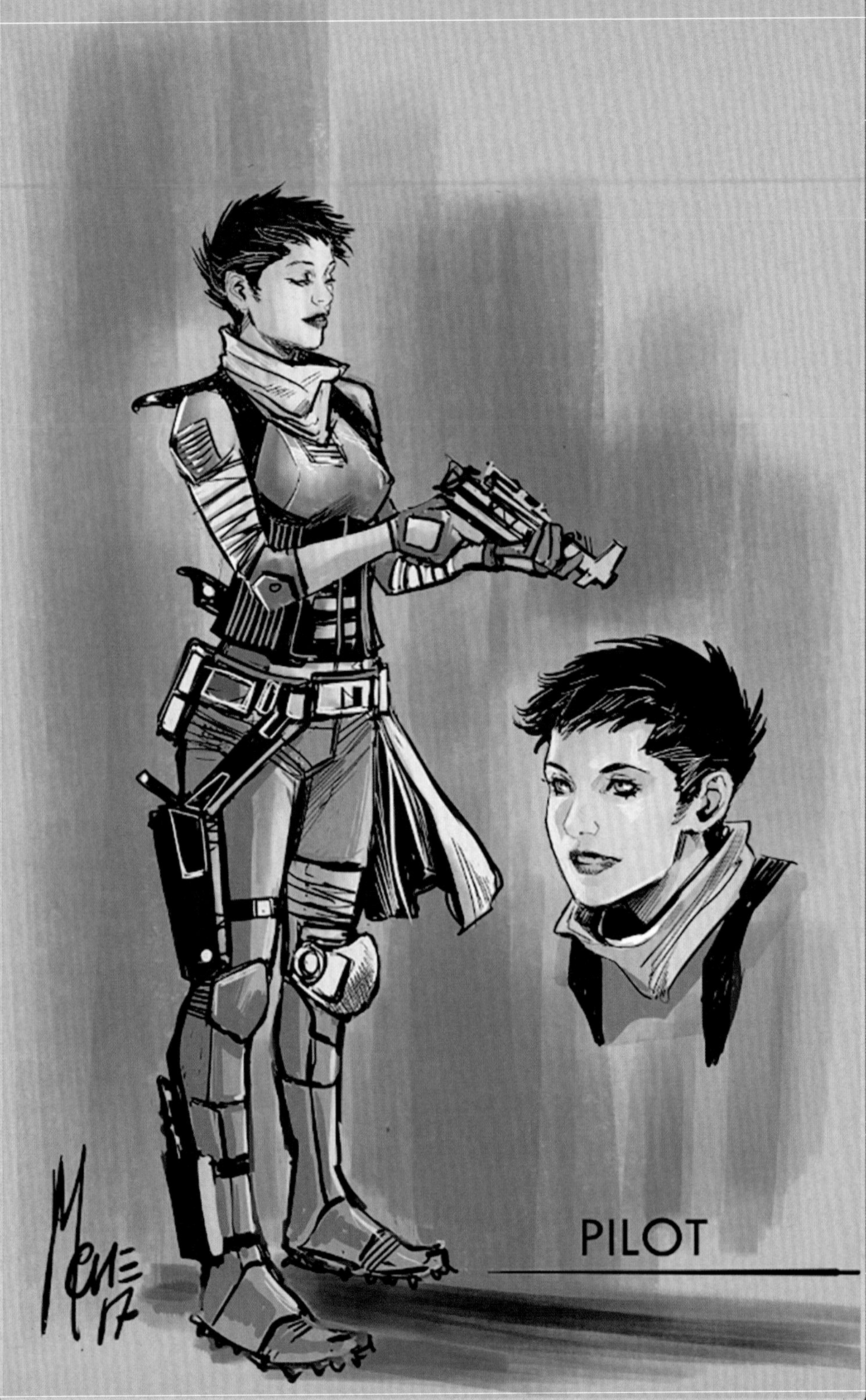
PILOT

HAN AND CHEWIE IN A RACE AGAINST TIME, THE EMPIRE AND THE FASTEST SHIPS IN THE GALAXY!

"This is the solo comic Han and *Star Wars* fans deserve."
— ComicVine.com

STAR WARS

HAN SOLO

LIU
BROOKS
VINES
OBACK

MARVEL

STAR WARS: HAN SOLO TPB
978-0785193210

ON SALE NOW

AVAILABLE IN PRINT AND DIGITAL WHEREVER BOOKS ARE SOLD

MARVEL Disney LUCASFILM

© & TM 2017 LUCASFILM LTD.

THE DARK LORD OF THE SITH'S FIRST DEADLY MISSION

**STAR WARS: DARTH VADER: DARK LORD OF THE SITH
VOL. 1: IMPERIAL MACHINE TPB**
978-1302907440

ON SALE NOVEMBER 2017
WHEREVER BOOKS ARE SOLD

TO FIND A COMIC SHOP NEAR YOU, VISIT COMICSHOPLOCATOR.COM

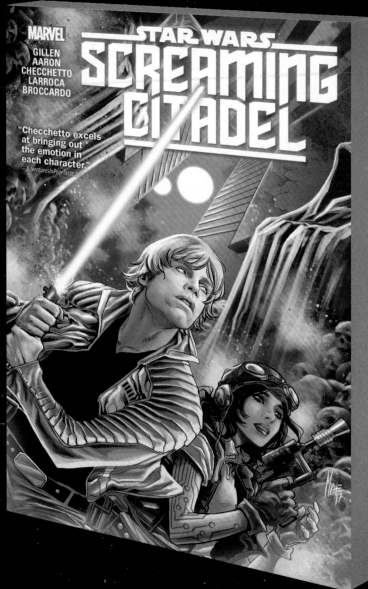